IMAGES
of America

Historic Movie Theatres of West Virginia

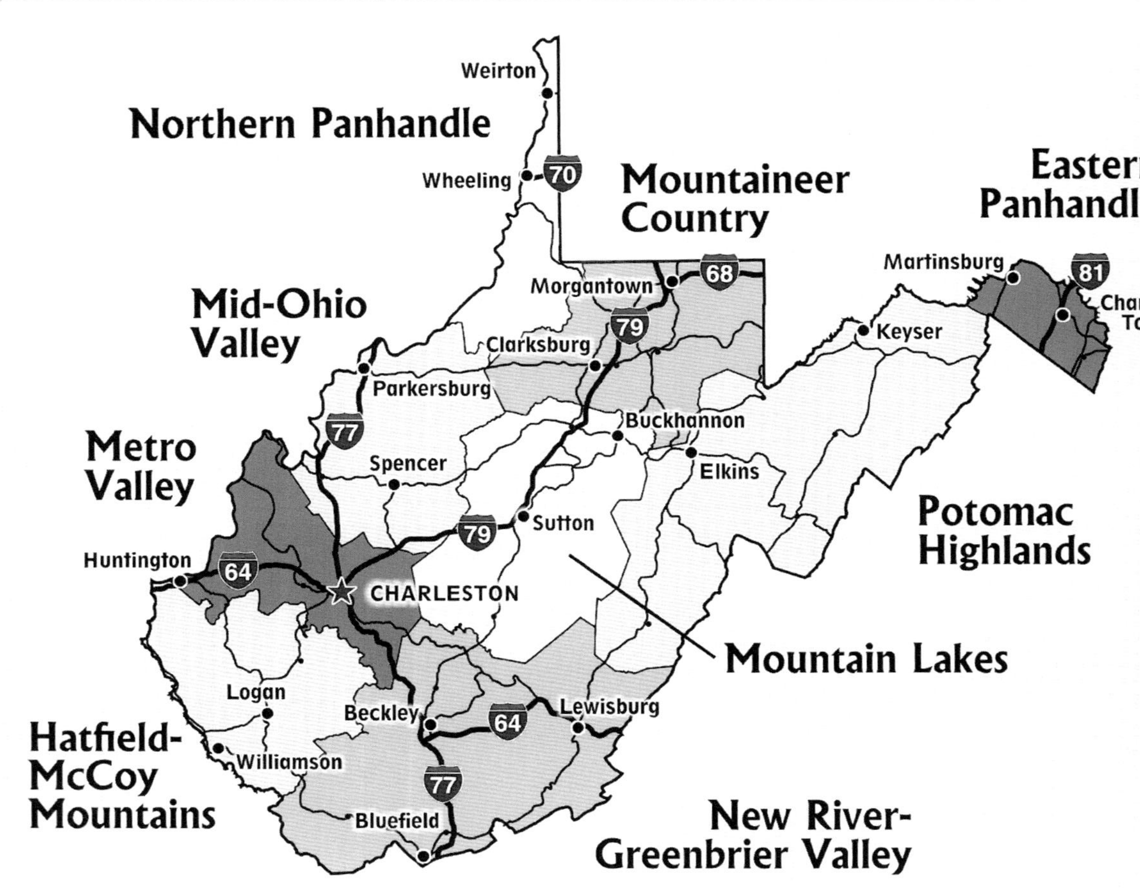

This map depicts the state's nine regions, as defined and marketed by the West Virginia Division of Tourism. These nine regions provide the organizational structure for the book, which covers one region per chapter. The map was created for the Preservation Alliance of West Virginia by graphic designer Peter Baxter, with approval from the Division of Tourism. (Author's collection.)

On the Cover: Designed by nationally famed theatre architect John Eberson for the Warner Bros. studio system's circuit, Morgantown's Warner Theatre opened in 1931. Future TV star Don Knotts ushered at the Art Deco venue with over 1,000 seats. In the 1970s, to compete with multiplexes, it added two screens, splitting the auditorium and separating the balcony. The Warner closed in 2010. (Courtesy of West Virginia & Regional History Center, West Virginia University [WVU] Libraries.)

IMAGES
of America

Historic Movie Theatres of West Virginia

Kelli Shapiro, PhD, and the
Preservation Alliance of West Virginia

ARCADIA
PUBLISHING

ISBN 978-1-4671-2850-6

Published by Arcadia Publishing
Charleston, South Carolina

Printed in the United States of America

Library of Congress Control Number: 2017954430

For all general information, please contact Arcadia Publishing:
Telephone 843-853-2070
Fax 843-853-0044
E-mail sales@arcadiapublishing.com
For customer service and orders:
Toll-Free 1-888-313-2665

Visit us on the Internet at www.arcadiapublishing.com

This book is dedicated to the individuals, organizations, and communities that have strived to keep West Virginia's historic theatres alive and vibrant.

Contents

Acknowledgments

This book was completed by Kelli Shapiro, PhD, for the Preservation Alliance of West Virginia (PAWV). Kelli is thankful to PAWV's other staff members and board for their invaluable support of the project over the past year. Kelli and PAWV would like to thank Arcadia Publishing for finding PAWV's West Virginia Historic Theatre Trail initiative online and suggesting the book concept, as well as for its editors' help throughout the process.

A great debt of gratitude goes out to the many museums, historical societies, archives, collectors, and theatre owners/operators across the state (and beyond) that provided the book's photographs and ephemera. In particular, the book was greatly enhanced by a plethora of items from the broad and impressive collections at West Virginia University's West Virginia & Regional History Center, the West Virginia State Archives, the Theatre Historical Society of America, and American Classic Images (americanclassicimages.com). A number of PAWV's Preserve WV AmeriCorps sites and its West Virginia Historic Theatre Trail members were also glad to assist with images and information.

Those who supplied historical information for the book are deserving of much appreciation. Kelli utilized local history books, newspapers, school yearbooks, city directories, clipping files, and other sources at multiple libraries and archives across the state; she would like to thank them for hosting and maintaining those important collections. Kelli also thanks the State Historic Preservation Office for putting all of the approved National Register of Historic Places nomination forms in the state online; those documents (especially those for National Register Historic Districts) provided much of use. Online newspaper databases were also a crucial source, especially Newspapers.com and the Library of Congress's Discover America's Story digitization project. Local history websites and crowdsourced theatre history databases were very helpful also, especially CinemaTreasures.org, Drive-ins.com, and Coalcampusa.com. A special thanks goes out to the creators, funders, and library partners behind the Media History Digital Library (mediahistoryproject.org); that nonprofit's massive digitization effort made decades' worth of entertainment industry trade journals both searchable and freely available. The multitude of facts about West Virginia theatres found in those journals significantly enriched the historical content throughout this book.

Introduction

Although this book's emphasis is on West Virginia's movie theatres, most of those auditoriums did not only show films. Many began as opera houses or vaudeville venues, with performances often continuing there after movies were added. Others were always multiuse facilities, especially in coal towns. Even those movie houses that began exclusively as such generally performed other community functions as well. They often held local organizations' meetings and fundraising events, wartime drives for bonds and scrap metal, holiday parties for schoolchildren, and more. Throughout the 20th century, they were an integral part of community life in West Virginia, far beyond simply being a place where people could go to watch a feature film (along with a cartoon, serial, and newsreel).

Still, the moviegoing experience was a powerful one. When West Virginians share their memories of attending the state's movie theatres, trends clearly appear regarding these buildings' sociocultural significance. Many people reminisce about how their very first date occurred at a local theatre. In college towns, former students recall seeing films as a relaxing break from classes and studying. Some citizens look further back to their childhoods, remembering attending Saturday matinees packed with kids, all enjoying munching on popcorn and candy (which they occasionally threw) while laughing at animated antics, booing at villains, and cheering for cowboys and other onscreen heroes. Certain people's memories include the excitement of sneaking into drive-in theatres, where they avoided payment (or tried to, although they were often caught) by hiding in cars' trunks. Still others look back at standing in long lines outside while waiting to see Hollywood blockbusters.

Many West Virginia residents' original perceptions of moviegoing were shaped by just one or two theatres, that often being all their communities could hold. That does not mean, however, that the state was not well-stocked in general. In the early years of the exhibition business, nickelodeons and other movie-oriented theatres sprang up statewide, spanning urban downtowns, small-town main streets, and often-ephemeral coal camps. However, many of the state's early theatres did not survive the coming of the "talkies" era, with its accompanying need for expensive sound equipment (and the creation of new, competing facilities that were designed for sound). According to the *Film Daily Year Book*'s first annual list of theatres by state across America, in 1926 (the year before Al Jolson's pioneering film *The Jazz Singer* was released), West Virginia contained over 390 movie venues. By 1933, when sound had become an expected feature, the state had 190 "wired" theatres, plus 211 silent-film theatres that were listed as closed.

That period also harkened the rise of the picture palaces—massive, elaborate venues against which many older, less amenity-filled theatres could not compete. Movie house closures were especially common during the Great Depression. That said, a number of theatres that shut down then were able to reopen once economic conditions improved. Also, with people seeking affordable enjoyment and escapism during those dark days, numerous new showplaces opened as well. By January 1942, a few weeks after America entered World War II, West Virginia had 342 movie theatres (34 of those shown as being closed).

It should be noted that, during this part of the 20th century, West Virginia's movie houses were segregated. Some did not allow African Americans to attend at all, while others offered seats for them in the balcony or at the back of the auditorium. A few film venues in the state, though, catered specifically to the black population during the segregation era. In 1934, four such facilities existed; 20 years later, that number had increased to 10. (The author was only able to find photographs of one: Charleston's Ferguson Theatre, located in an African American neighborhood called the Block.)

Postwar life brought changes that impacted the exhibition industry, including the growth of a more automobile-focused society and an increasing shift of families from cities and small towns to suburbs (or at least outlying neighborhoods in urban areas). That led to the rapid expansion of not only neighborhood theatres but also drive-in theatres. Drive-ins increased in West Virginia from only one in the *Film Daily Year Book*'s 1947 list (the Open Air Drive-in Theatre in Beckley) to 77 in 1969. This correlated to the closure of various downtown movie houses— their precarious situation also made worse by television's arrival (followed by cable TV and the VCR).

In most of America, the coming of the multiplex movie theatre then became a major factor in the obsolescence of both historic, single-screen theatres and newer drive-ins. However, in the relatively multiplex-scarce West Virginia, it was less of a problem. Still, some larger downtown theatres did turn themselves into twins or triplexes by dividing their spaces, while others closed once their circuits opened multiplexes nearby. The national trend of drive-ins being razed for replacement by more valuable subdivisions and shopping centers was also less prevalent in the state, with its often rural and mountainous environment; while redevelopment did occur in many cases, other former drive-ins' land simply remained vacant. West Virginia's widespread, postindustrial job losses and its resultant population exodus were, of course, key culprits behind many drive-in and indoor theatres' shutdowns.

Theatres in circuits (known in other businesses as chains) typically fared better than others during changing times. This was partially due to their collective management and joint film-booking and equipment-buying ability. Still, circuits came and went. The state's most prominent circuit, the Kingwood-based Alpine, was founded in the 1930s and had 25 West Virginia movie houses (all but seven of them named the Alpine Theatre) at its height, from 1944 to 1950. By 1956, it only had eight left, and in 1961, Alpine sold its last theatre. One rare, historic circuit that still survives is that operated by the Hyman family, which started in 1910 in Huntington. Over the years, the Hymans owned at least eight single-screen (indoor and drive-in) theatres in the Huntington area. As of this writing, their Greater Huntington Theatre Corporation still has three theatres in West Virginia (plus one in Ohio), all multiplexes.

In 1957, the final time that the *Film Daily Year Book* published its comprehensive list of states' movie theatres, West Virginia had less than 290. As of 2018, West Virginia offers barely half a dozen indoor, historic movie houses that show films regularly, as well as five seasonally operated drive-ins. Almost 20 other historic former film venues now host live performances, such as plays and concerts. The Mountain State also has approximately 20 open multiplexes.

This book attempts to reconstruct the history of the state's individual, single-screen movie houses and drive-ins. While it cannot come close to being comprehensive, it does contain photographs of (and historical information about) well over 200 separate theatres. For the reader's ease of use, these theatres are organized into regional chapters, utilizing the nine regions delineated by the West Virginia Division of Tourism. Each chapter's material is then arranged alphabetically by town (except for a few images on chapters' introductory pages).

Overall, the Preservation Alliance of West Virginia hopes that reading this book will inspire West Virginians not just to reminisce about lost movie houses but also to support those that still exist, attending events at operational historic theatres and championing the restoration and reopening (or at least the architecturally sensitive adaptive reuse) of those that currently sit vacant.

One

Eastern Panhandle

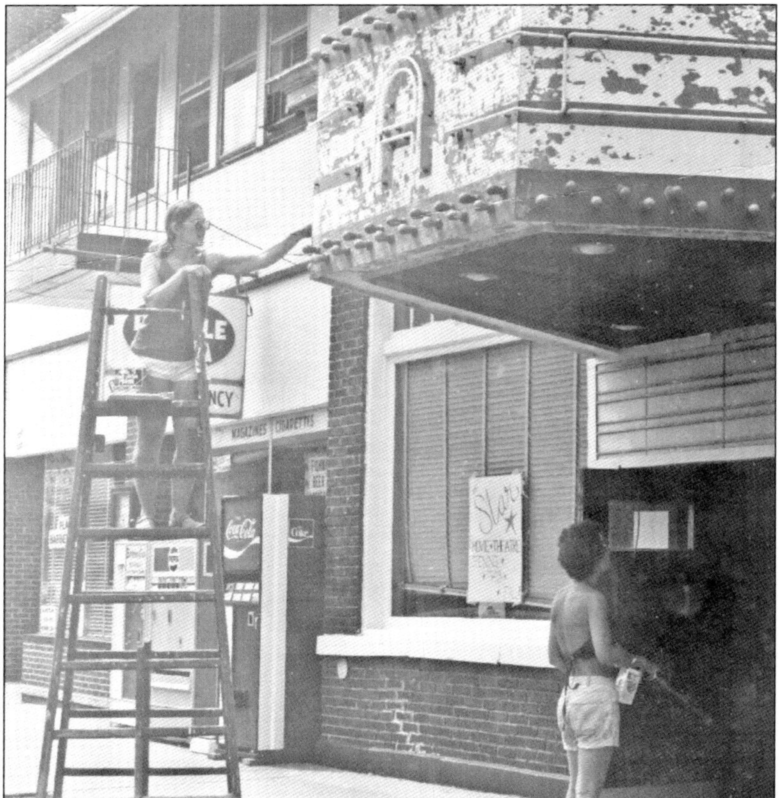

Ernest Johnson's 250-seat Berkeley Theatre opened in 1928 in a converted automobile garage in Berkeley Springs. In 1949, the Alpine theatre circuit remodeled it and renamed it the Alpine Theatre. After a 1970s stint as the Lynn Theatre, the movie house became the Star Theatre. The Star's co-owner, Jeanne Mozier, is seen here repainting the marquee after her 1977 purchase. The Star plays recent films every weekend. (Courtesy of Jeanne Mozier.)

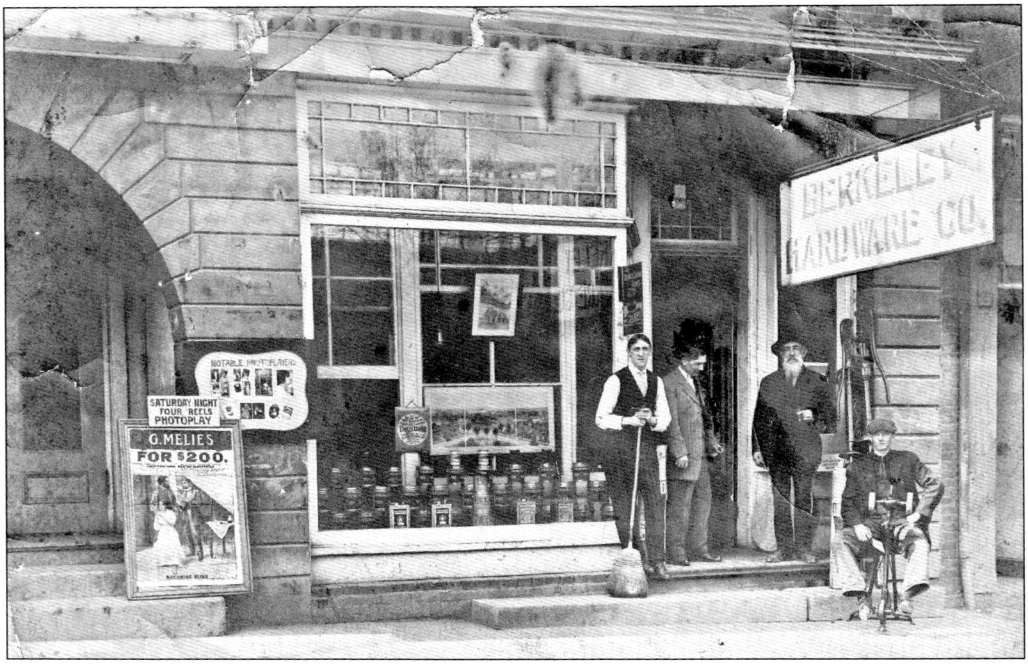

Berkeley Springs' 450-seat Opera House opened in 1906 and, like its competitor, underwent multiple identity changes. When it became a film venue in 1909, it was renamed the Palace Theatre. Later, it became the New Theatre (1925), the Carter Theatre (1936), and the Ideal Theatre (1939). The Ideal disappeared from listings in the mid-1950s. In 1974, the theatre's entire block of Fairfax Street burned down. (Courtesy of Jeanne Mozier and Betty Lou Harmison.)

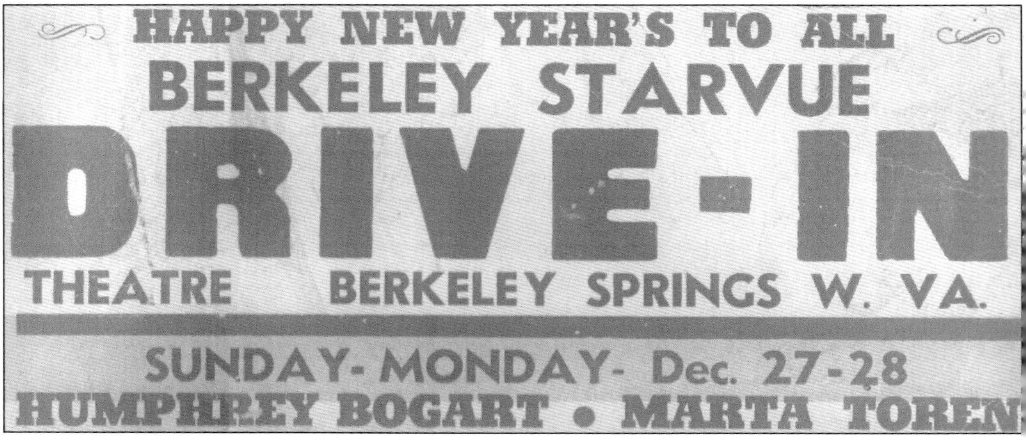

The StarVue Drive-in was a short-lived theatre along Johnsons Mill Road in Berkeley Springs. The Pierce family owned and operated it from its 1953 launch until its 1963 closure. Opening night, when only 20 cars showed up, was indicative of the 200-space drive-in's struggles. Despite offering family-friendly films, a playground, and freshly made food, attendance remained low. This poster was made close to the StarVue's end. (Courtesy of Jeanne Mozier.)

The New Opera House, designed by architect T.A. Mullett, opened in 1911, after Annie G. Packette raised $50,000 to enhance Charles Town's cultural opportunities. The 750-seat performance venue was showing movies by 1915, continuing until its 1948 closure. After decades of commercial reuse, the building was donated in 1973 to the Old Opera House Theatre Company, which restored the landmarked facility and returned it to its original use. (Author's collection.)

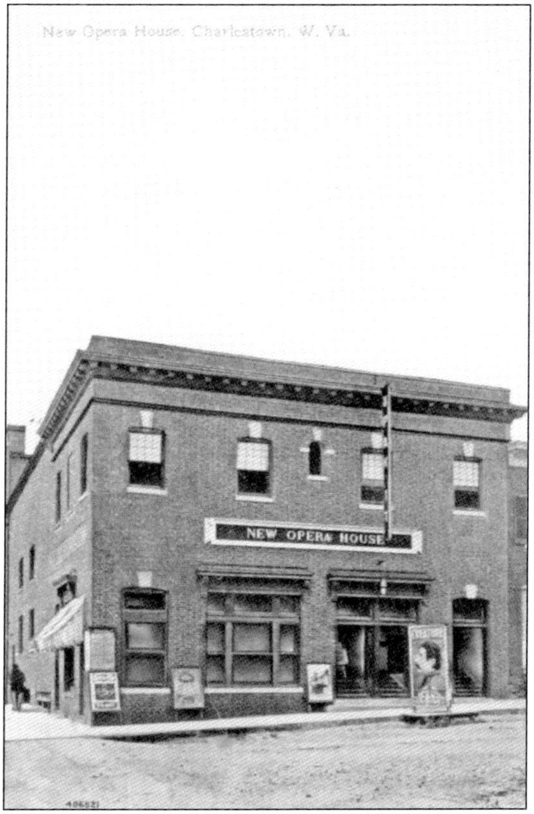

Charles Town's Pitts-Jefferson Theatre, visible on the right, was constructed in 1931 and remodeled and expanded in 1939. The Pitts Theatres circuit operated the movie house, which began with 600 seats and ended with over 750. It hosted events like Red Cross benefits and the Kiwanis Club's annual Christmas party for schoolchildren. It closed by 1964. The brick Art Deco building now hosts the American Legion. (Courtesy of Jefferson County Museum.)

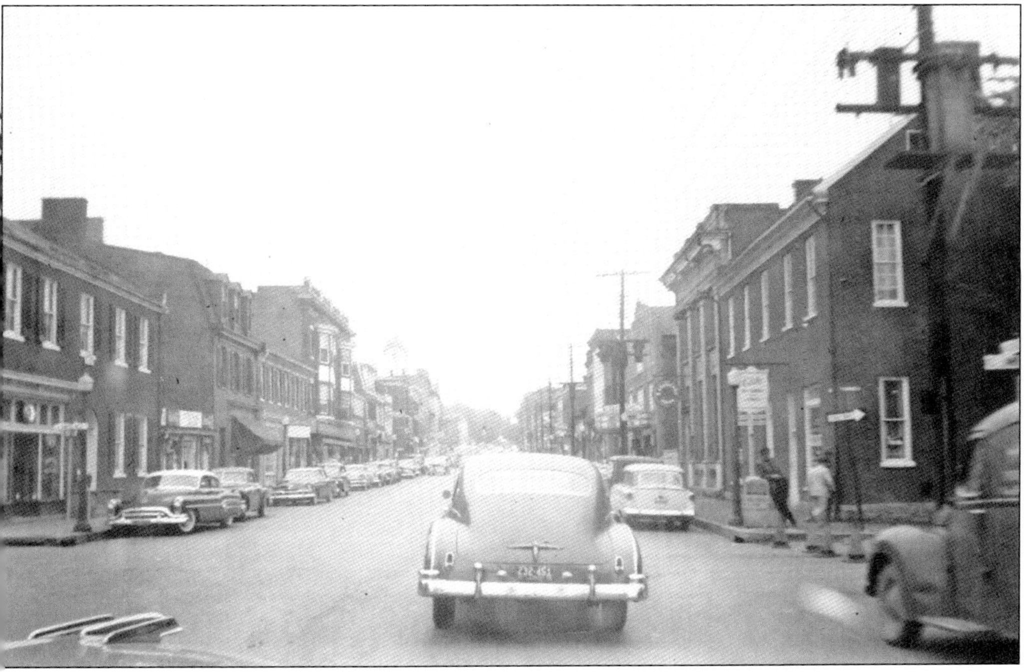

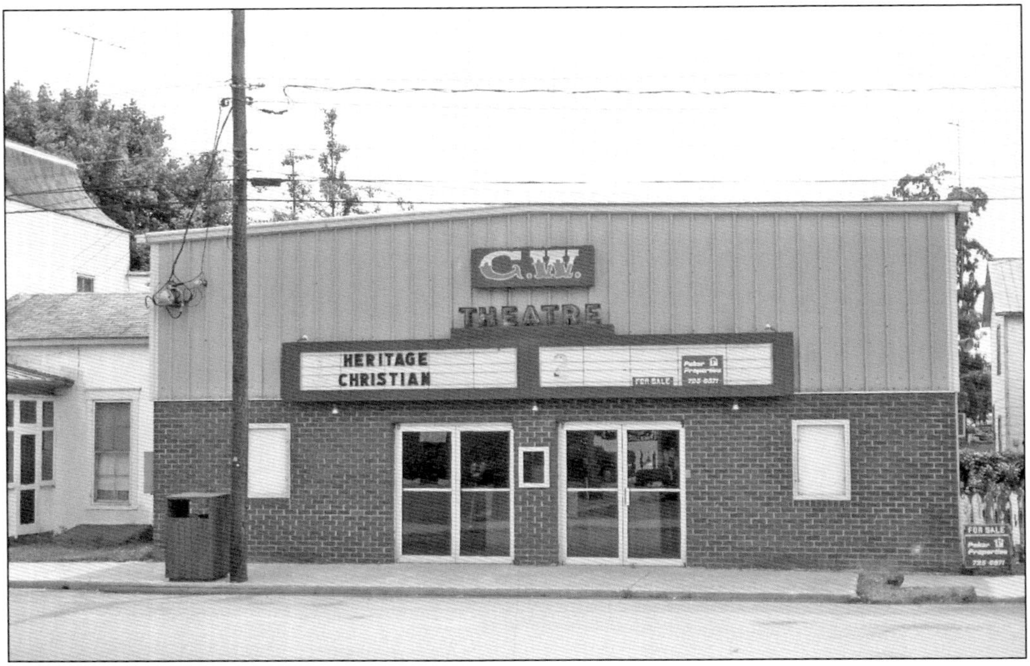

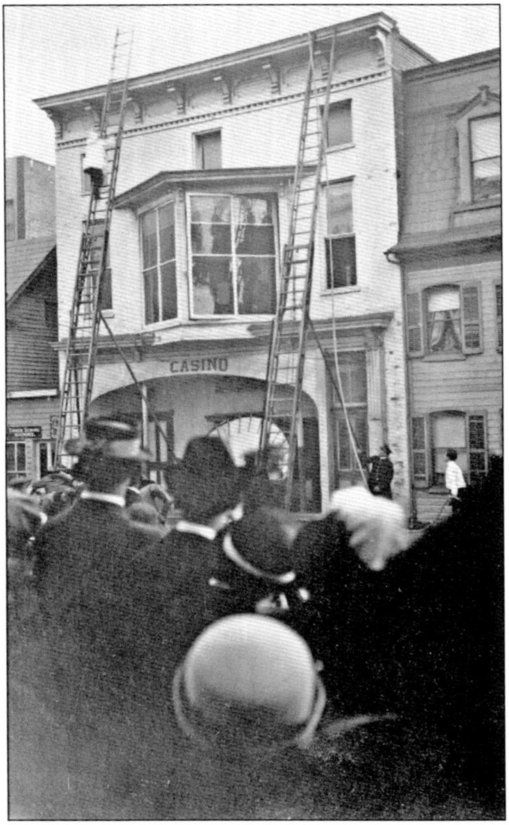

After the forced 1977 closure of Ranson's Charles Washington Theatre, owner Wayne Rankin moved the seats and equipment to a prefabricated metal building in Charles Town. Its name shortened to C.W. Theatre, the cinema, which Rankin intended to later "twin," did not last long. When this 1987 photograph was taken, it was reused and for sale. Its seats were sold in 1990. The structure is currently vacant. (Courtesy of American Classic Images.)

This image shows a fire drill at Martinsburg's Casino Theatre, which opened in early 1911 on the 200 block of West King Street. A 1914 directory revealed that the nickelodeon was managed by W.E. Crawford, had 535 seats, and offered 5¢ and 10¢ admission. By late 1914, Fred Wright had taken over. The Casino had closed by the mid-1920s. (Courtesy of West Virginia State Archives, G. Walter Kibler Collection.)

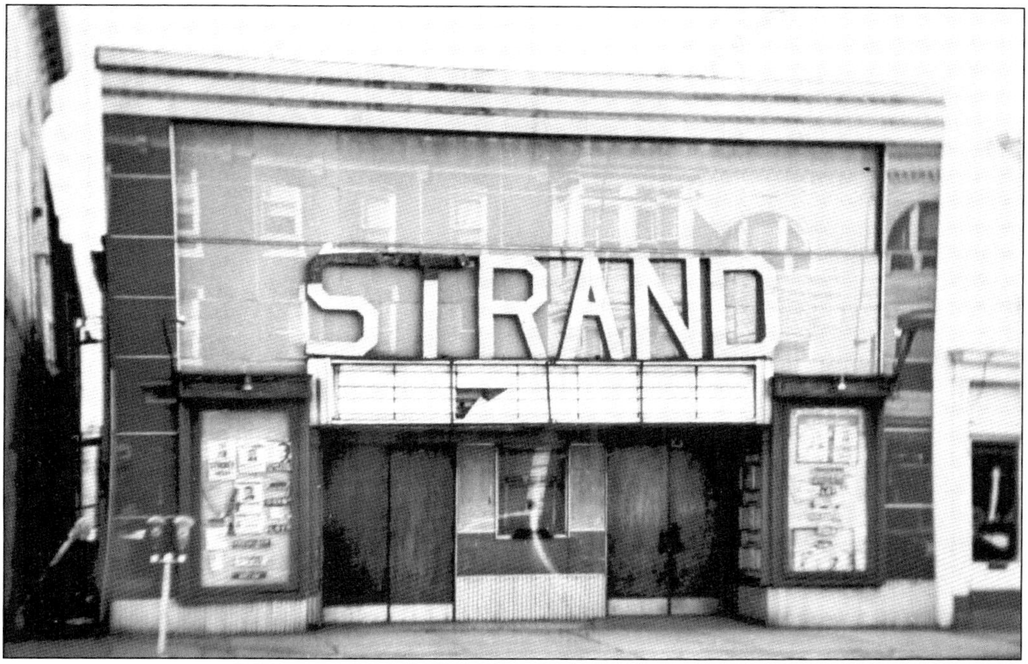

Martinsburg's Strand Theatre opened in 1903. By 1920, it was part of Harry M. Crandall's movie theatre chain; it later joined the Warner Bros. circuit. In 1939, it received a full remodel, including a new facade, new projection and sound equipment, and 400 new seats. In 1962, the still-operational theatre's back section burned. The Strand never reopened. It was later demolished. (Courtesy of West Virginia State Archives, Jeff Hollis Collection.)

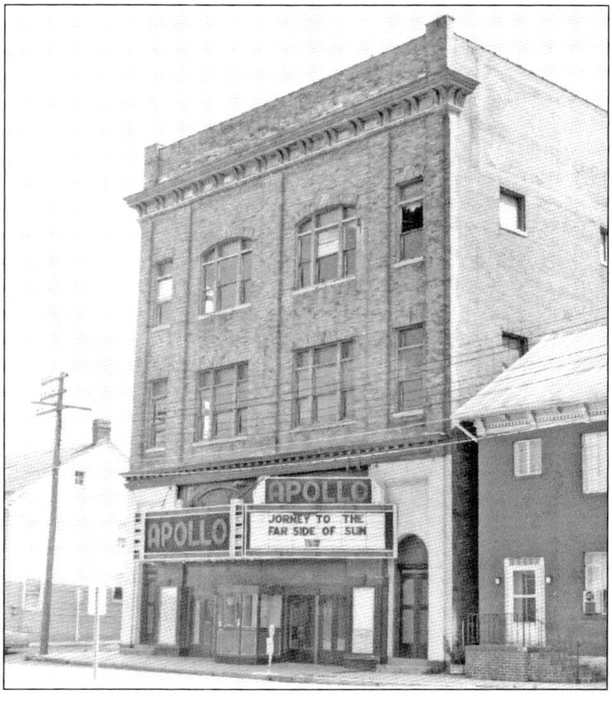

H.P. Thorn's 1,000-seat Apollo Theatre, designed by Reginald Geare for film and stage shows, opened in 1914 in Martinsburg. Stars like Will Rogers and Tex Ritter performed there before their films. It moved away from live events in the 1940s, primarily showing movies until the Berkeley County Civic Theatre purchased it in 1975. The Apollo has since served as a performance venue. (Courtesy of Theatre Historical Society of America, Editor's Collection.)

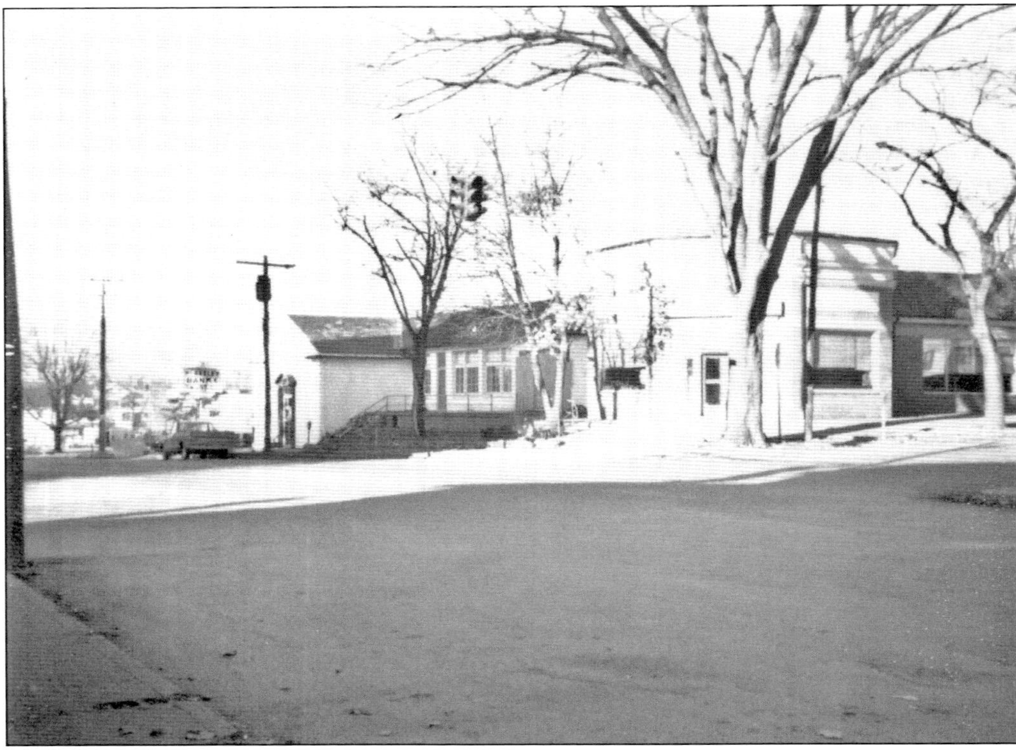

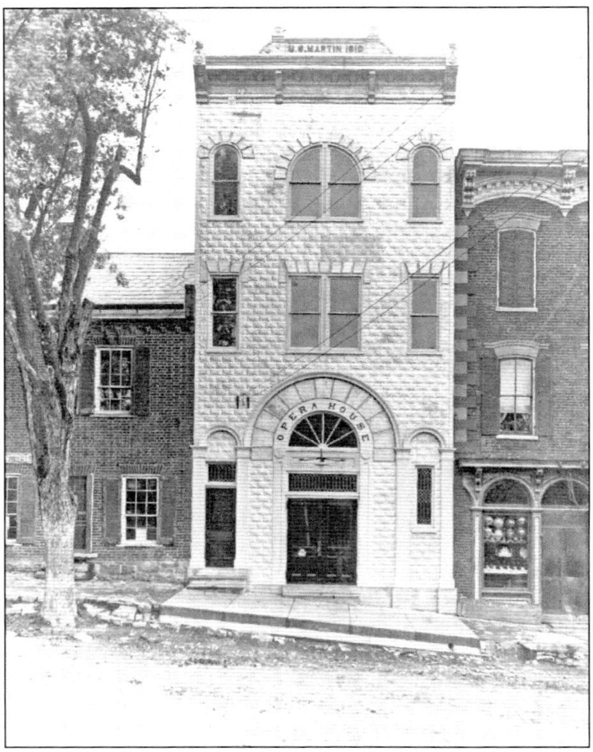

The Charles Washington Theatre opened in 1949 in Ranson's new Charles Washington Shopping Center. Named after adjacent Charles Town's founder, the movie house featured 600 seats and a 300-foot well to provide cool air. It operated until 1977, when the center's owners decided to raze the building (seen in this photograph forming the left end of the center's L-shaped design). The rest of the center remains. (Courtesy of Jefferson County Museum.)

Shepherdstown's mayor, U.S. Martin, opened the Opera House in 1909 and sold it that year to the Musser family, who showed films nightly. Articles claim the Opera House was West Virginia's first theatre to play sound films in 1928. The Mussers closed it in 1956. It sat vacant until, following restoration, it reopened in 1992 with 135 seats. The Opera House is now a music venue. (Courtesy of Historic Shepherdstown Commission.)

Two

Hatfield-McCoy Mountains

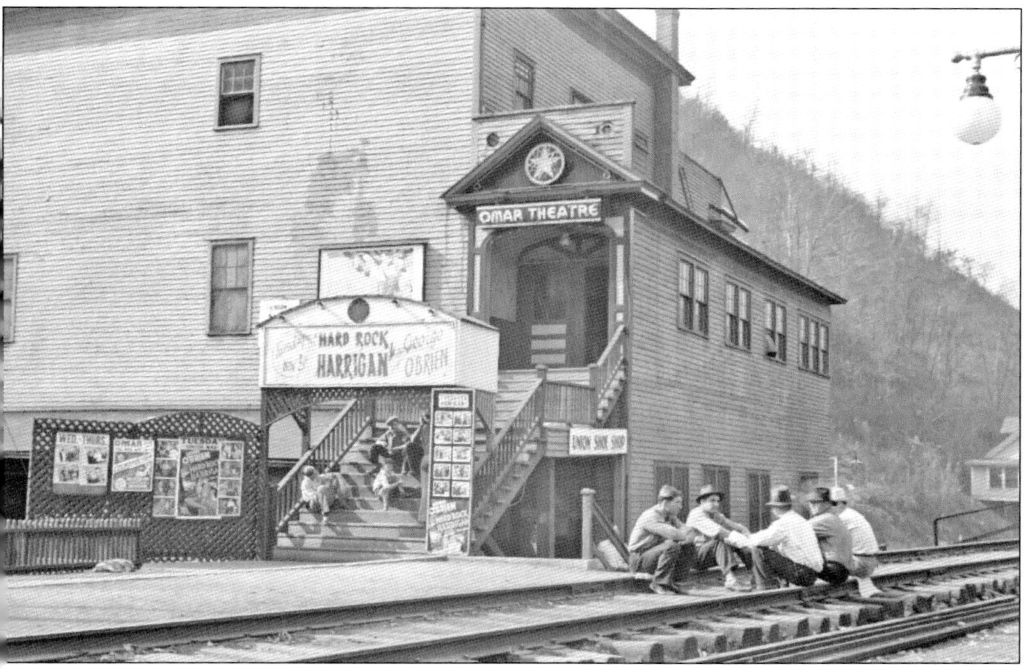

In the coal mining company town of Omar, a company-built, multipurpose structure along the railroad tracks housed the Omar Theatre as early as 1926. Shown here offering 10¢ admission in 1935, the segregated, second-floor movie house had 400 seats. It was operated by J.C. Newbold's circuits from 1934 to at least 1959. The Omar Theatre building was destroyed by a fire in February 1964. (Courtesy of Library of Congress.)

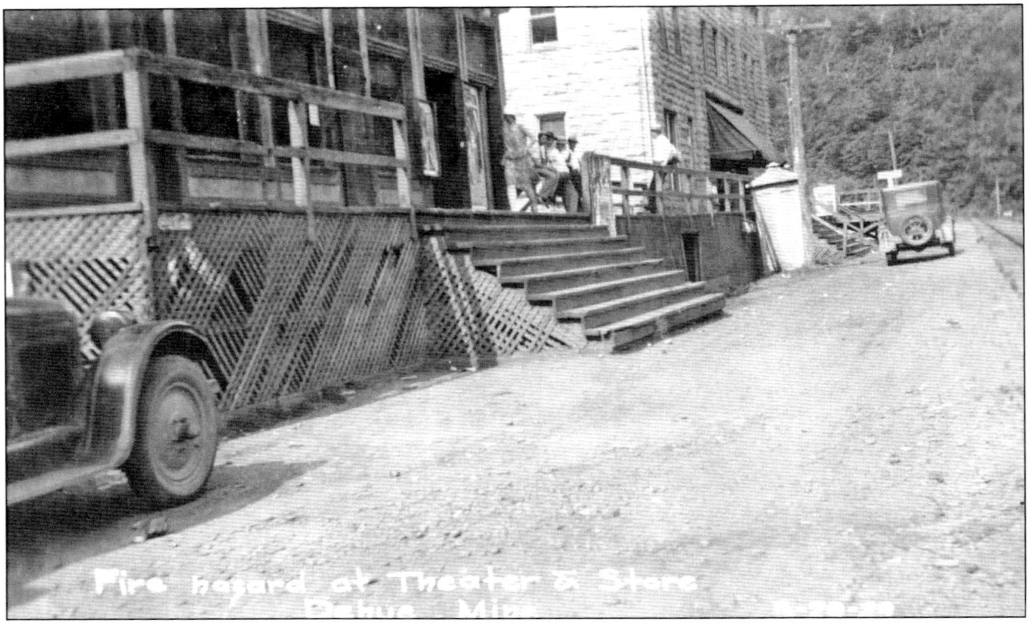

This 1929 photograph shows movie poster boards on the Dehue Theatre's building in the Dehue coal camp, near Logan. Opening prior to 1926, the 100-seat, segregated auditorium was on the second floor. Owned by Youngstown Mining, it closed temporarily during a 1939 miners' strike. The Dehue Theatre was operational until at least 1957. The vacant structure burned down in 1988. (Courtesy of West Virginia State Archives, Dolores Riggs Davis Collection.)

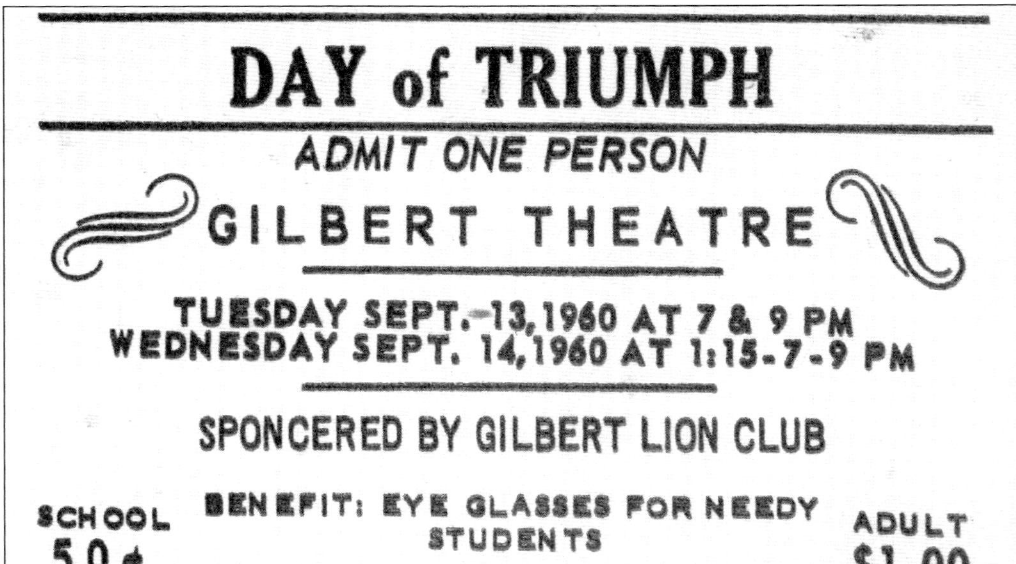
DAY of TRIUMPH

ADMIT ONE PERSON

GILBERT THEATRE

TUESDAY SEPT. 13, 1960 AT 7 & 9 PM
WEDNESDAY SEPT. 14, 1960 AT 1:15-7-9 PM

SPONCERED BY GILBERT LION CLUB

SCHOOL 50¢

BENEFIT: EYE GLASSES FOR NEEDY STUDENTS

ADULT $1.00

Earl Miller's Gilbert Theatre opened on Central Avenue in Gilbert, a Mingo County town, in late 1940 or early 1941. Built expressly as a movie house, it had a Simplex projector, a Walker screen, and over 200 seats. The Gilbert Theatre operated until at least 1960, as this ticket to a benefit screening reveals. After the venue's closure, the adjoining Ward Hardware expanded into its building. It still stands. (Author's collection.)

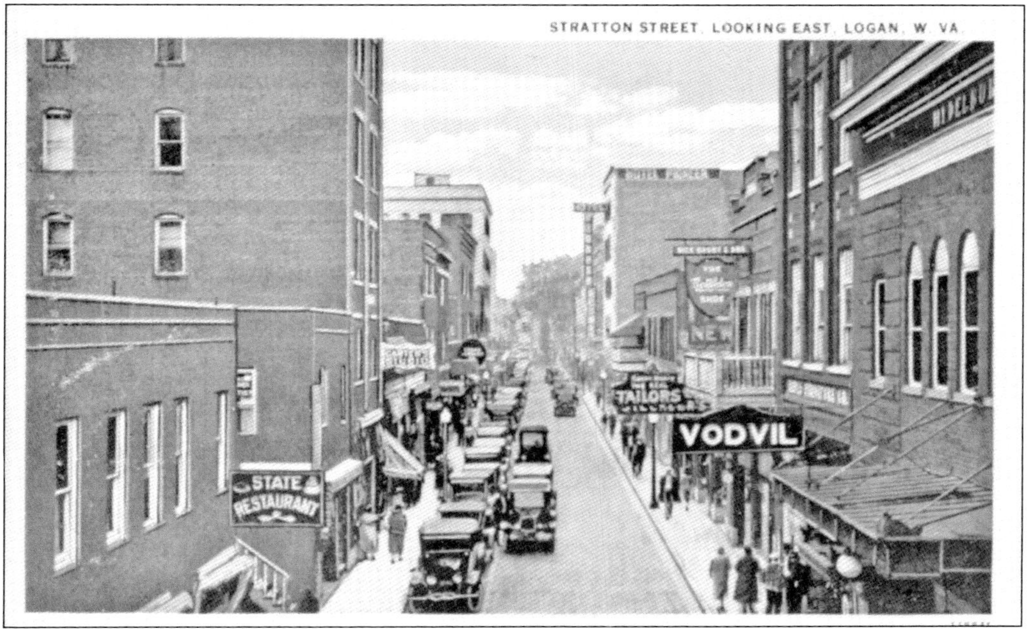

Cincinnati architects C.C. and E.A Weber designed Ferd Midelburg's 800-seat Midelburg Theatre in 1918. The venue, at Stratton and Dingess Streets in Logan, offered film and vaudeville (or, as its sign read, "Vodvil"). Known for playing Westerns, it marketed itself as "Logan's action house" in 1956. It had closed by 1963. After years holding a discount department store, the vacant building is for sale. (Courtesy of West Virginia State Archives, Archives Collection.)

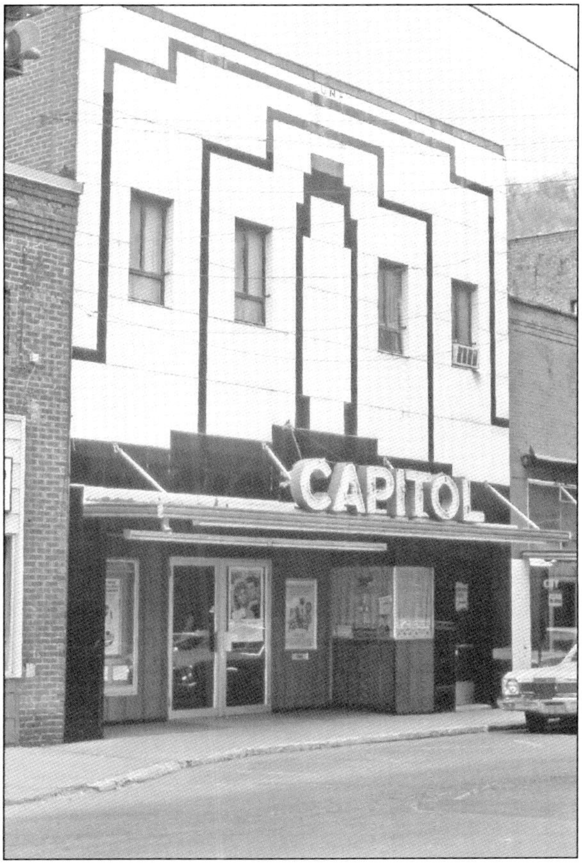

Logan's first Capitol Theatre, part of Ferd Midelburg's circuit, opened in 1925 on Main Street and operated until at least 1963. In the early 1970s, longtime Capitol employee Alex DeFobio opened the second Capitol in this Art Deco storefront on Stratton Street. Showing mostly second-run films, the 174-seat auditorium had a flat floor. It survived until around 1996. The building, its Vitrolite tiles removed, once again has commercial uses. (Courtesy of American Classic Images.)

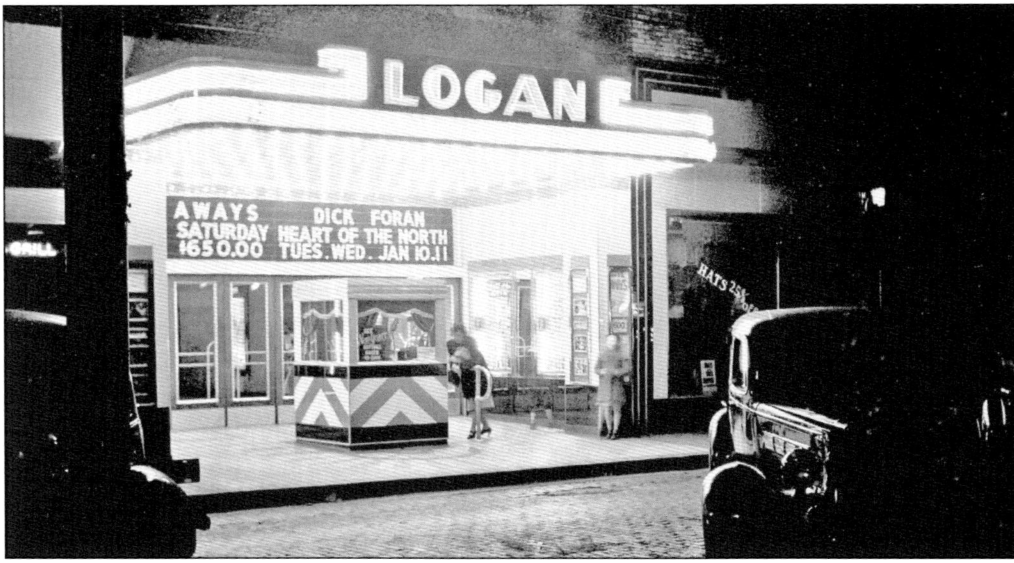

The 1,300-seat, $150,000 Logan Theatre was opened by Ferd Midelburg in October 1938 with *Sing, You Sinners.* Advertisements called it "West Virginia's finest theatre." Designed by Meanor and Handloser, the Art Deco picture palace featured air-conditioning and fire sprinklers—plus a balcony for "colored" patrons. Open into the 1980s, it now serves as a nonprofit music venue, the Coalfield Jamboree. (Courtesy of West Virginia State Archives, Bob Spence Collection.)

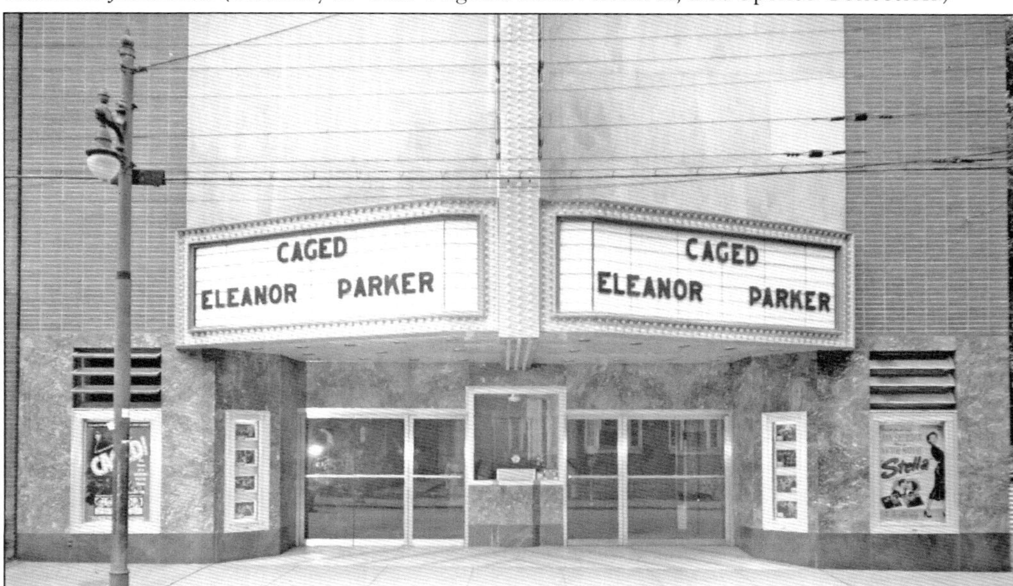

The Newbold-Keesling circuit's short-lived Guyan Theatre opened on Logan's Main Street in 1950. Designed by architect Alex Mahood, the marble-fronted Late Moderne building was billed as a "deluxe first run theatre." Its 1,000-seat auditorium featured massive murals by Chicago's Hanns Teichert Studios, depicting regional history and industry. The Guyan Theatre was remodeled into commercial space in 1960. Its site is now a parking garage. (Courtesy of Eastern Regional Coal Archives.)

This 1950 letter from the Rogers circuit gave Elizabeth Drewry, the state legislature's first elected African American woman, an annual pass to its five movie houses. Those venues included the Man Theatre in the Logan County town of Man. The Man was operating as early as 1926. It then had 200 seats, later expanding to 275. In 1969, the Man was part of the Moore circuit. (Courtesy of Eastern Regional Coal Archives.)

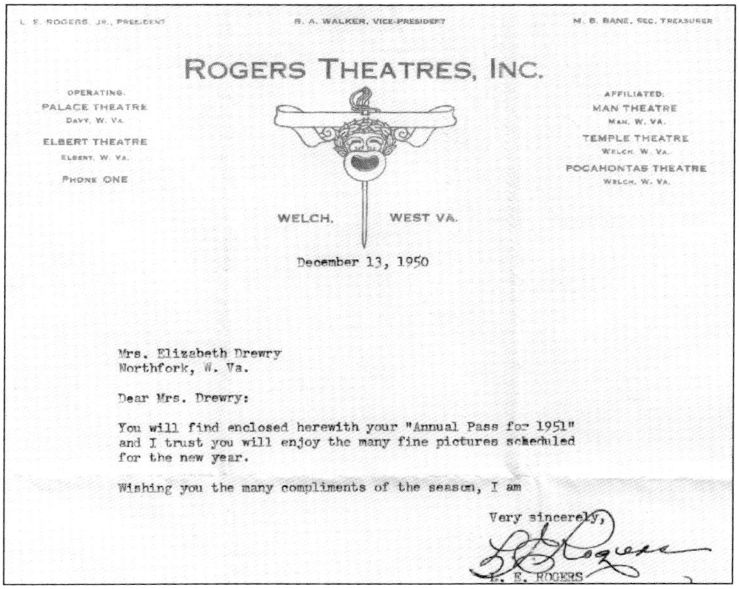

L. E. ROGERS, JR., PRESIDENT R. A. WALKER, VICE-PRESIDENT M. B. BANE, SEC. TREASURER

ROGERS THEATRES, INC.

OPERATING:
PALACE THEATRE
DAVY, W. VA.
ELBERT THEATRE
ELBERT, W. VA.
PHONE ONE

AFFILIATED:
MAN THEATRE
MAN, W. VA.
TEMPLE THEATRE
WELCH, W. VA.
POCAHONTAS THEATRE
WELCH, W. VA.

WELCH, WEST VA.

December 13, 1950

Mrs. Elizabeth Drewry
Northfork, W. Va.

Dear Mrs. Drewry:

You will find enclosed herewith your "Annual Pass for 1951" and I trust you will enjoy the many fine pictures scheduled for the new year.

Wishing you the many compliments of the season, I am

Very sincerely,

L. E. ROGERS

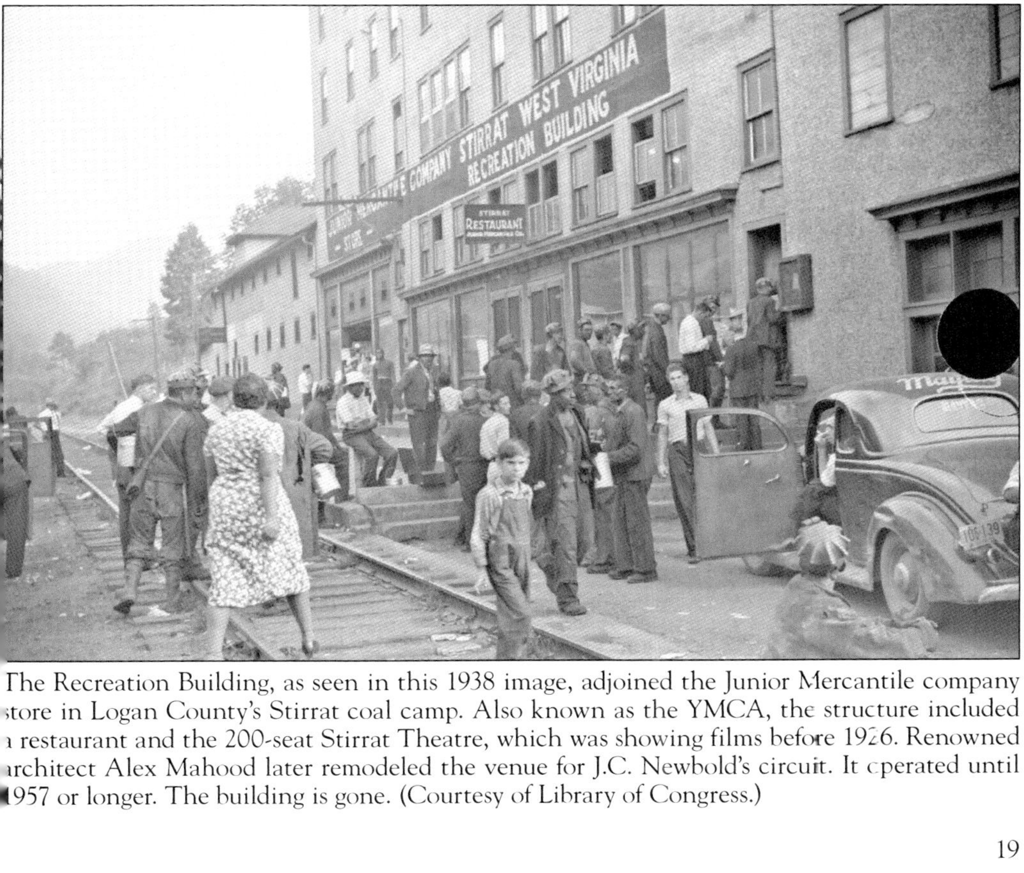

The Recreation Building, as seen in this 1938 image, adjoined the Junior Mercantile company store in Logan County's Stirrat coal camp. Also known as the YMCA, the structure included a restaurant and the 200-seat Stirrat Theatre, which was showing films before 1926. Renowned architect Alex Mahood later remodeled the venue for J.C. Newbold's circuit. It operated until 1957 or longer. The building is gone. (Courtesy of Library of Congress.)

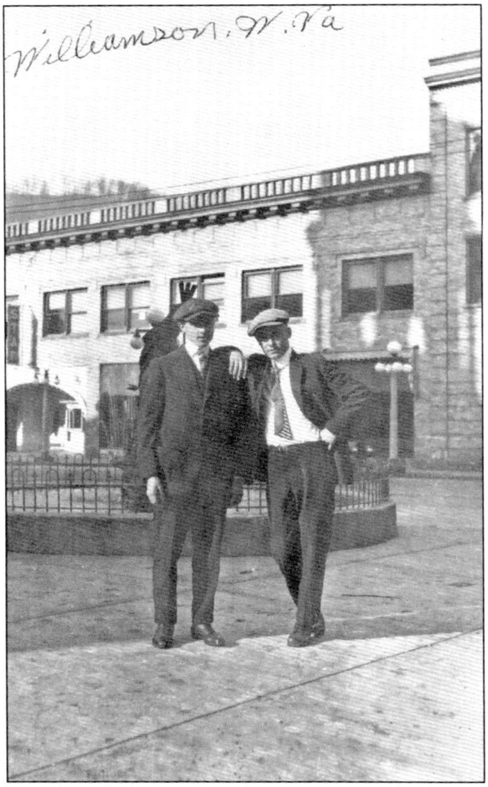

E.R. Leroy owned the short-lived Star Theatre in Williamson. It opened after the 1911 opening of the city's first nickelodeon, the Hippodrome. In 1915, Leroy announced that he was closing the Star and buying its competitor instead. This photograph shows the Star behind employees of brickmason Thoney Pietro's Morgantown-based company, which paved much of Williamson in 1915. (Courtesy of West Virginia & Regional History Center, WVU Libraries.)

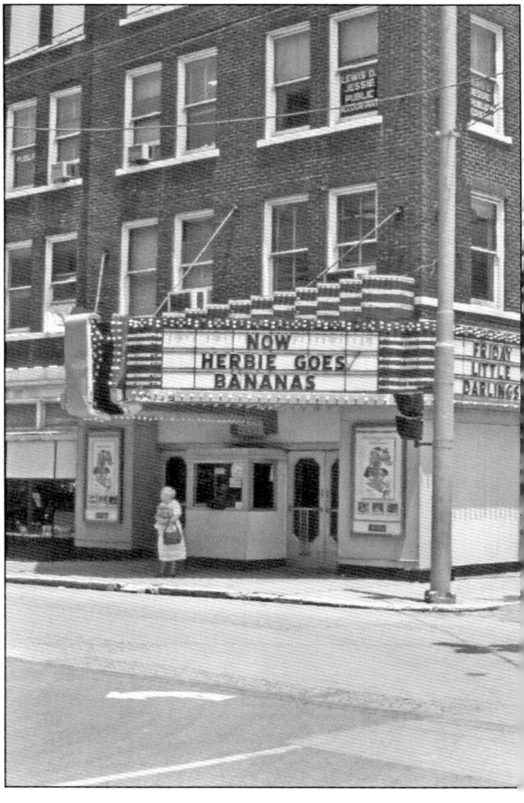

In 1921, Hyman Banks closed the Hippodrome and opened the 1,000-seat Cinderella Theatre in the new Patterson Building. The Cinderella closed in 1984 after flooding in Williamson; its seats were removed and its floor leveled. In 1998, a couple leased the space to reopen it as the Cinderella Opry House but faced financial and logistical challenges. The venue is vacant, except for some usage as a bingo hall. (Courtesy of American Classic Images.)

Three

Metro Valley

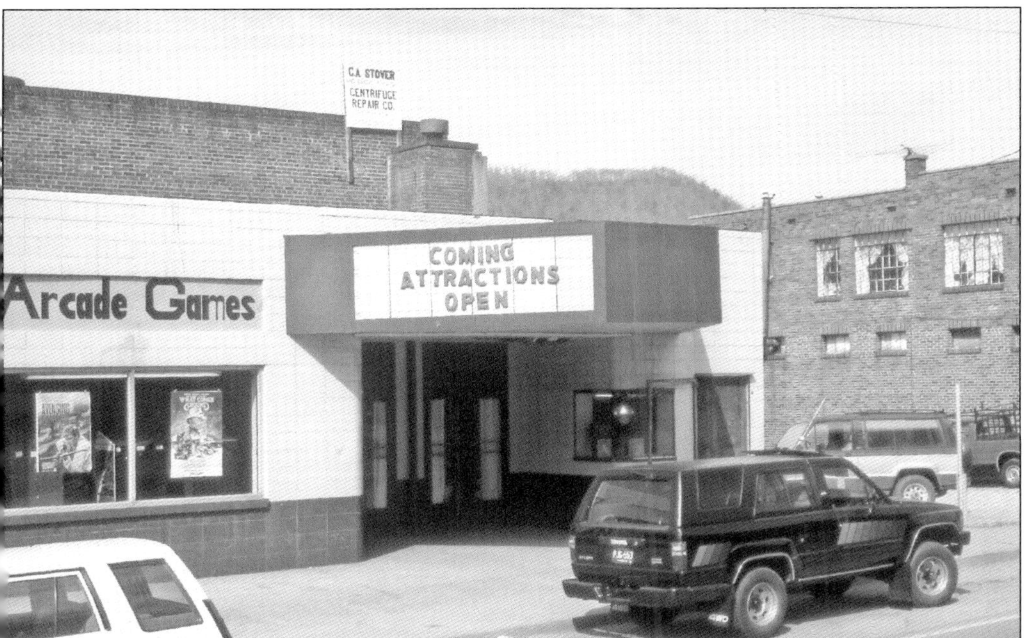

In 1933 in Cabin Creek, D.E. Brown purchased Robert Wilson's 300-seat Wilson Theatre and renamed it. Listings then showed it as the Brown, Brown's, or Browns Theatre. A 1941 fire destroyed the movie house's entire block. Brown's rebuilt venue operated into the 1970s, when it was briefly called the Seventh Heaven Theatre. The building has since hosted commercial uses, like the video store in this 1985 image. (Courtesy of American Classic Images.)

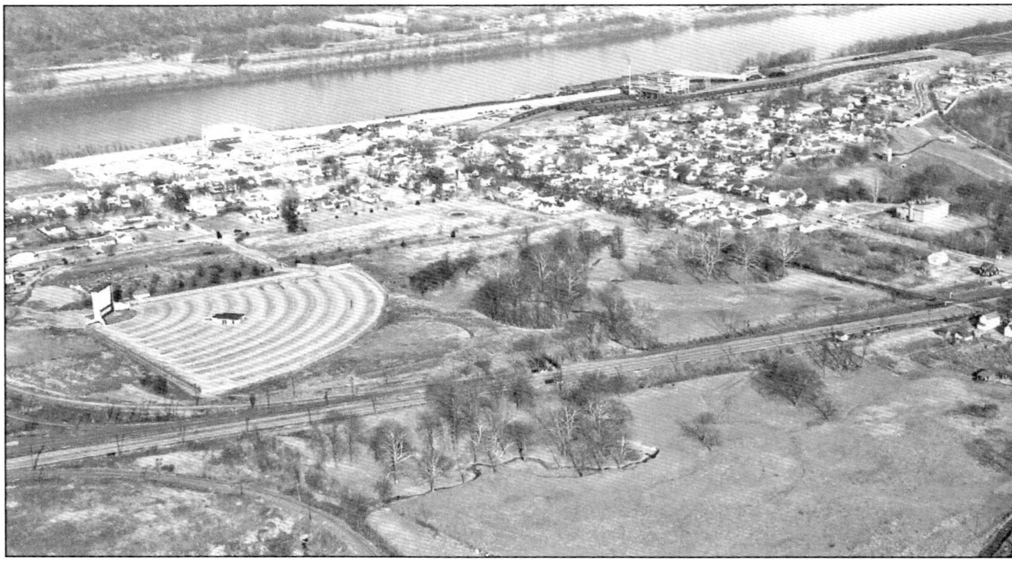

This aerial photograph shows the Ceredo Drive-in Theatre, located along Route 60 in the Huntington suburb of Ceredo. The area's very first drive-in, it opened on a former golf course's site in June 1948. Holding 750 cars, it was part of the Hyman family's regional theatre circuit. The Ceredo Drive-in closed in 1975, replaced by the Ceredo Plaza Shopping Center. (Courtesy of *Herald-Dispatch*.)

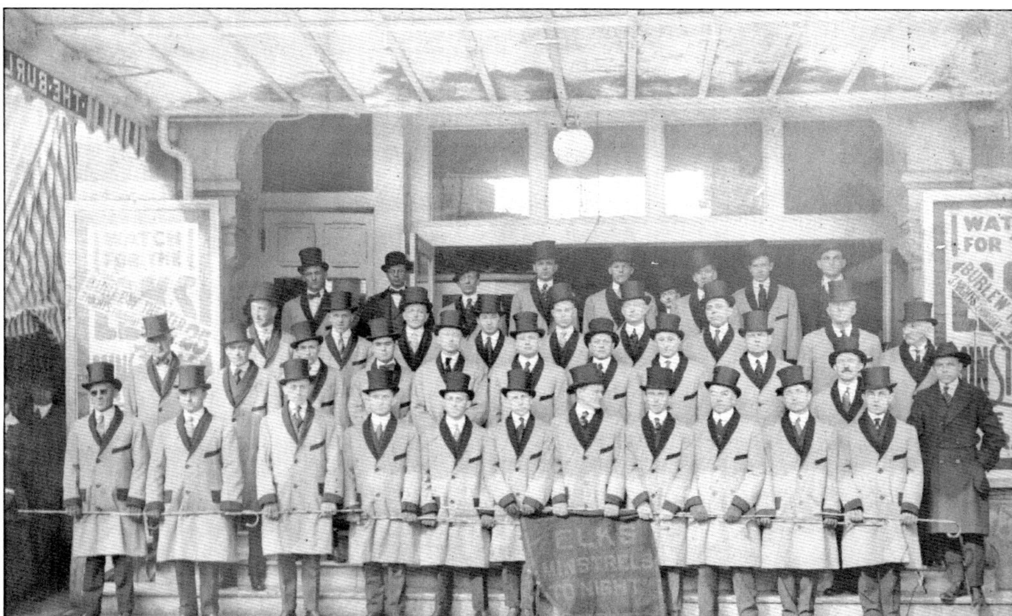

Charleston's Burlew Opera House, later the Burlew Theatre, was opened in 1891 by Gen. N.S. Burlew. In addition to live entertainment, it began showing films in 1906. In 1918, T.L. Kearse took over, announcing a remodel and an expansion from 1,600 to 2,000 seats. Its June 1919 reopening promised a 16-piece orchestra accompanying "the highest type of photoplay." Nonetheless, the Burlew soon closed, and it was demolished by 1920. (Author's collection.)

Dreamland, one of Charleston's earliest movie venues, was on Capitol Street's 200 block (adjacent to Hotel Fleetwood, on the left). A 1907 *Billboard* issue relayed, "Business good with songs and moving pictures." A 1908 update stated that it was "drawing crowded houses with electric pictures and illustrated songs" (involving the audience singing along to onscreen lyrics). The nickelodeon did not last long. (Courtesy of Theatre Historical Society of America, Editor's Collection.)

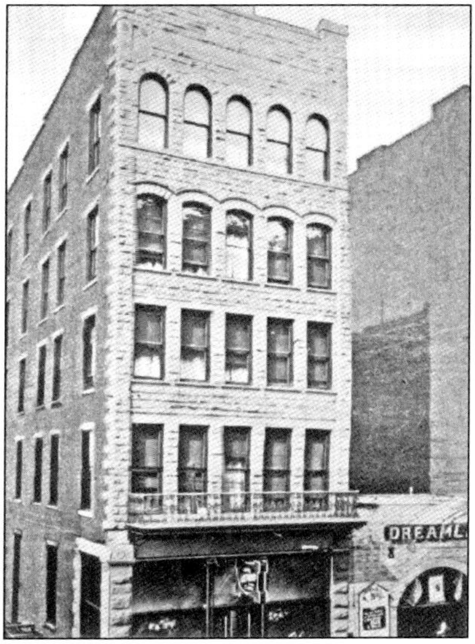

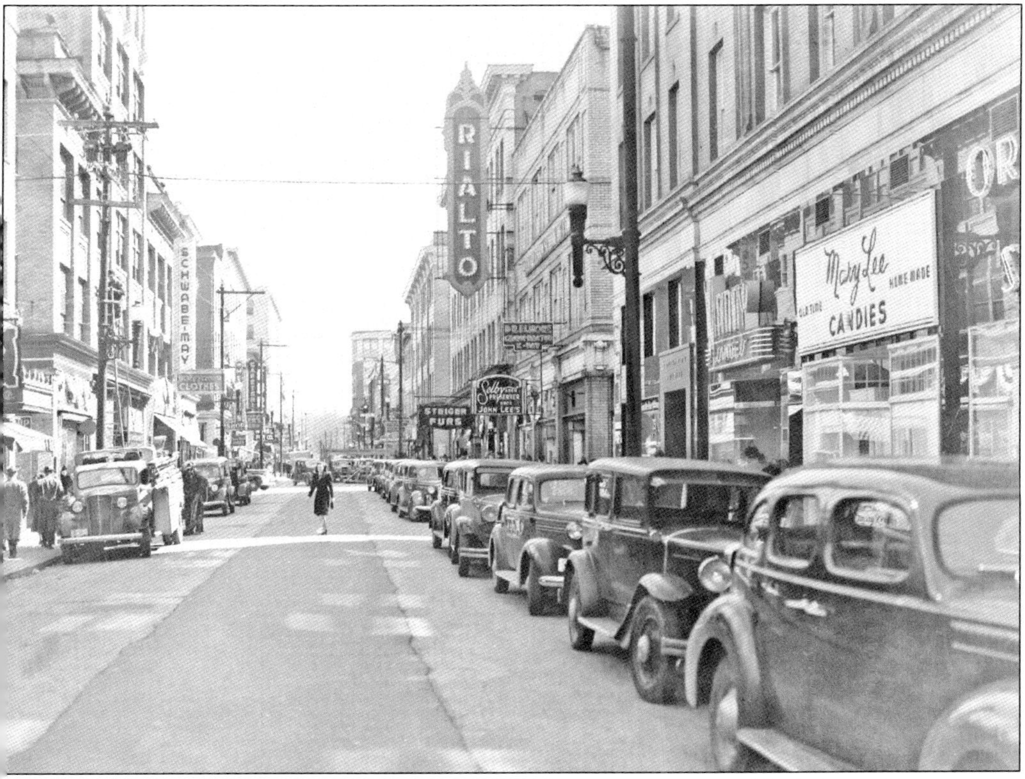

Built in 1917, the 800-seat Rialto Theatre in Charleston was operated by Warner Bros. and its spin-offs from 1930 until 1968—when the theatre showed adult movies. The Charleston Repertory Cinema opened there in 1969, closing in 1970. Owens Midtown Theatre then came in; before its 1975 closure, it was playing both mainstream and X-rated films. The theatre's Morrison Building, located at 815 Quarrier Street, is part of the Downtown Charleston Historic District. (Courtesy of West Virginia State Archives, W.E. Mohler Collection.)

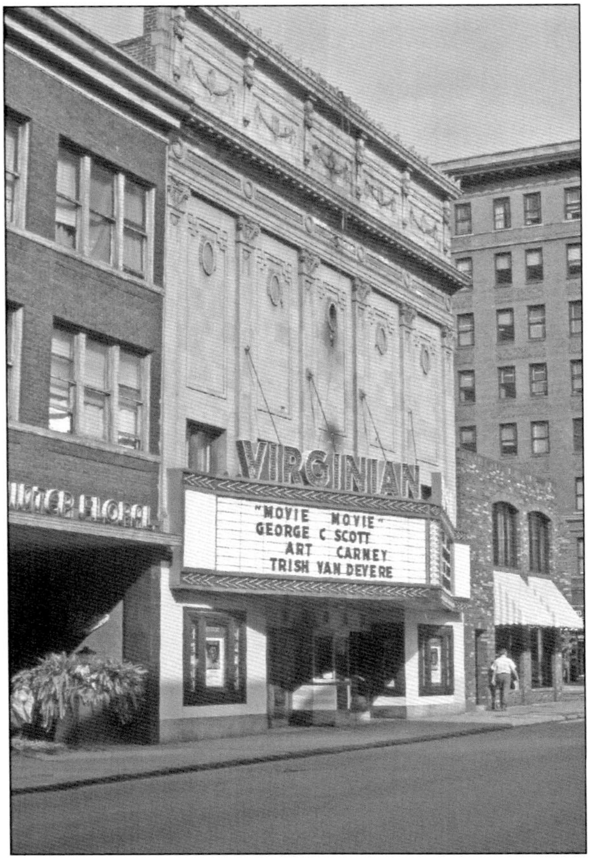

Charleston's Virginian Theatre opened on November 20, 1922, showing *Smilin' Through*. The 1,100-seat Classical Revival venue on Lee Street featured a pipe organ, marble floors, and Charleston's biggest electric sign. In 1983, the Cinemette circuit closed the Virginian and sold it to a developer—who, in 1989, announced plans to raze the vacant building for a parking lot. Preservationists encouraged maintaining or salvaging the facade, but the Virginian soon fell. (Courtesy of American Classic Images.)

T.L. Kearse opened Charleston's Strand Theatre on a prominent Summers Street corner in 1916. The movie house was known for its silent-film orchestra. By 1931, it was renamed the New Greenbrier Theatre, which operated until at least 1956. In the early 1960s, it was known as the Temple Theatre. Its block was destroyed in 1965 for a bank's parking facility. (Courtesy of West Virginia and Regional History Center, WVU Libraries.)

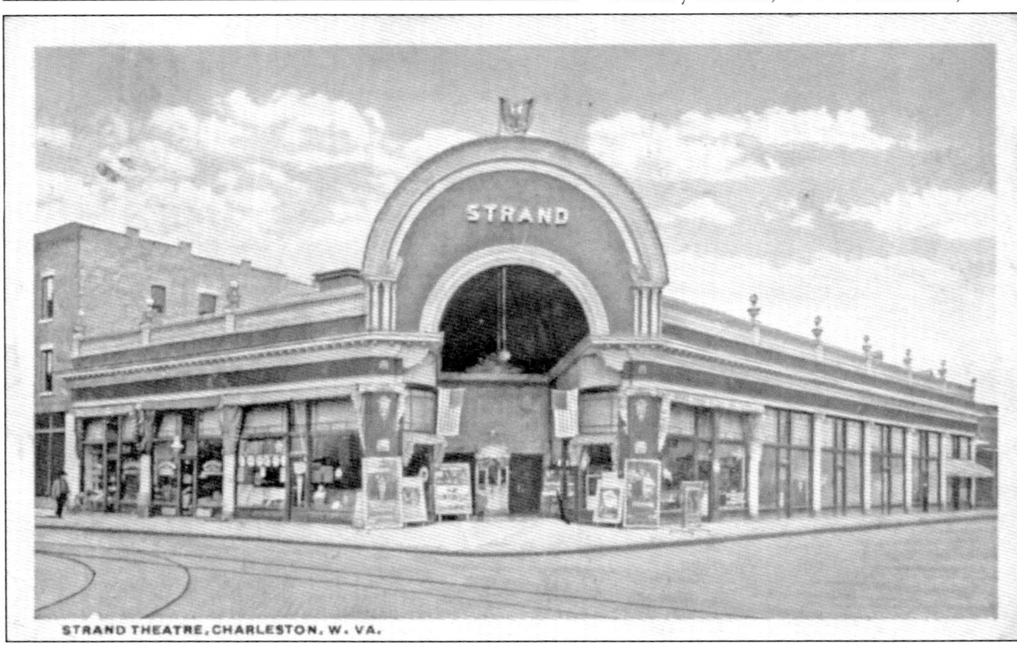

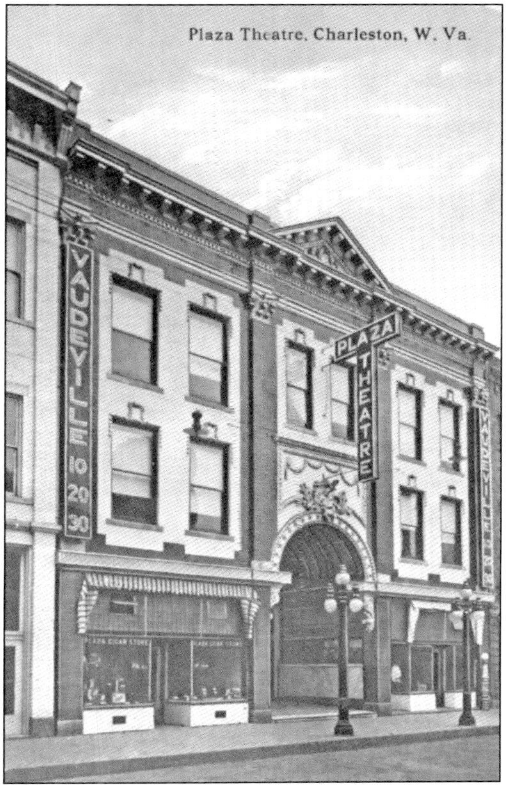

Charleston's 1912 Plaza Theatre has had multiple incarnations. The Classical Revival vaudeville venue closed in 1919, reopening in 1921 as the Capitol Theatre. Additions included a projection room, Wurlitzer pipe organ, marquee, and 30-foot-high blade sign. More remodeling occurred in 1923 and 1956. The 1,165-seat movie theatre closed in 1982. In 1985, it became Capitol Plaza Music Hall. After the performing arts center's 1991 closure, the property was donated to West Virginia State College (now University). Called WVSU Capitol Center, the 800-seat auditorium then hosted student plays, the annual West Virginia International Film Festival, and rentals. In 2018, the university sold the operational facility to a local church, which plans to use it as a sanctuary while also continuing its usage as a rental venue. (Right, courtesy of West Virginia State Archives, Archives Collection; below, courtesy of American Classic Images.)

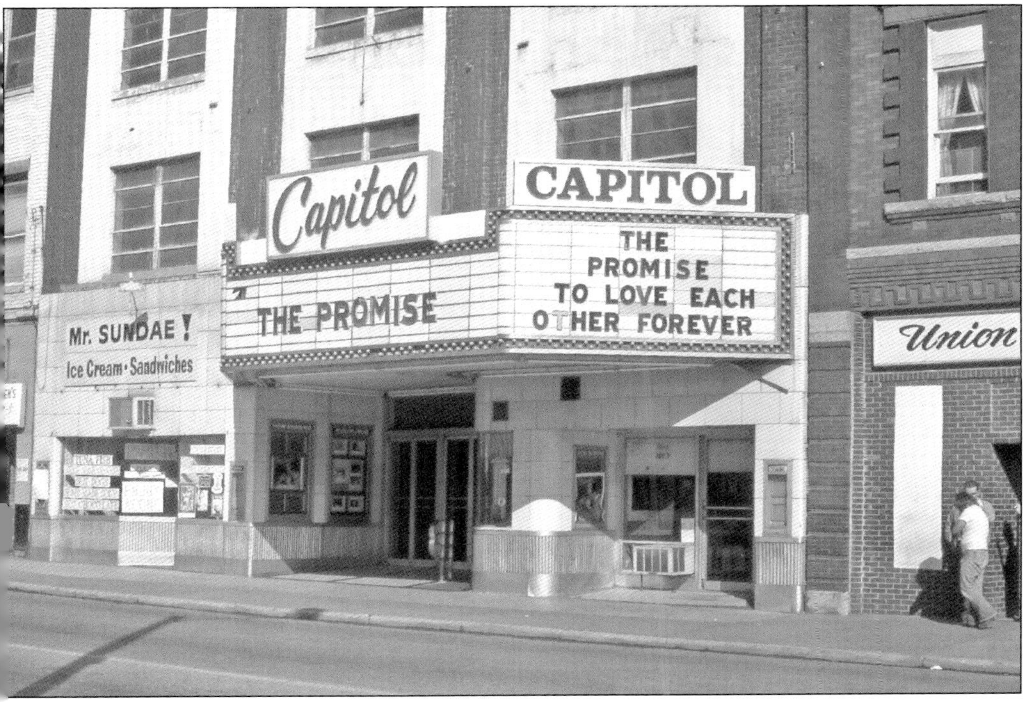

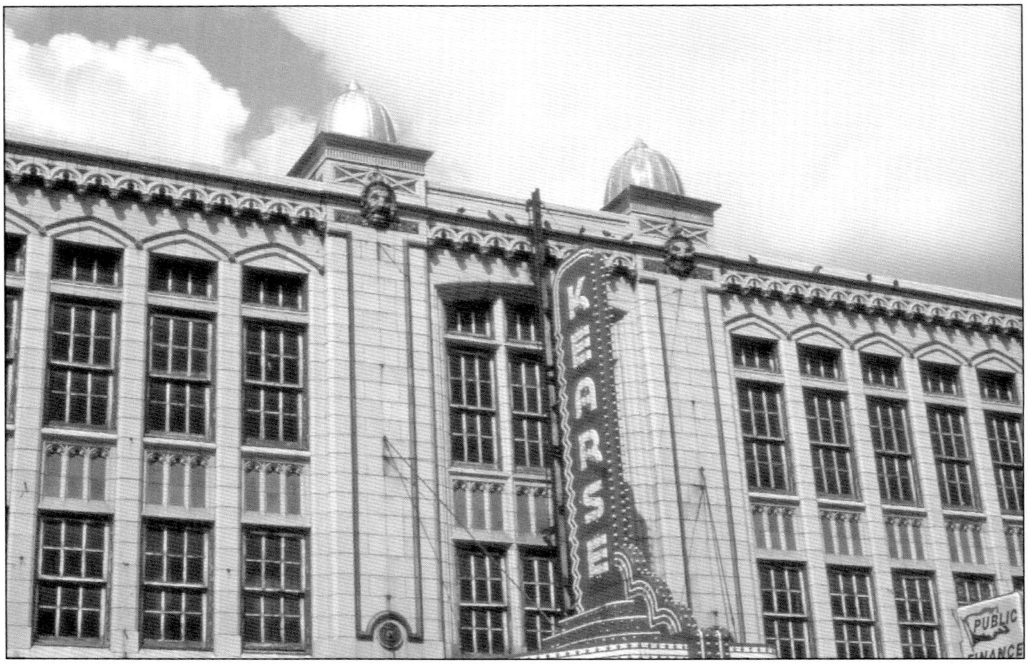

With its 1922 opening on Charleston's Summers Street, T.L. Kearse's 2,000-seat Kearse Theatre became West Virginia's largest movie theatre (containing the state's biggest theatre pipe organ). Architects Mills and Millspaugh's Gothic picture palace, featuring decorative terra-cotta, ornamental plasterwork, and marble accents, received an Art Deco marquee and blade sign in 1938. The Kearse closed in 1979. Preservationists could not stop its 1982 destruction for parking. (Courtesy of Michael Gioulis.)

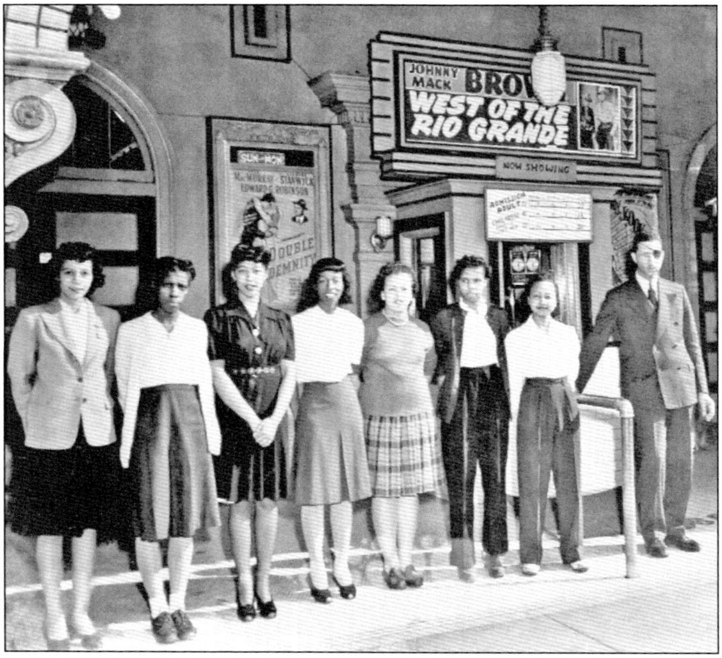

John C. Norman, West Virginia's first African American licensed architect, designed the Ferguson Theatre as part of the 1922 Ferguson Hotel building. Located in the Block, a segregated neighborhood, the movie house was frequented by Charleston's black population. This photograph shows theatre employees around 1944. The venue, with over 350 seats, operated until around 1956. The Ferguson Hotel burned in 1966 and was demolished. (Courtesy of West Virginia State Archives, L. Bernidean Brown Collection.)

The Lyric Theatre opened on Charleston's Summers Street in 1923. The Bramwell Theatres circuit purchased it in 1938, giving it new equipment and an Art Deco remodel by Alex Mahood. This 1939 image depicts the 500-seat movie house touting its first-run films. About 1969, the Lyric began showing X-rated films, continuing that policy until it caught fire in 1975 and was bulldozed. (Courtesy of West Virginia State Archives, W.E. Mohler Collection.)

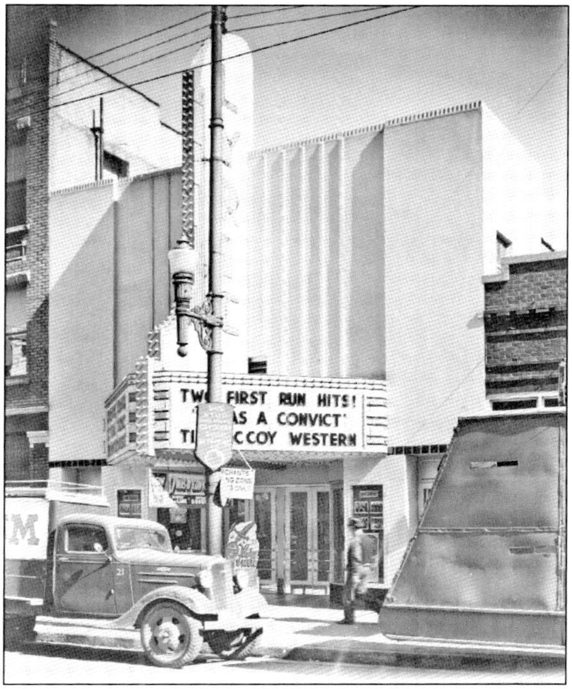

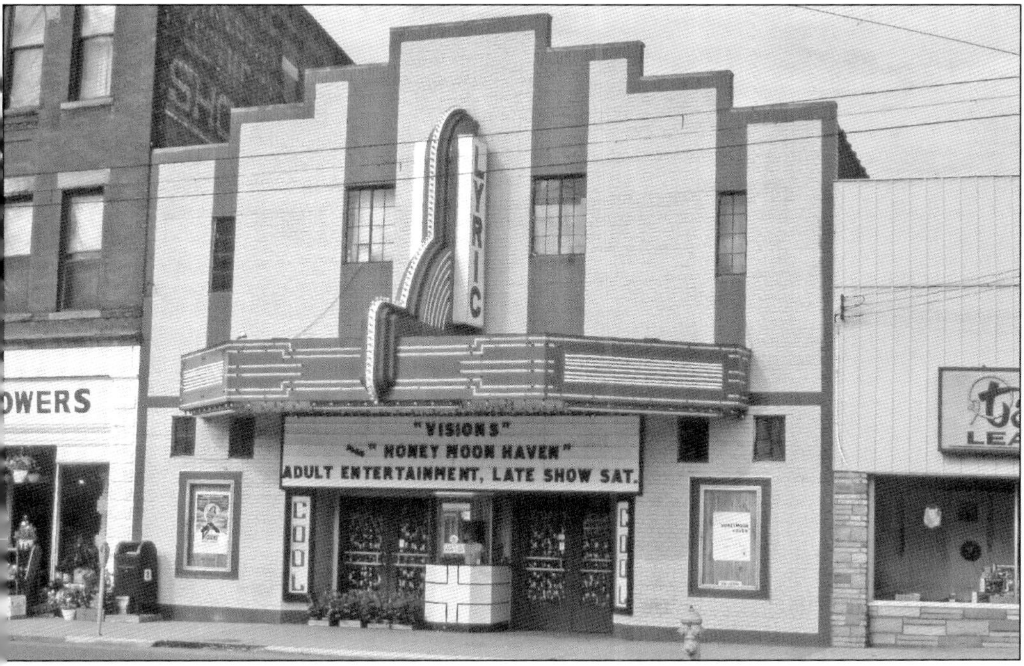

Charleston's 550-seat Custer Theatre, built in 1938, changed names multiple times, first to the Robinson Theatre in 1972 and then to the West Side Cinema. In 1975, despite protests, the burned Lyric Theatre's adult-movie operation moved there. Called the New Lyric, it operated until around 1985. By then, a metal slipcover (since removed) hid its Art Deco facade. The building—now offices—is part of the Elk City Historic District. (Courtesy of American Classic Images.)

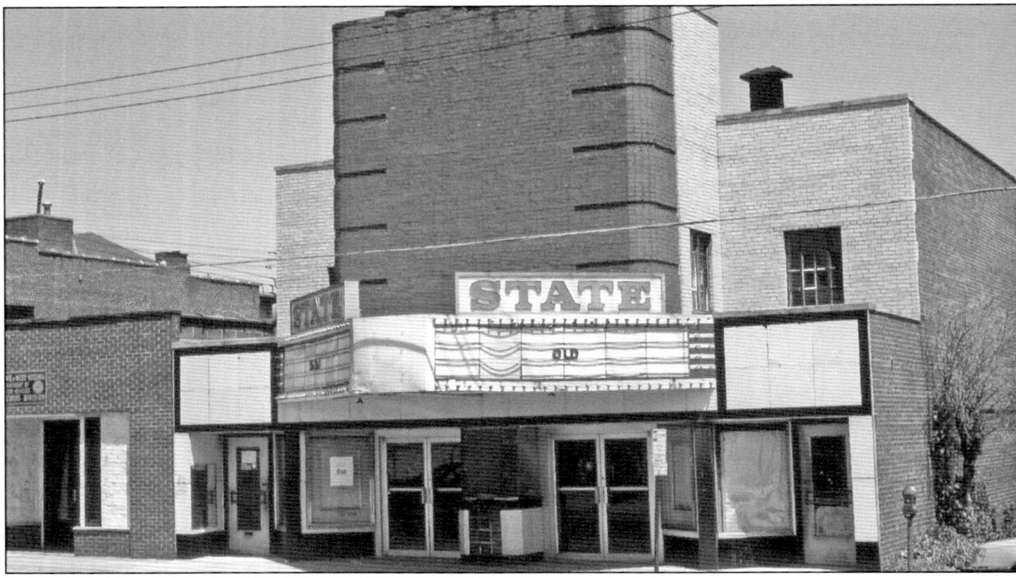

The State Theatre opened on September 13, 1939, offering air-conditioning and 25¢ admission for *Love Affair*. The 680-seat Art Deco neighborhood theatre in Charleston's East End closed in 1983. It was vacant (as seen in this 1986 photograph) until 2005. It then became offices following a facade restoration, which included replacing the State's Vitrolite tiles and replicating its original blade sign, entry doors, and ticket booth. (Courtesy of American Classic Images.)

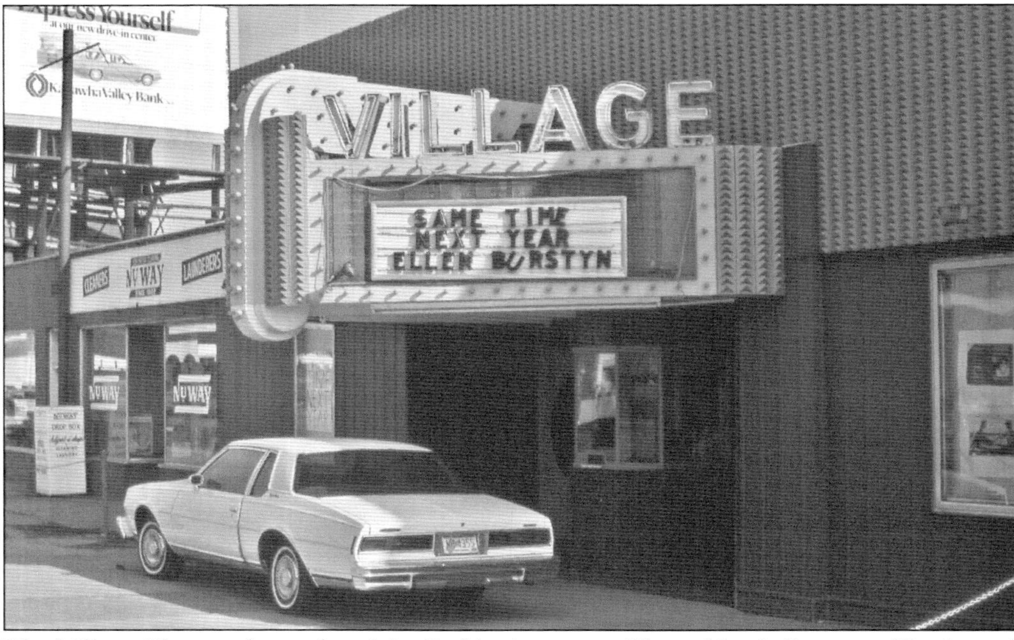

The Village Theatre, located on MacCorkle Avenue at Thirty-Ninth Street in Charleston's Kanawha City neighborhood, opened on April 2, 1941, with a screening of *Rhythm on the River*. The 500-seat movie house featured loveseats, air-conditioning, and a nursery room. By the time of this 1979 image, a metal slipcover rested on the Village's facade. Its marquee sat empty by 1985. The now-reused building is unrecognizable. (Courtesy of American Classic Images.)

Huntington's Lyric Theatre, the first venue in Abe and Sol Hyman's major circuit, was built in 1910. During construction, two men working on the Fourth Avenue nickelodeon's facade died when scaffolding broke. In 1913, the theatre survived a major flood. Following a 1915 interior remodel, it received a $100,000 addition designed by Meanor and Handloser in 1921. The 1,000-seat Lyric closed in 1931. (Courtesy of Marshall University Archives and Special Collections, 1975.0099.10.03.02.)

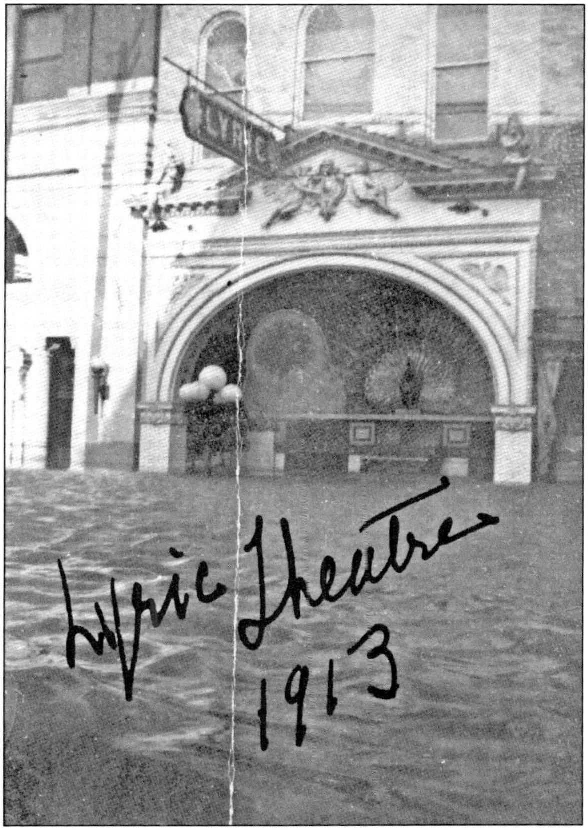

In this 1914 image, a band plays in front of the Huntington Hippodrome's stage. A vaudeville venue as early as 1909, it was playing movies by 1918. In 1919, it burned down. The Hippodrome was rebuilt and was later operated by the Hymans' circuit. It stopped appearing in listings around 1929, not making the transition to sound films. (Courtesy of Marshall University Archives and Special Collections, 1979.01.0255.24.12.01.)

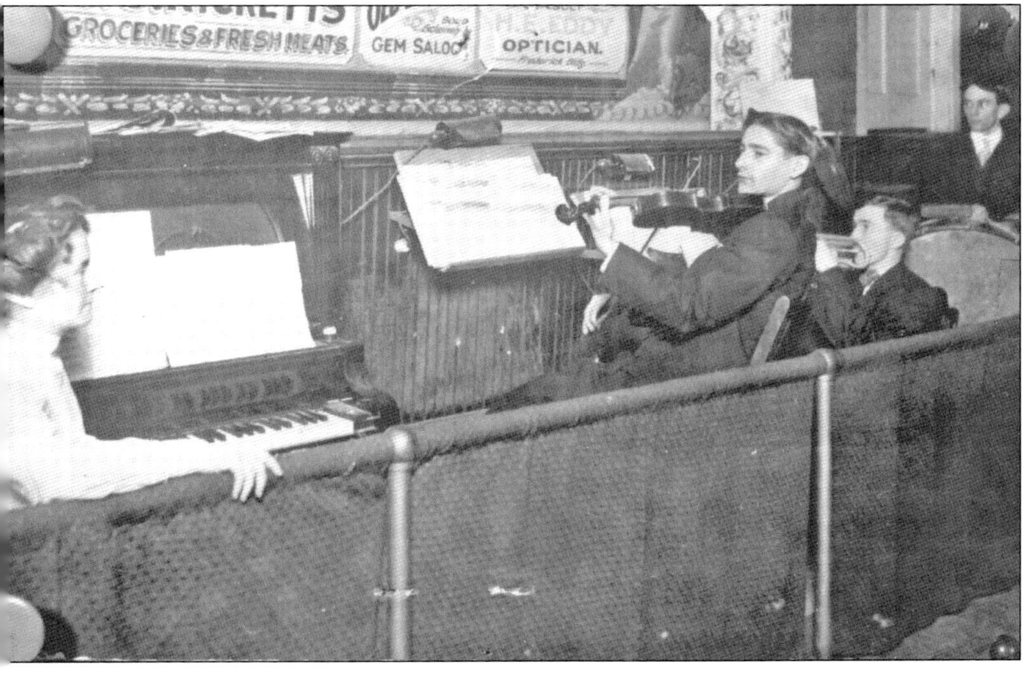

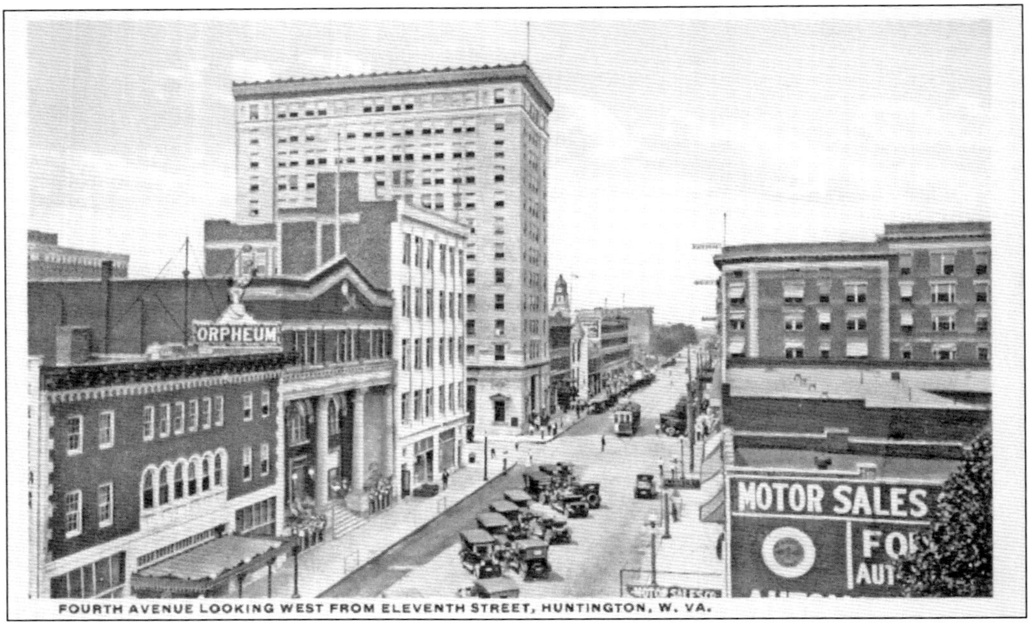

FOURTH AVENUE LOOKING WEST FROM ELEVENTH STREET, HUNTINGTON, W. VA.

The Orpheum Theatre opened in Huntington in March 1916 with the film *Peggy*. Architect Verus T. Ritter designed the vaudeville and film venue for his cousin, owner Charles Lloyd Ritter. A year later, the Hyman family took control. In 1930, the 1,200-seat Orpheum was remodeled; among other enhancements, it gained a marquee with space for film titles (unlike its earlier canopy, shown above). Sometime between 1965 and 1969, the Orpheum was renamed as the Cinema Theatre. The many-windowed historic building also received a massive remake, giving its facade the plain, boxlike appearance seen below. Later, the Cinema was multiplexed, divided into four screening areas. By the time Derek Hyman closed it in 2011, it was operating as a discount second-run movie house. Today, still looking like this 1985 photograph, the structure holds a church. (Above, author's collection; below, courtesy of American Classic Images.)

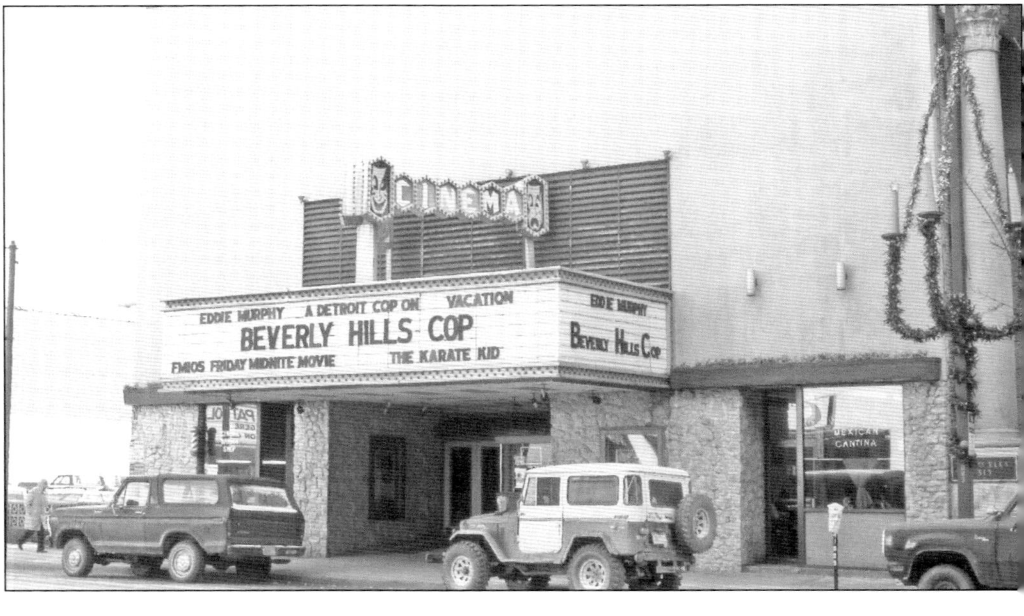

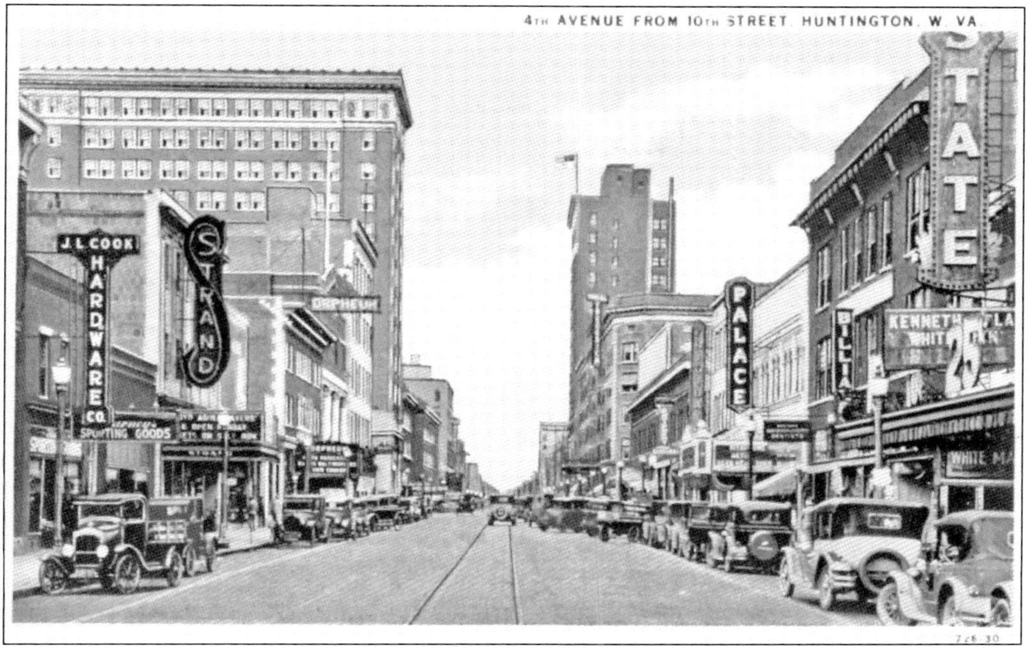

In the above postcard, the Strand Theatre stands among three other Huntington movie houses on one entertainment-filled block of Fourth Avenue. The 900-seat Strand opened on July 7, 1924. *Moving Picture World* noted that 2,500 people crammed themselves into "every nook and corner of the beautiful new house" in order to see an unnamed "photoplay bill" and musical performances. The Strand added Vitaphone sound equipment in 1927 and became part of Smith Amusement's circuit in 1930. It had closed by 1933, when C. Bertram Hukle bought, remodeled, and renamed it. It reopened in August as the Roxy Theatre, featuring Katharine Hepburn's first film, *Bill of Divorcement*. A 1952 fire, seen below, caused the Roxy's closure. The building later housed a bank; a parking lot finally replaced it. (Above, courtesy of Theatre Historical Society of America, Postcard Collection; below, courtesy of *Herald-Dispatch*.)

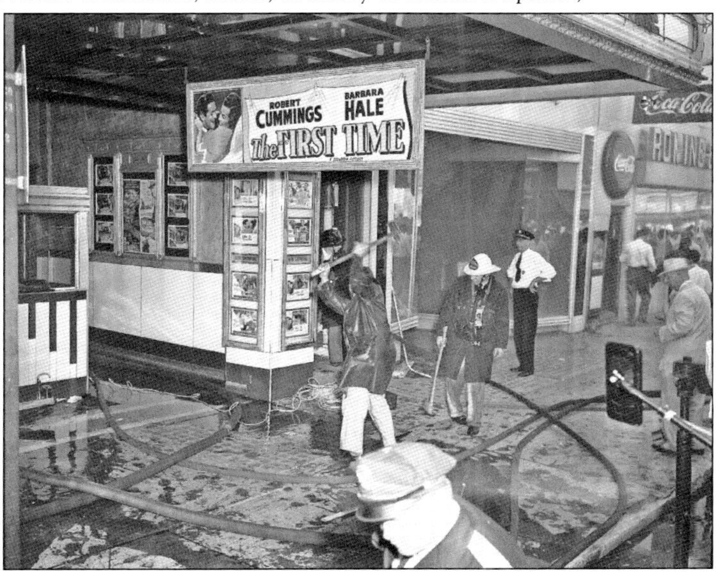

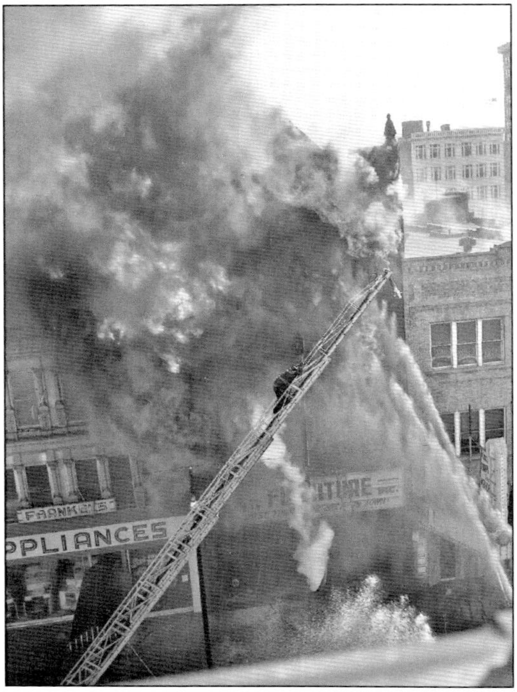

This undated photograph shows Huntington's Rialto Theatre (right), with its marquee surrounded by smoke from the adjacent furniture store's fire. The 450-seat movie house, owned by L.G. Mantho, opened in May 1926. Before the Rialto got sound equipment in 1930, music teacher Gertrude Riley played the piano during silent films. The Rialto was still operating in 1956. Its building on Third Avenue's 1000 block is now gone. (Courtesy of *Herald-Dispatch*.)

The 800-seat State Theatre is seen here during the Great Ohio River Flood of 1937. (The State and other Huntington movie houses wisely removed their seats and equipment when waters starting rising.) A 1943 fire caused $20,000 damage to the State, which opened around 1923. The venue, part of the Hyman family's circuit, no longer appeared under their name by 1965. (Courtesy of Marshall University Archives and Special Collections, 1978.0227.02.07.03.)

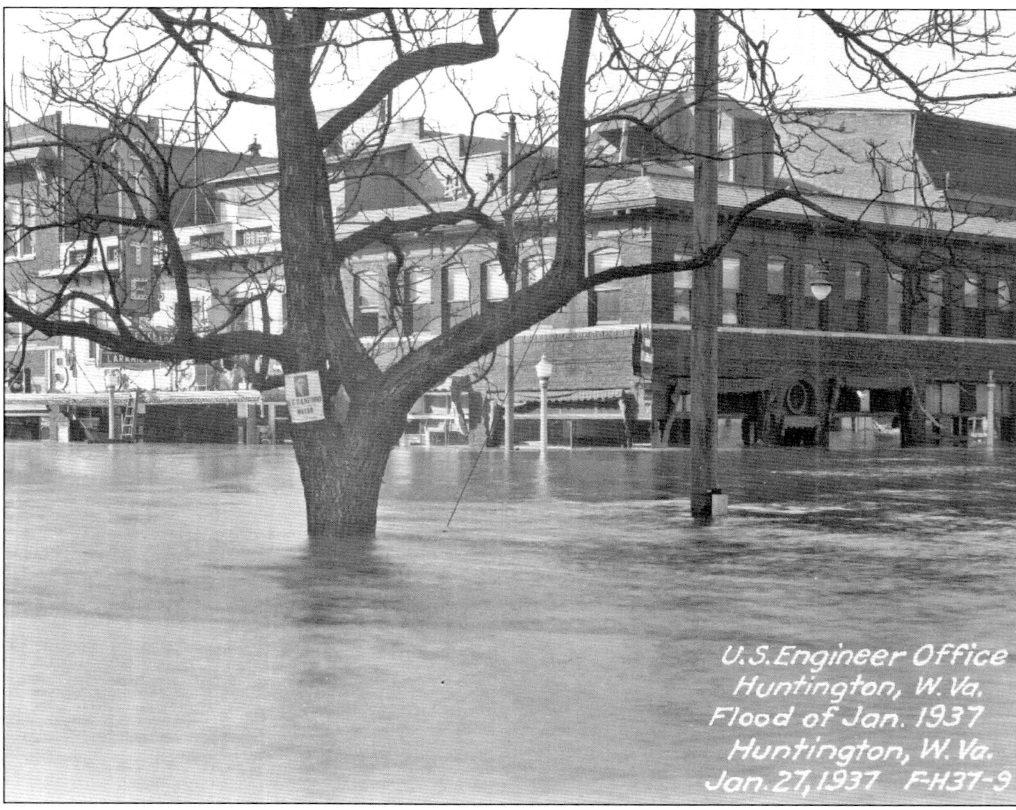

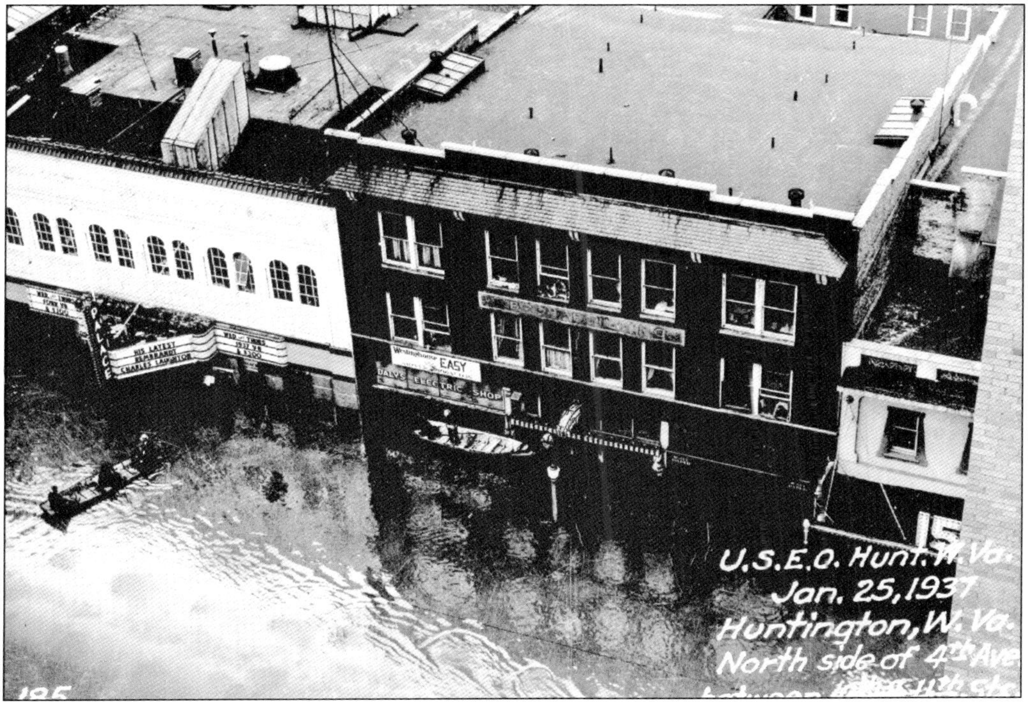

In the above 1937 flood photograph, the 1,390-seat Palace Theatre's marquee advertises not just a film but giveaways. The prizes probably related to the movie house's $15,000 redesign, finished a week earlier. The Smith Amusement circuit's Huntington venue opened on November 15, 1925, with marble trim on the walls, bronze poster cases, and a box office accented with bronze and gold. The streamline moderne marquee was likely added during the 1937 remodel. Between 1969 and 1976, the Hyman circuit renamed the Palace the Camelot, redoing its façade with the knight theme seen in the 1985 image below. Facing competition from a new multiplex, the Camelot closed in 2006. Fourth Avenue Arts now holds dance classes and performances inside The building's original brickwork was recently uncovered. (Above, courtesy of Marshall University Archives and Special Collections, 1975.0099.11.18.03; below, courtesy of American Classic Images.)

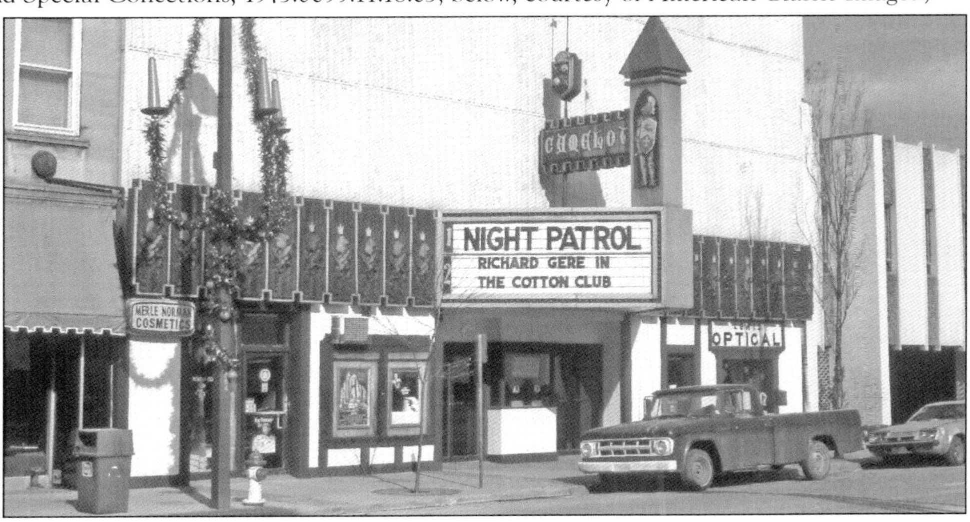

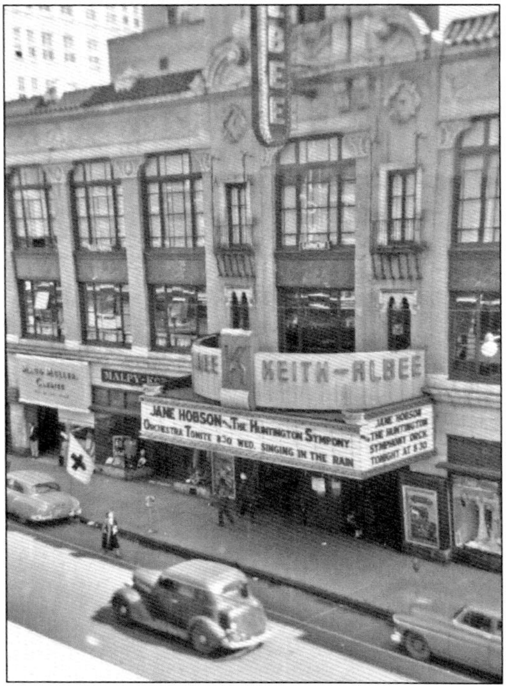

The Hyman brothers opened Huntington's $2 million Keith-Albee Theatre, named after the Keith-Albee vaudeville circuit, on May 8, 1928. Thomas Lamb, one of the nation's most renowned movie theatre architects, created the 2,622-seat Spanish baroque picture palace. Its "atmospheric" auditorium replicated a courtyard setting, complete with a star-covered ceiling. The Keith-Albee hosted film premieres and preview screenings for movies about, or written by, West Virginians (1969's *Bridge at Remagen*, 1988's *Rain Man*, and 2006's *We Are Marshall*). In the 1970s, its auditorium was carefully split to hold three screens. The Hymans closed the theatre in 2006, donating it to a foundation. Today, its auditorium restored and its Wurlitzer pipe organ reinstalled after being absent for decades, it serves as the Keith-Albee Performing Arts Center. (Left, courtesy of Marshall University Archives and Special Collections, 1981.05.0332.06.25.01; below, courtesy of West Virginia State Archives, Keith-Albee Collection.)

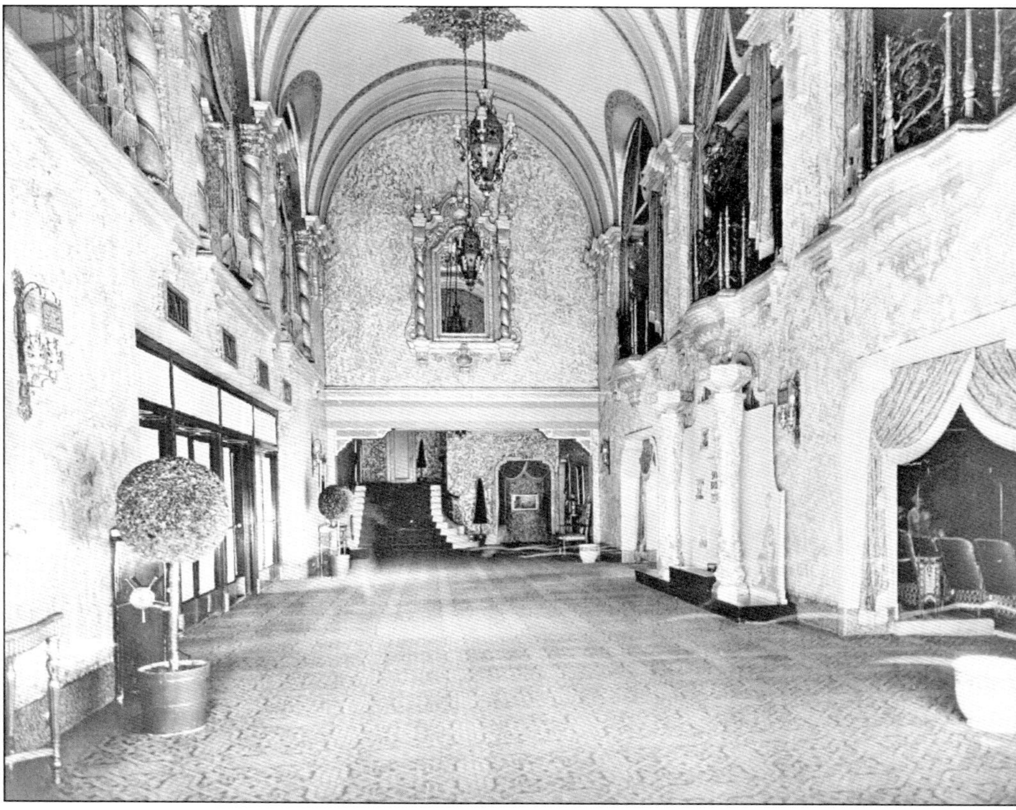

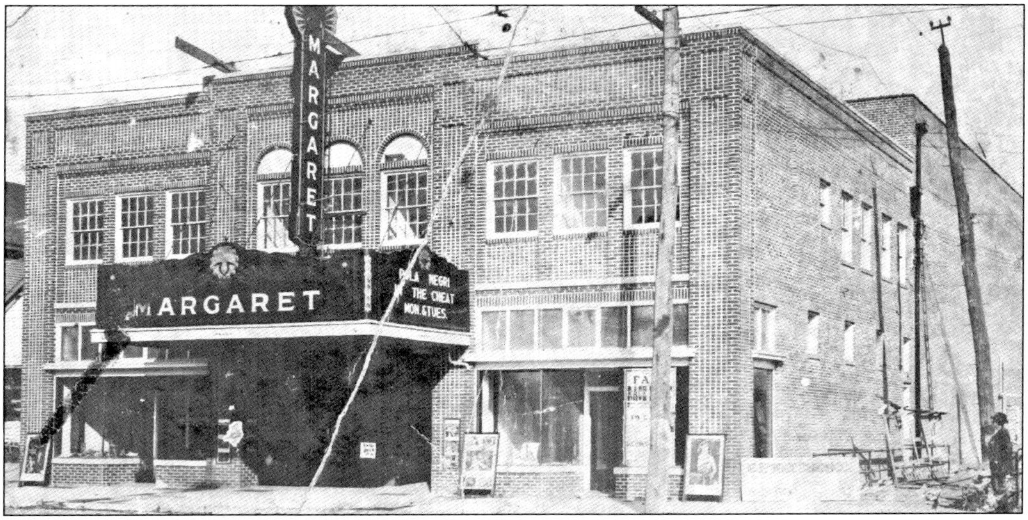

The Margaret Theatre, a Huntington neighborhood movie house, was at the corner of Twentieth Street and Eighth Avenue. William E. Deegans opened the 500-seat, $75,000 venue, named after his wife, in 1923. It played first-run fare until its renaming as the Uptown Theatre around 1940. Known for Westerns and serials, the Uptown survived into the 1950s. The building had commercial uses until 2016; it is now vacant and for sale. (Courtesy of Skip Deegans.)

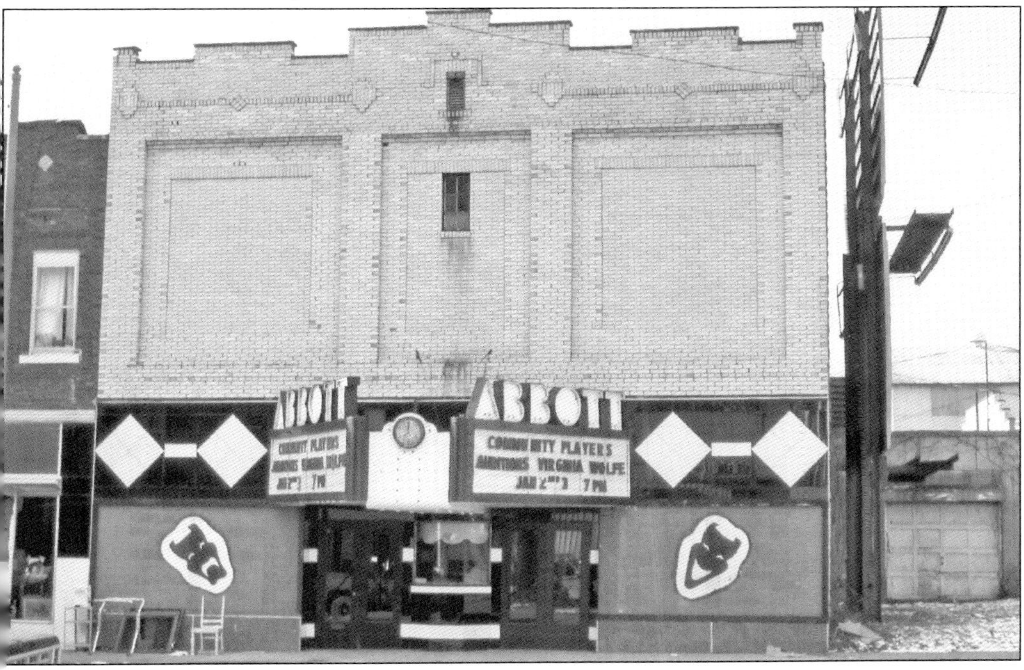

W.E. Neal's $17,000 Abbott Theatre opened in 1938 on Fourteenth Street in Huntington's West End neighborhood. The 300-seat Art Deco movie house played second-run films until 1951. Shortly thereafter, it became the Community Players' playhouse, hosting performances until the early 1990s. After the vacant building suffered two fires and vandalism, it was condemned in 1994. Attempts to find a buyer or restorer were unsuccessful, and the Abbott fell. (Courtesy of American Classic Images.)

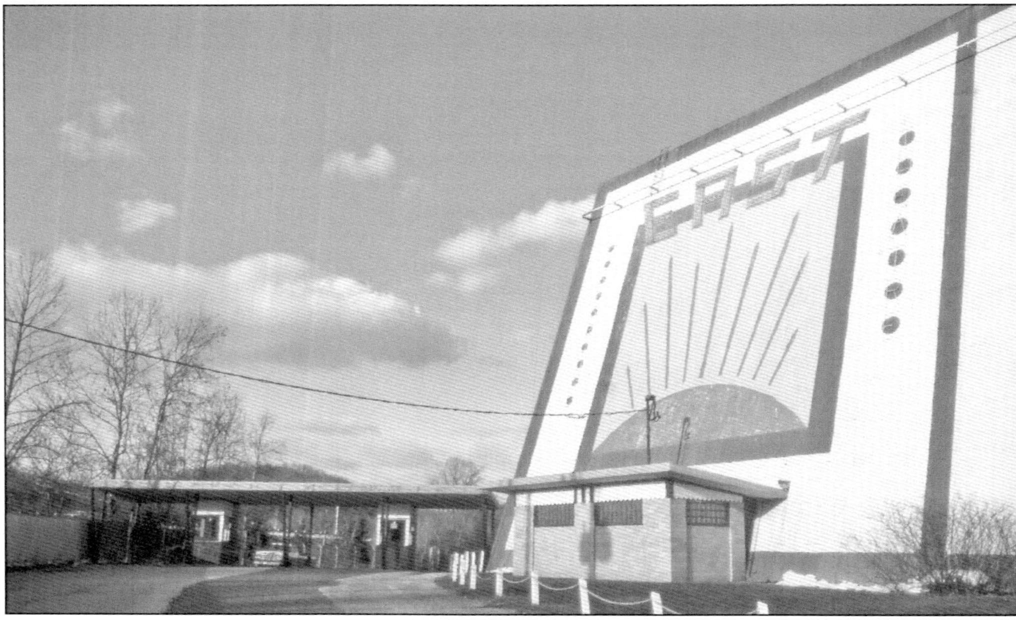

Huntington's 1,000-car East Outdoor Theatre opened in 1951 along Route 60 East. Its grand opening featured fireworks and free kids' rides (including on miniature fire engines). In 1980, its speaker poles were replaced by radio sound. Although the drive-in stayed popular, its location by an interstate exit made the massive property desirable for other uses. In 1993, the East closed in order to be replaced by Walmart. (Courtesy of American Classic Images.)

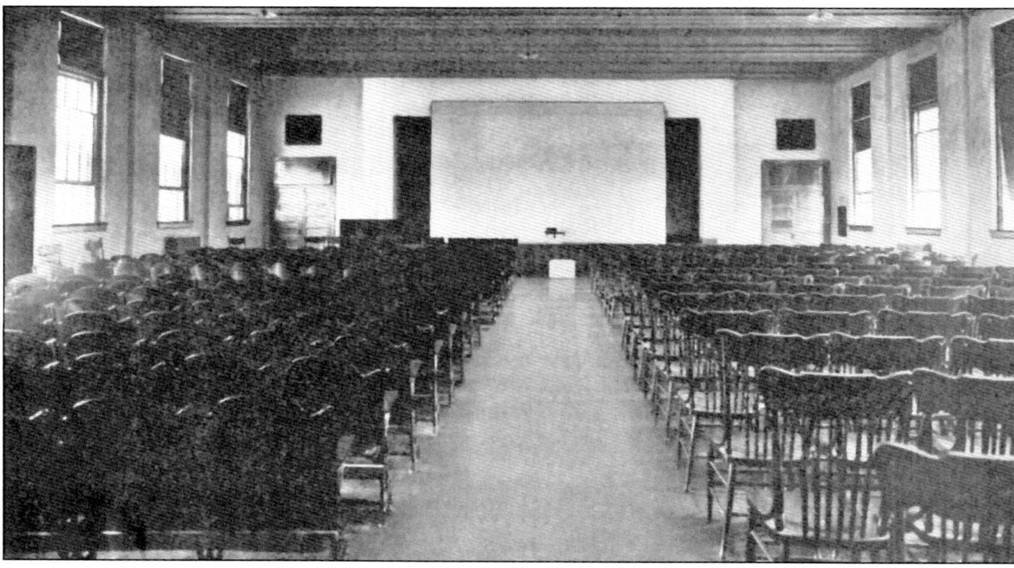

This photograph shows the Amusement Hall at Huntington's West Virginia Asylum (now Mildred Mitchell-Bateman Hospital), established in 1897 for the mentally ill. The site's Building 5—built in 1911 of brick and Berea sandstone—featured a 600-seat entertainment facility. In 1914, state documents listed the patients' regular schedule, which included, "Friday: 1:30 to 2:30 p.m. picture show in Amusement Hall." (Courtesy of West Virginia & Regional History Center, WVU Libraries.)

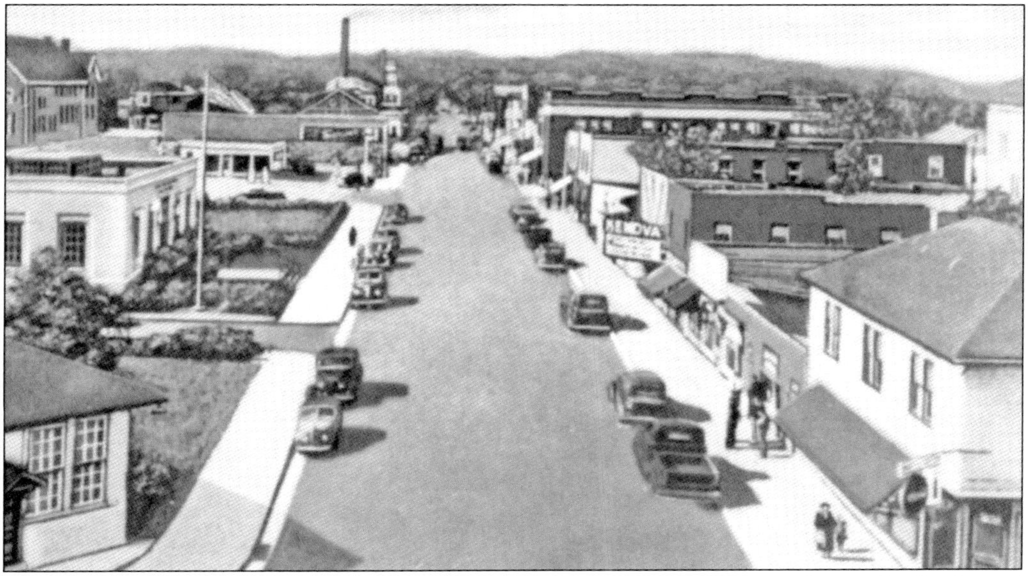

This postcard shows the Kenova Theatre in Huntington's suburb of Kenova. Originally the Strand Theatre, it was playing films as early as 1921. In 1945, Milt Levine and William Thalheimer bought the Strand and renamed it. The 300-seat Kenova was painted to look like light beams were shining up from its marquee. The theatre operated into the early 1970s. After a retail reuse, the building was razed. (Courtesy of Michael Gioulis.)

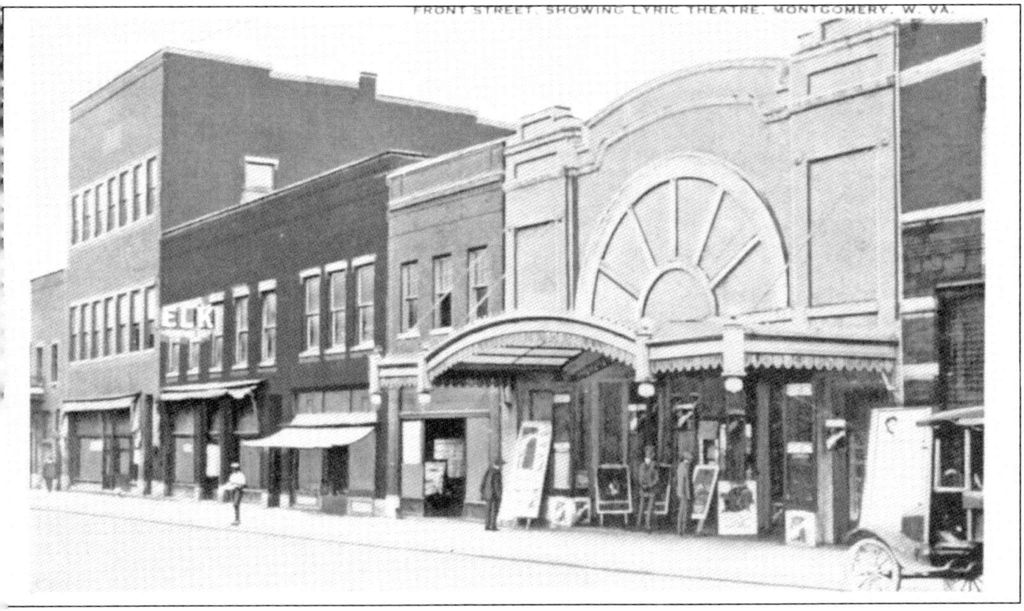

Montgomery's 400-seat Lyric Theatre was showing films by 1922. In 1929 or 1930, it gained Movie-Phone sound and was renamed the Avalon Theatre. In 1932, a fire injured operator Thomas Cosgrove and caused $4,000 in damages. Designer Billy ZeVan remodeled the movie house's interior in 1939. Between approximately 1942 and 1959, the Kayton circuit controlled the Avalon, which the nearby New River State College often used for events. The building no longer stands. (Author's collection.)

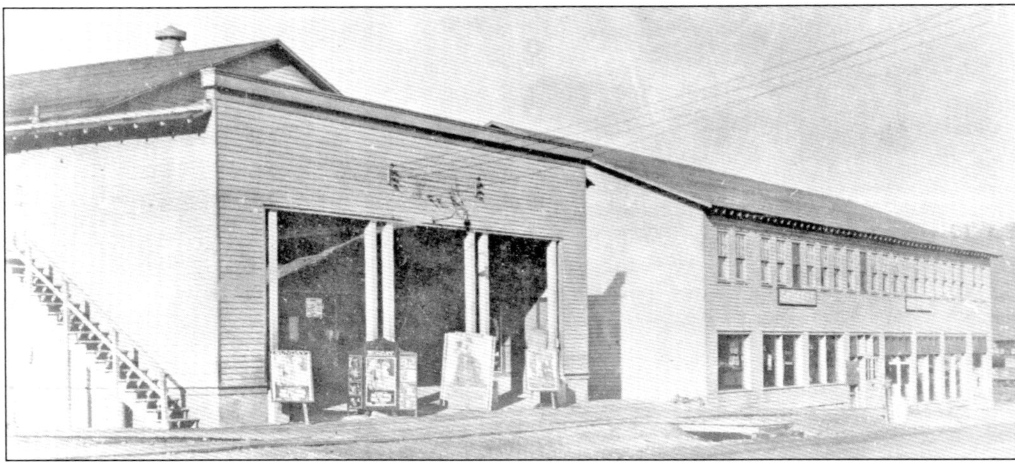

In 1927, the first Nitro Theatre (above), which opened by 1919 on Nitro's Twenty-First Street, was renamed the Lyric Theatre. Frank J. Nalley bought the 300-seat Lyric in 1932. Nalley also owned the second Nitro Theatre, which was built nearby in 1940. He and his wife operated both movie houses until their 1945 retirement. The Lyric Theatre survived until 1957 or later. (Courtesy of West Virginia State Archives, William D. Wintz Collection.)

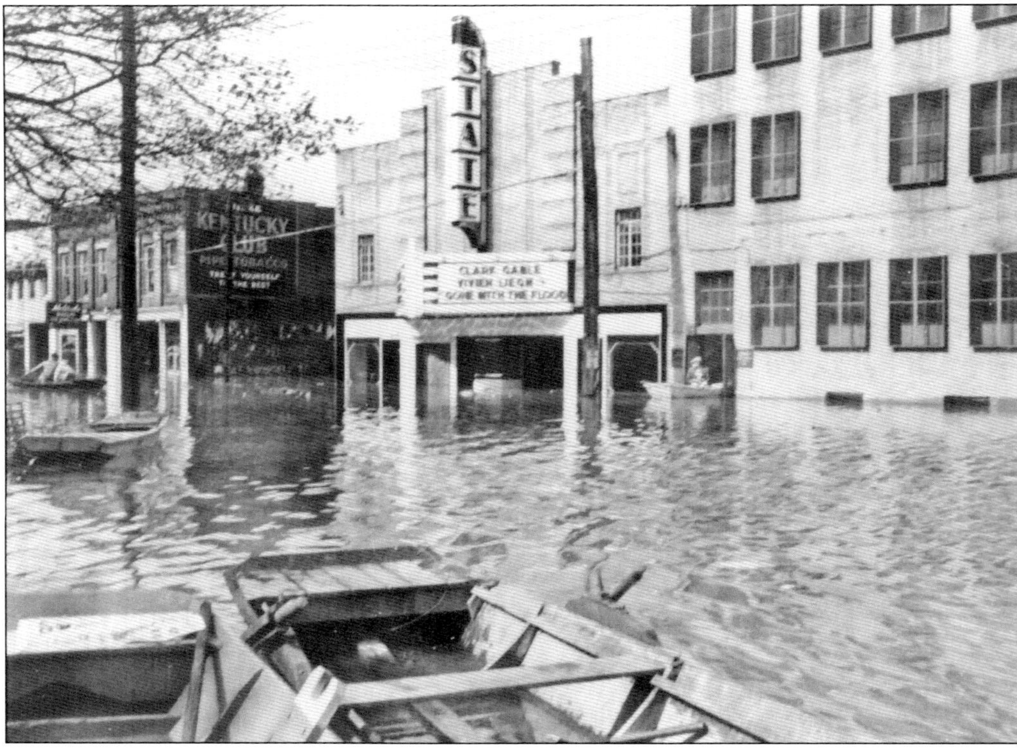

Point Pleasant's second State Theatre opened in 1942. (The first was renamed the Alpine by the Alpine circuit in 1936.) It survived this photographed 1948 disaster, with its marquee humorously advertising "Gone with the Flood." The 300-seat Art Deco movie house remained operational into the early 1980s and reopened during the 1990s. It has been vacant since 2003, except during special events. (Courtesy of West Virginia & Regional History Center, WVU Libraries.)

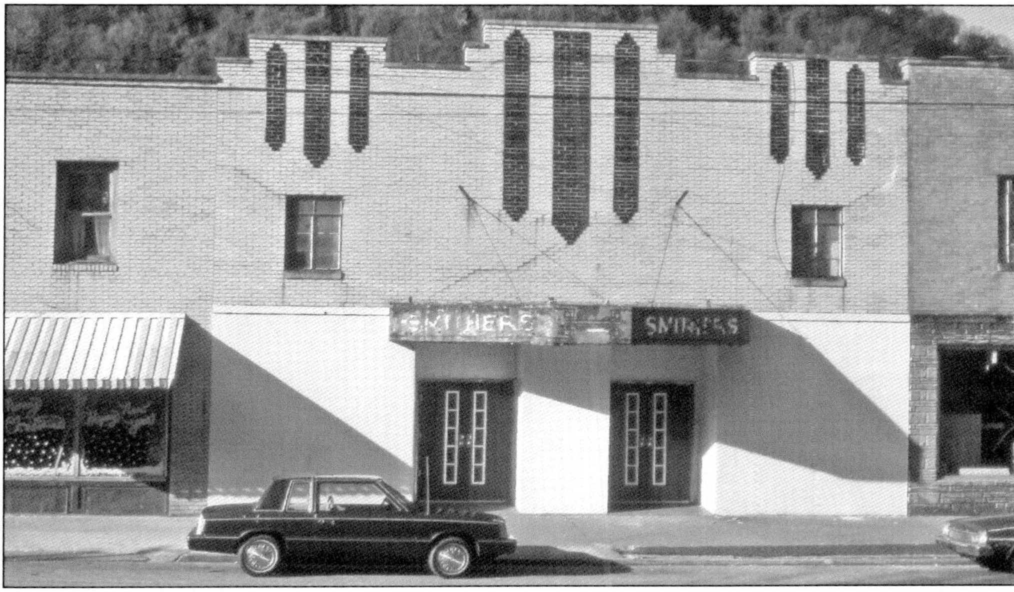

The Smithers Theatre opened in 1938 along the 100 block of Michigan Avenue in Smithers. Its opening gave the Black Diamond Theatre Company circuit more than 10 in-state movie houses. The 350-seat Art Deco facility operated into the 1970s. When this 1984 photograph was taken, it was sitting vacant. The building, which has been completely remodeled but is still somewhat recognizable, currently functions as a church. (Courtesy of American Classic Images.)

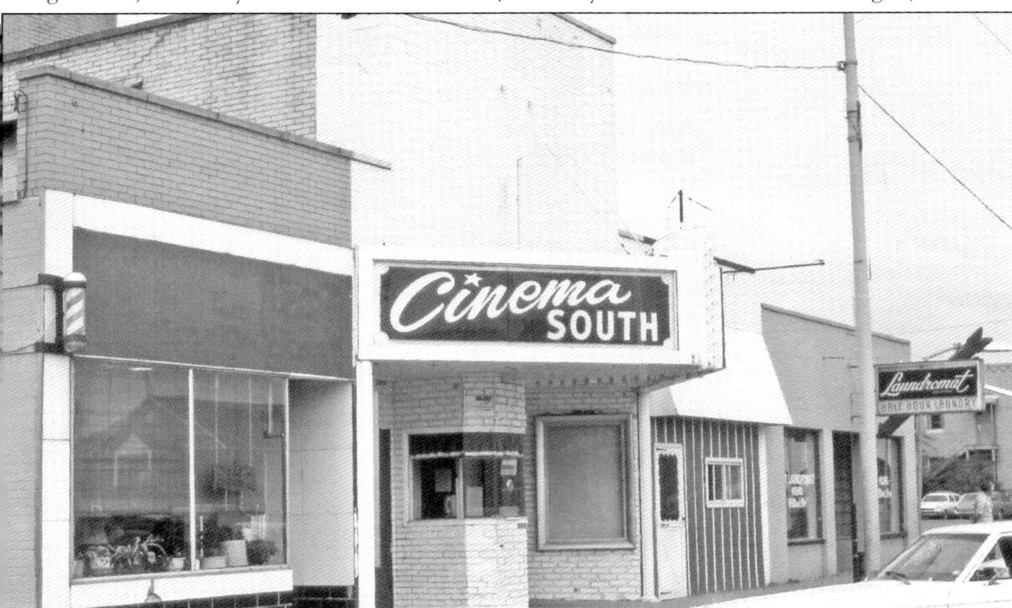

Walter B. Urling's LaBelle Theatre opened in 1939 in South Charleston. In 1967, it was remodeled, becoming the Cinema South; it closed in 1979. The city bought the theatre in 2003 after years as a church, renovating it and even replicating the LaBelle's original neon marquee and blade sign. The 300-seat auditorium is now a rental venue, while the lobby holds the South Charleston Convention and Visitors Bureau. (Courtesy of American Classic Images.)

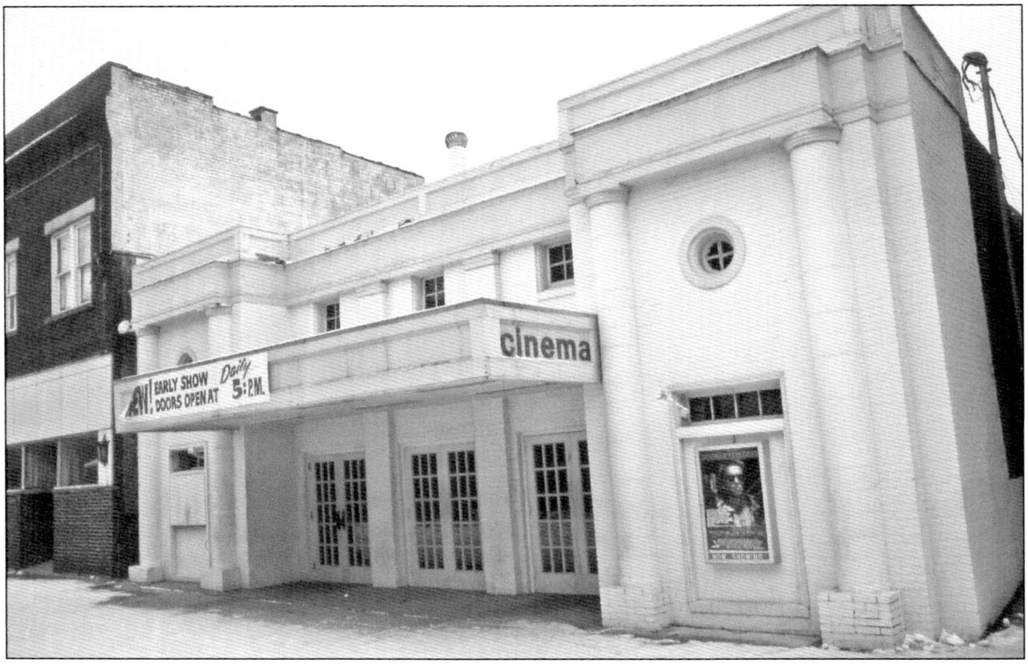

The 500-seat Colonial-style Alban Theatre, owned by O.B. Pierce, opened in 1938 in St. Albans. Later, the Alban featured promotions like free coffee and admitting women at children's prices during *Monday Night Football*. It closed around 1986. After a longtime church reuse, the vacant movie house was purchased by the city in 2007. It now serves as a nonprofit community playhouse, the Alban Arts and Conference Center. (Courtesy of American Classic Images.)

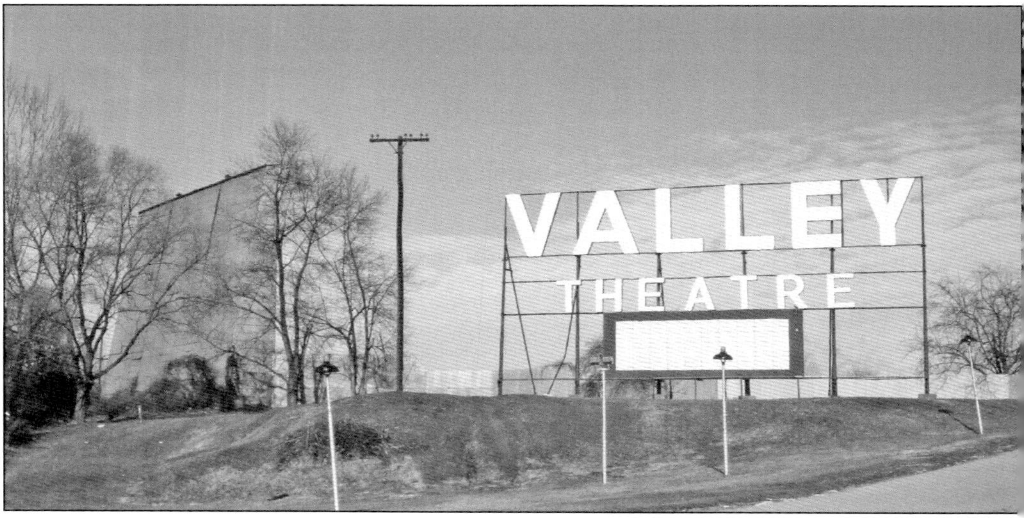

E.R. Custer opened the Charleston area's second outdoor theatre, St. Albans's Valley Drive-in, ir 1948. The Valley had space for 400 cars, later expanding to 700. It always maintained a family-friendly environment, with a playground, free children's admission, and more. It was the Metr Valley's last operational drive-in, closing in 1996. The site is now occupied by 84 Lumber, wit the Valley's screen surviving and serving as the store's giant billboard. (Courtesy of America Classic Images.)

Four

MID-OHIO VALLEY

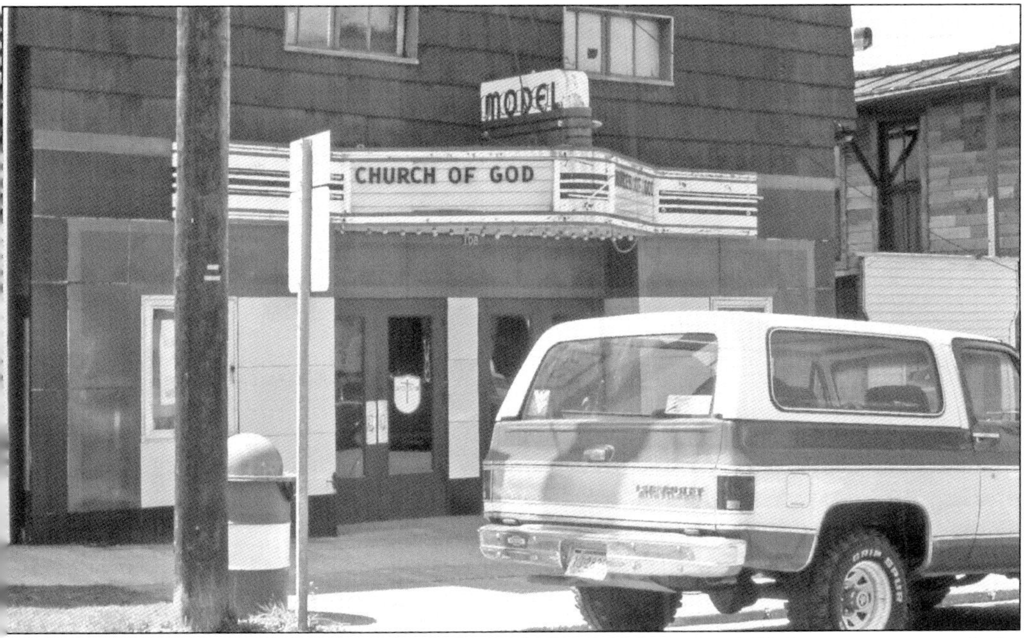

Harrisville's 200-seat Electric Theatre was open before 1926. Around 1940, it was renamed the Model Theatre and remodeled in the Art Deco style. In later years, it was operated by prominent local attorney, judge, and WVU College of Law professor David Hanlon. By the time of this 1983 photograph, the Model had closed, with its building being reused as a church. It was demolished in 1984. (Courtesy of American Classic Images.)

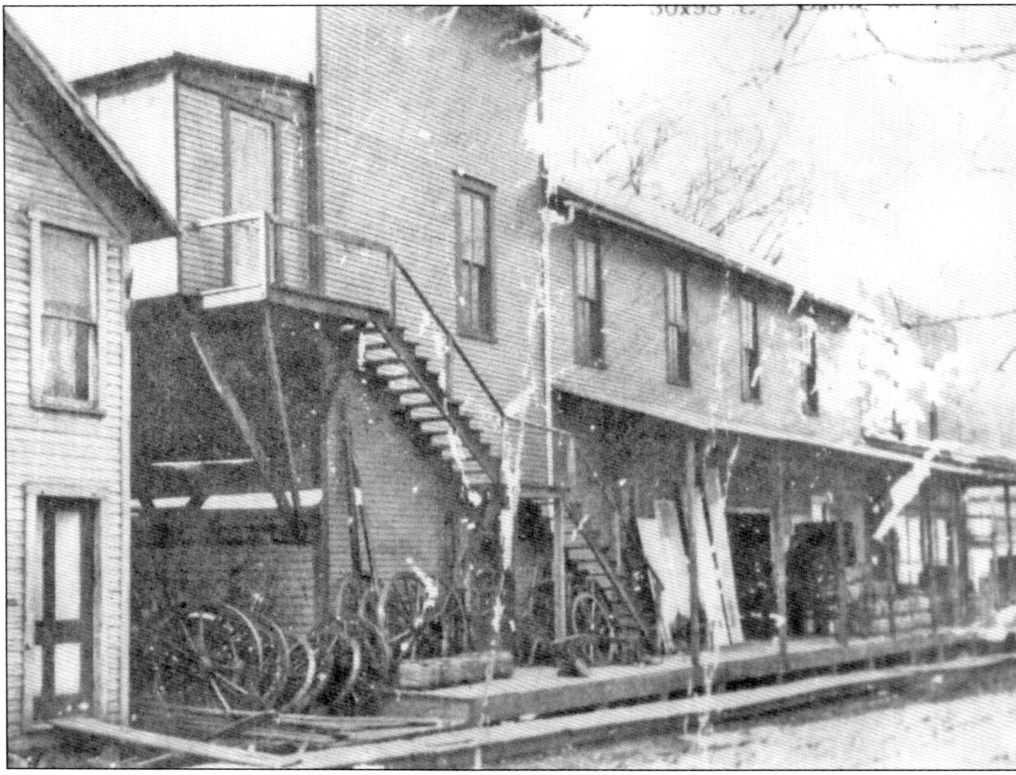

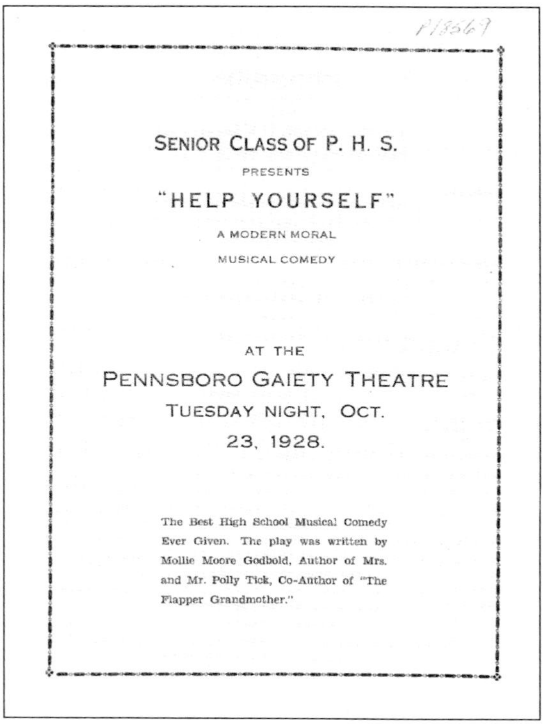

SENIOR CLASS OF P. H. S.

PRESENTS

"HELP YOURSELF"

A MODERN MORAL

MUSICAL COMEDY

AT THE

PENNSBORO GAIETY THEATRE

TUESDAY NIGHT, OCT.

23, 1928.

The Best High School Musical Comedy Ever Given. The play was written by Mollie Moore Godbold, Author of Mrs. and Mr. Polly Tick, Co-Author of "The Flapper Grandmother."

In the Ritchie County town of Cairo, the 250-seat Opera House was on a commercial building's second floor. The older theatre was showing movies by 1922, when Winfield McGregor sold it to John Lemon. During the Great Depression, it temporarily closed at several points, including in 1930 and from around 1933 to 1936, before apparently being shut down permanently by 1938. (Courtesy of West Virginia & Regional History Center, WVU Libraries.)

The Gaiety Theatre, located on the second floor of the Farmers and Merchants Bank building in Pennsboro, opened in 1906 with vaudeville. Films played regularly there by 1914. After its 1930s renaming as the Penn Theatre, it gained a prefabricated neon marquee above its miniscule downstairs entry. The 250-seat Penn operated into the 1950s. The structure now hosts a church. (Courtesy of West Virginia & Regional History Center, WVU Libraries.)

Former US senator Johnson Newlon Camden's 1,400-seat Camden Theatre opened in 1902 on the 700 block of Market Street in Parkersburg. Along with a three-level auditorium with boxes, the venue featured a marble-floored foyer with stained glass. The Smoot Amusement Company began showing films there for a nickel in 1912. Parkersburg's worst fire ever started at the Camden in 1929, destroying it and multiple other buildings. (Courtesy of Artcraft Studio.)

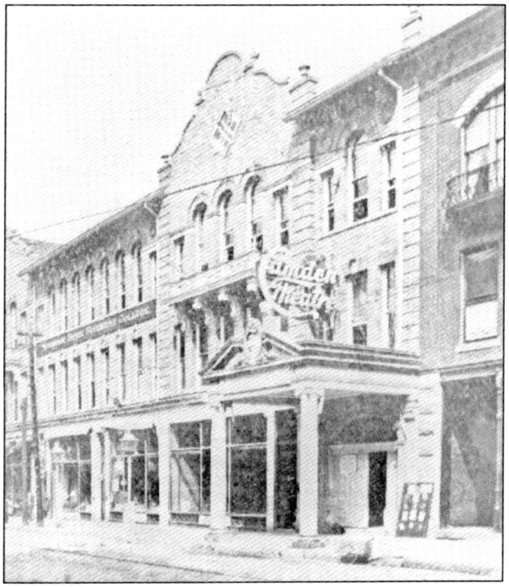

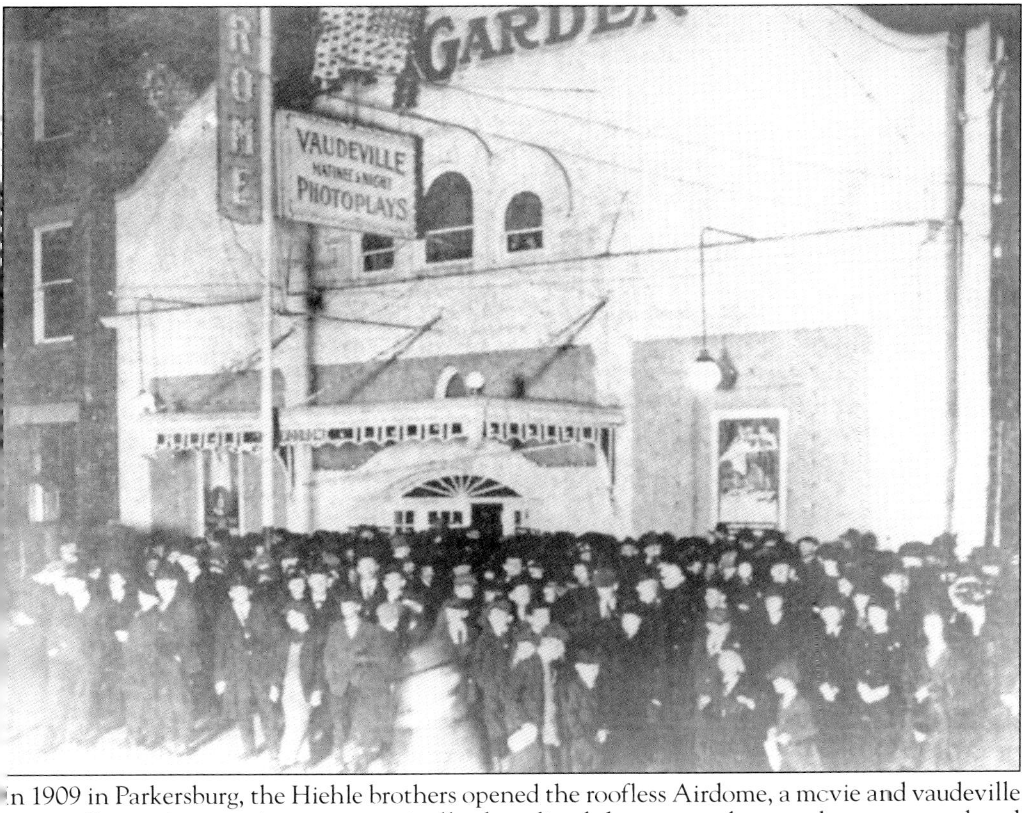

In 1909 in Parkersburg, the Hiehle brothers opened the roofless Airdome, a movie and vaudeville venue. Open-air operations were typically short-lived due to weather, so they soon enclosed their facility and reopened it in November 1910 as the Hippodrome. Sometimes called the Hipp Garden Theatre, it was promoted as "Parkersburg's family amusement house." Later part of F.C. Smoot's circuit, it was demolished in 1925 for the Smoot Theatre's construction. (Courtesy of Artcraft Studio.)

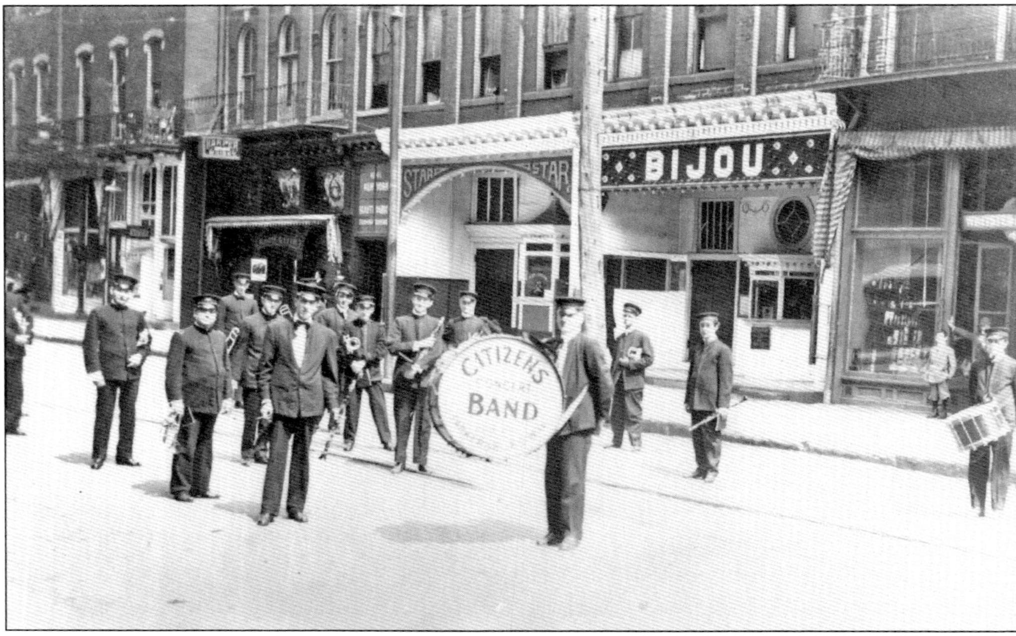

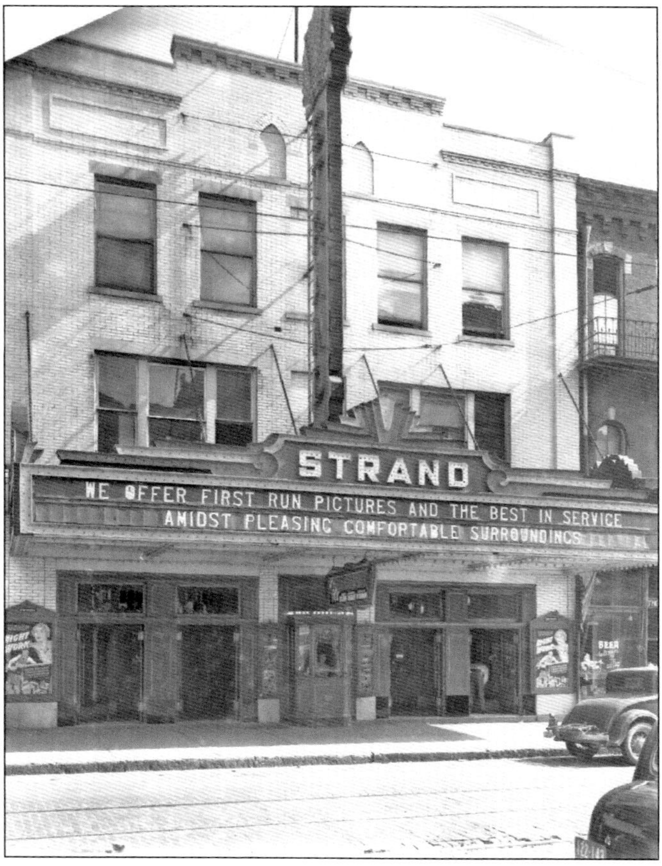

In a 1909 advertisement, F.L. Harris's Bijou Theatre offered 5¢ admission for "two reels of first run motion pictures," with patrons "cooled by big electric fans." By 1912, the Bijou's building on Market Street's 400 block also hosted another nickelodeon: Percy W. Barrett's 300-seat Star. In 1916, Barrett bought his adjacent competitor in order to combine the two into a larger, nicer movie house. The result was the 500-seat Strand Theatre (later enlarged to 725 seats). Billing itself as "the pride of progressive Parkersburg," it claimed it was "home of the best pictures made." It was part of Warner Bros.' circuit from 1930 until the early 1950s, when the Jur circuit took over. The Strand closed around 1956. Its building has since had commercial uses. (Above, courtesy of West Virginia & Regional History Center, WVU Libraries; left, courtesy of Artcraft Studio.)

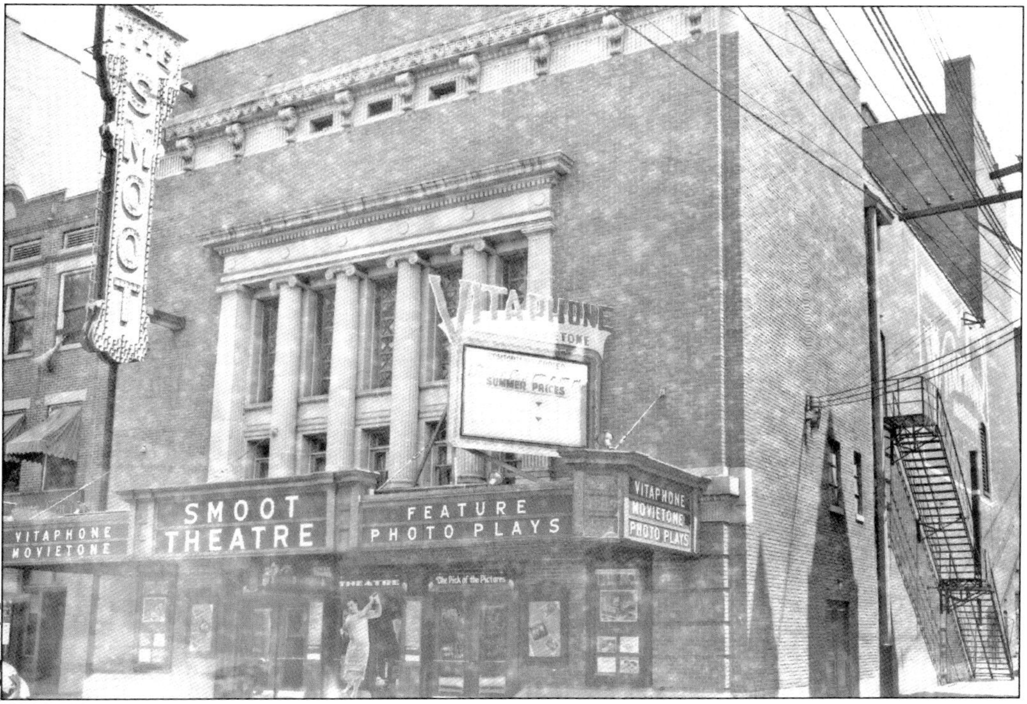

After Parkersburg's Hippodrome was demolished, the vaudeville-focused Smoot Theatre opened on its site in 1926. Architect Fred W. Elliott of Columbus, Ohio, designed the neoclassical style brick and terra-cotta building. In 1930, the venue joined the Warner Bros. film studio's theatre circuit and got an Art Deco interior remodel. The Smoot then began showing movies using Warner's Vitaphone sound system. The auditorium also continued to host live events over the years—such as a 1931 performance by the Singer Midgets, who later portrayed the Munchkins in 1939's *The Wizard of Oz*. The ornate 720-seat Smoot closed in 1986; a preservation campaign saved it weeks before its scheduled 1989 demolition. The restored theatre features historic elements like chandeliers, beveled lobby mirrors, and mahogany doors. The Smoot serves as a nonprofit performing arts center. (Both, courtesy of Artcraft Studio.)

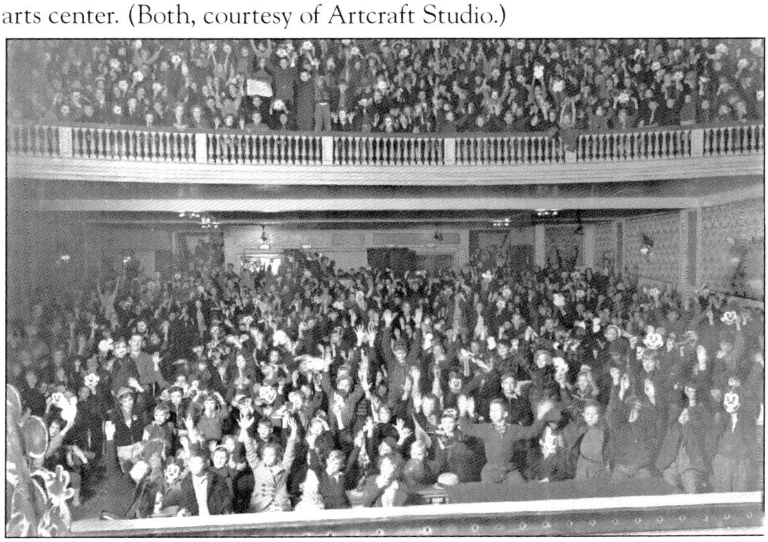

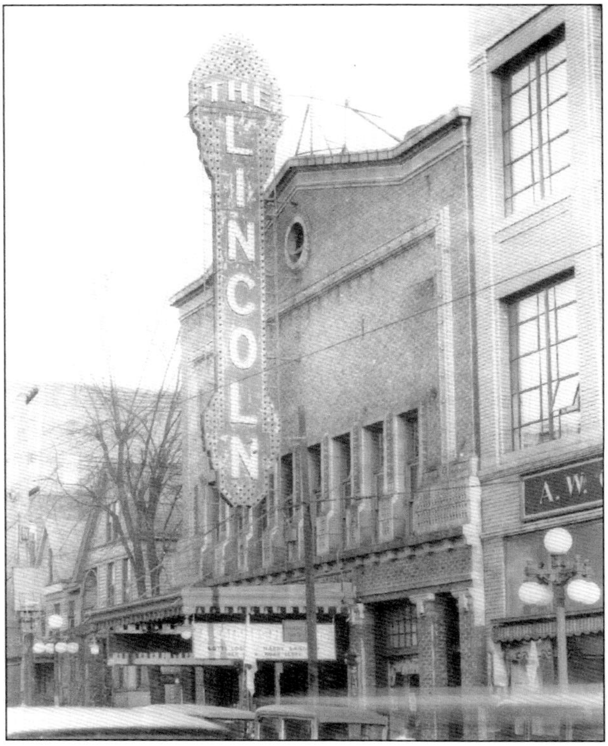

F.C. Smoot's Lincoln Theatre, designed by Fred W. Elliott, opened in 1920 with Mary Pickford's film *Pollyanna*. It advertised that it offered "supreme photoplays—maximum entertainment at minimum cost." In 1930, Warner Bros. bought the 900-seat Lincoln, closing it only two years later. From 1936 until 1972, J.C. Penney reused the building. It has since served as the playhouse for the nonprofit Actors Guild of Parkersburg. (Courtesy of Artcraft Studio.)

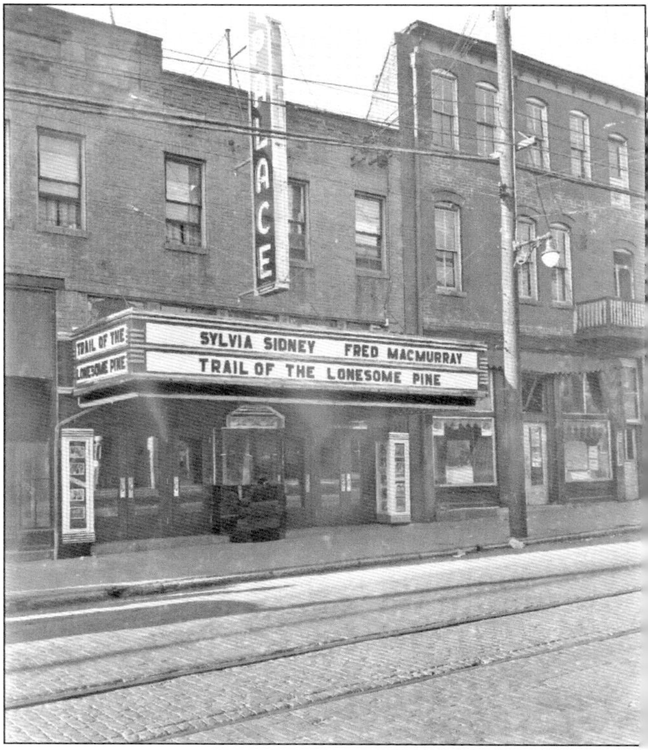

The Palace Theatre opened around 1928 in a former grocery store at Seventh and Lynn Streets in Parkersburg. George and Pete Angelos leased it to Rose Thomas, who bought it in 1931. Rebuilt after a 1936 fire, the Palace closed in the 1960s. By 1974, the reopened venue was showing X-rated films as the Playboy Theater, later known as the Swingers Theatre. It is no longer standing. (Courtesy of Artcraft Studio.)

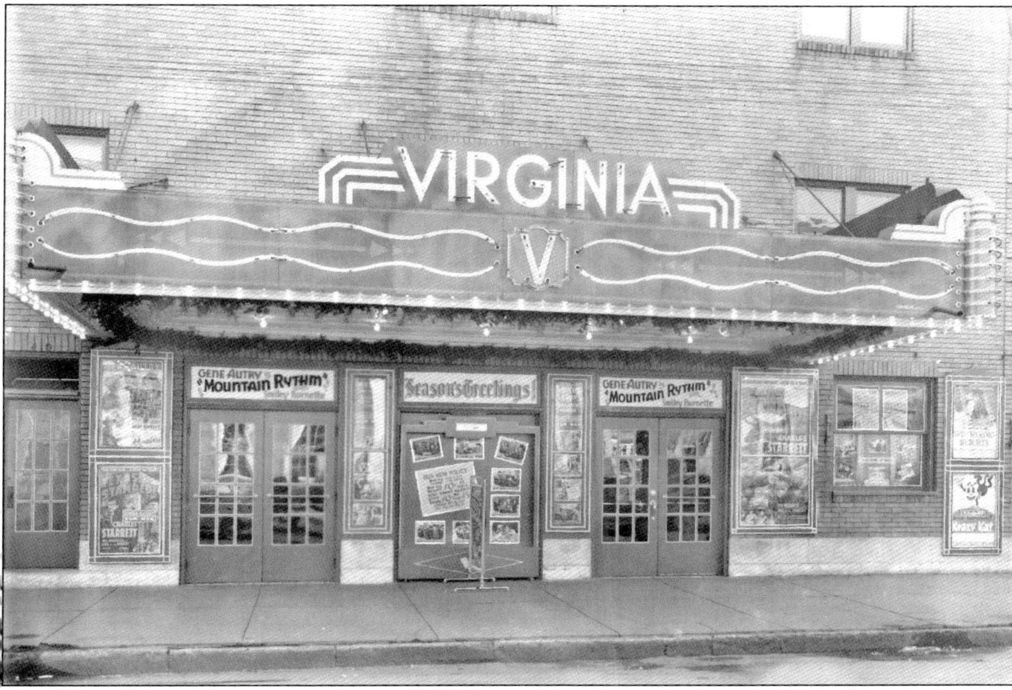

Parkersburg's Virginia Theatre, located along the 400 block of Juliana Street, was opened by Charles B. Hall in 1928. It was known for playing Westerns. One local recalled that his parents forbade him from going there due to its "tough" clientele. The 900-seat Virginia closed in 1957. In the 1960s, it and its adjacent buildings were razed for a bank with a parking lot. (Courtesy of Artcraft Studio.)

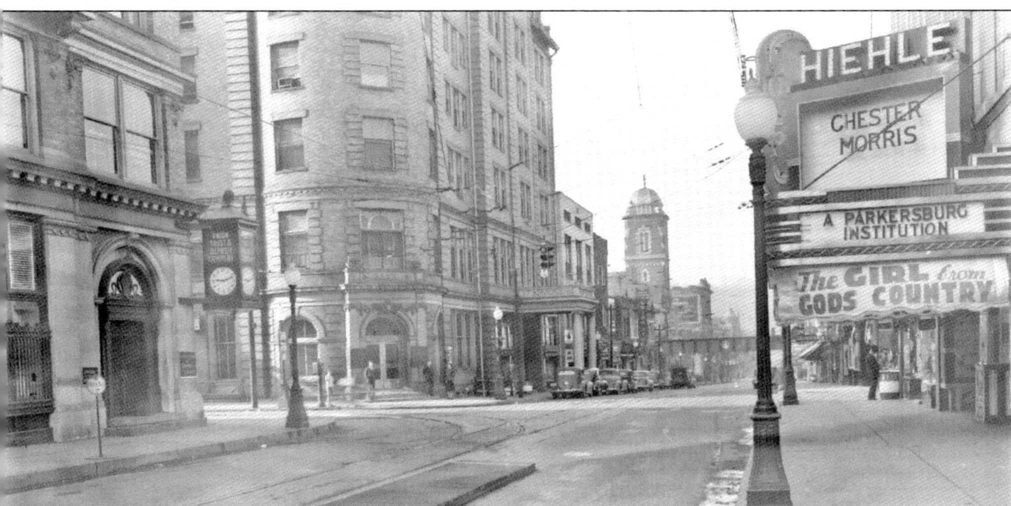

R.J. Hiehle's Hiehle Theatre opened in 1930 on the same Market Street block in Parkersburg where the Camden Theatre had previously burned down. The $50,000 second-run movie house featured geometric Art Deco designs throughout. Due to its lot's shape, the 392-seat Hiehle had a narrow, long auditorium, upstairs bathrooms, and a balcony far back from the screen. It closed in the early 1960s; its building is unrecognizable today. (Courtesy of Artcraft Studio.)

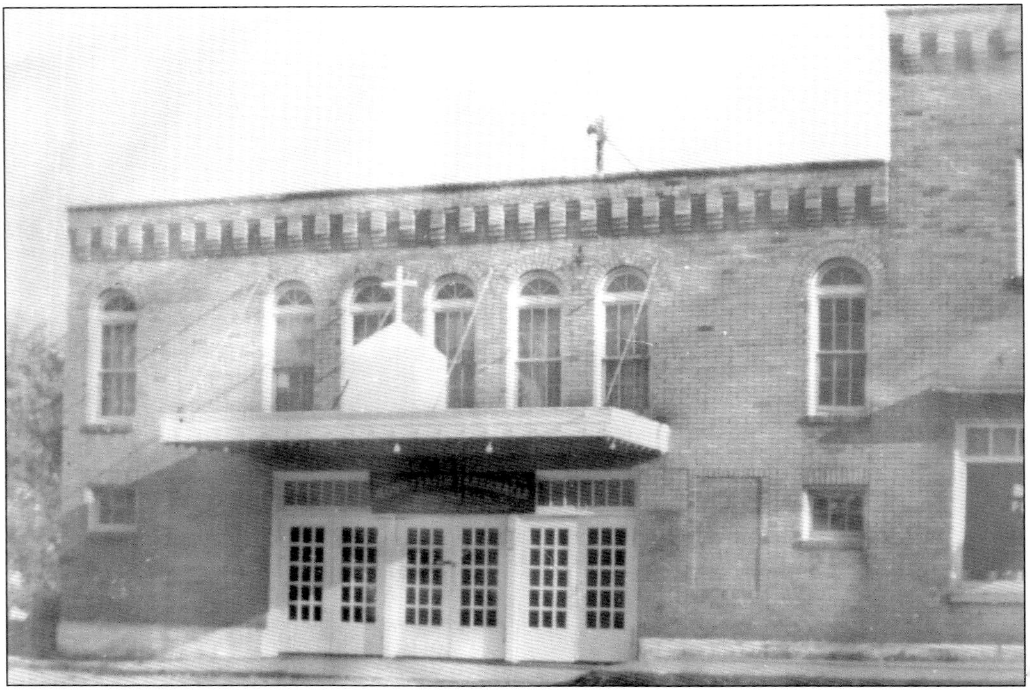

In south Parkersburg, the Broadway Theatre opened on its namesake thoroughfare (around Tenth Avenue) in 1936. The next year, the 350-seat movie house went out of business (possibly due to the Great Depression). The Broadway reopened around 1941, having expanded to 500 seats. However, it did not last long. By the late 1950s, the building had undergone a church conversion, as seen here. It was eventually demolished. (Courtesy of Artcraft Studio.)

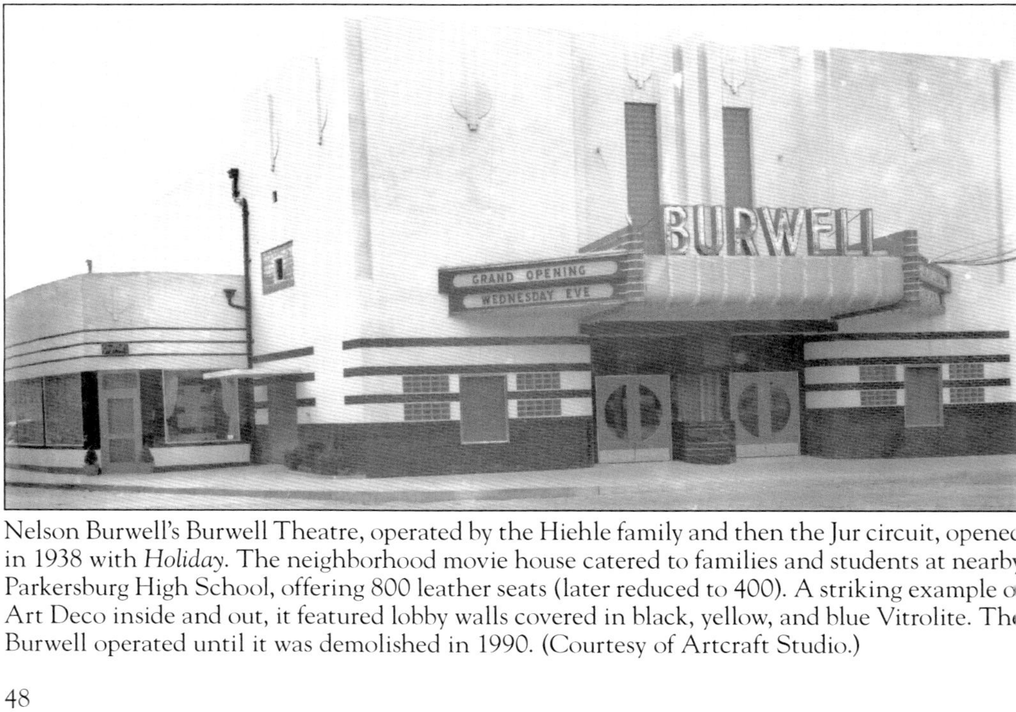

Nelson Burwell's Burwell Theatre, operated by the Hiehle family and then the Jur circuit, opened in 1938 with *Holiday*. The neighborhood movie house catered to families and students at nearby Parkersburg High School, offering 800 leather seats (later reduced to 400). A striking example of Art Deco inside and out, it featured lobby walls covered in black, yellow, and blue Vitrolite. The Burwell operated until it was demolished in 1990. (Courtesy of Artcraft Studio.)

The 600-seat Parker Theatre almost adjoined the Lincoln Theatre on Parkersburg's Market Street. Its Art Deco facade covered one storefront on a larger structure. Along with mainstream films, it played B-movie fare, as shown here around 1945. The Parker was operated by Rose Thomas from its 1939 opening to 1961, followed by the Jur circuit. It closed around 1974. The YMCA reuses the building. (Courtesy of Artcraft Studio.)

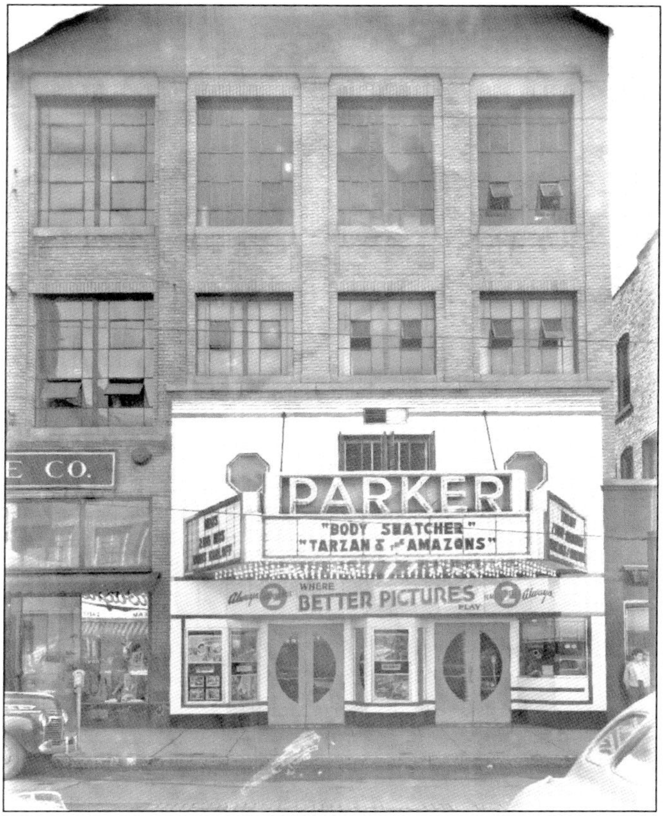

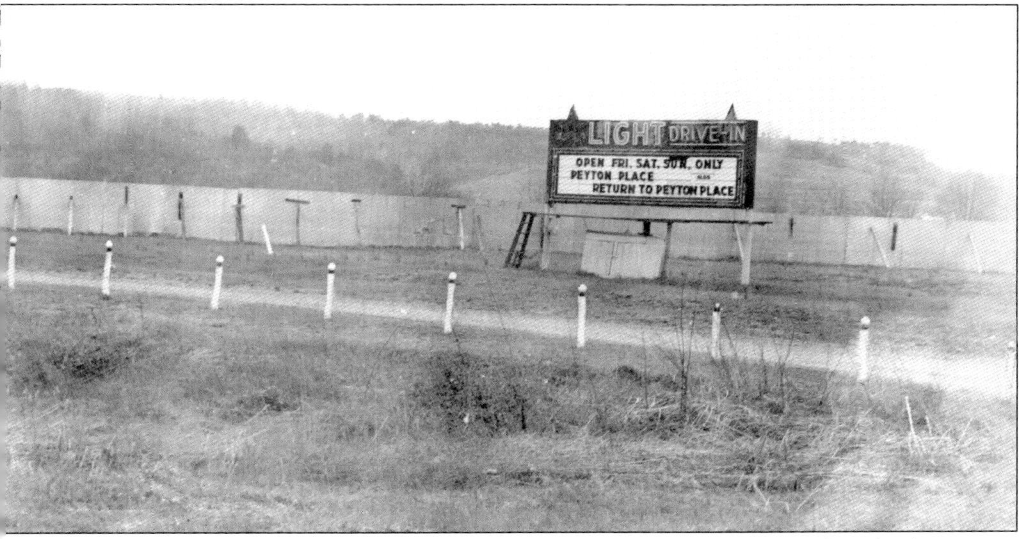

Parkersburg's Starlight Drive-in Theatre, at the intersection of Gihon Road and Pike Street, opened in July 1951 with 50¢ adult admission and 25¢ children's admission. Often advertised as the "Starlite," the 600-car facility offered walk-up patrons the opportunity to see movies as well. Operated from the early 1950s by the Jur circuit, it shut down around 1974 and was replaced by a shopping center. (Courtesy of Artcraft Studio.)

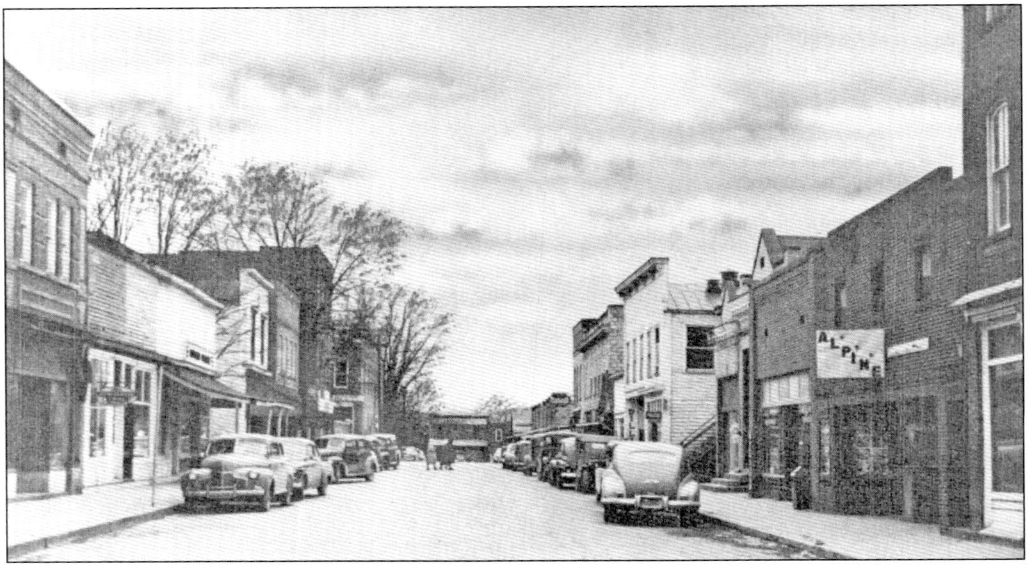

In 1937 in Ravenswood, the Alpine circuit built the 300-seat Alpine Theatre. The Jur circuit leased the venue in 1951. Nonetheless, the theatre kept its Alpine name until the late 1950s, when it was retitled the Jur Theatre. The Jur Theatre later became part of the Moore circuit, which operated it until at least 1969. Its building no longer exists. (Courtesy of West Virginia State Archives, Washington Lands Collection.)

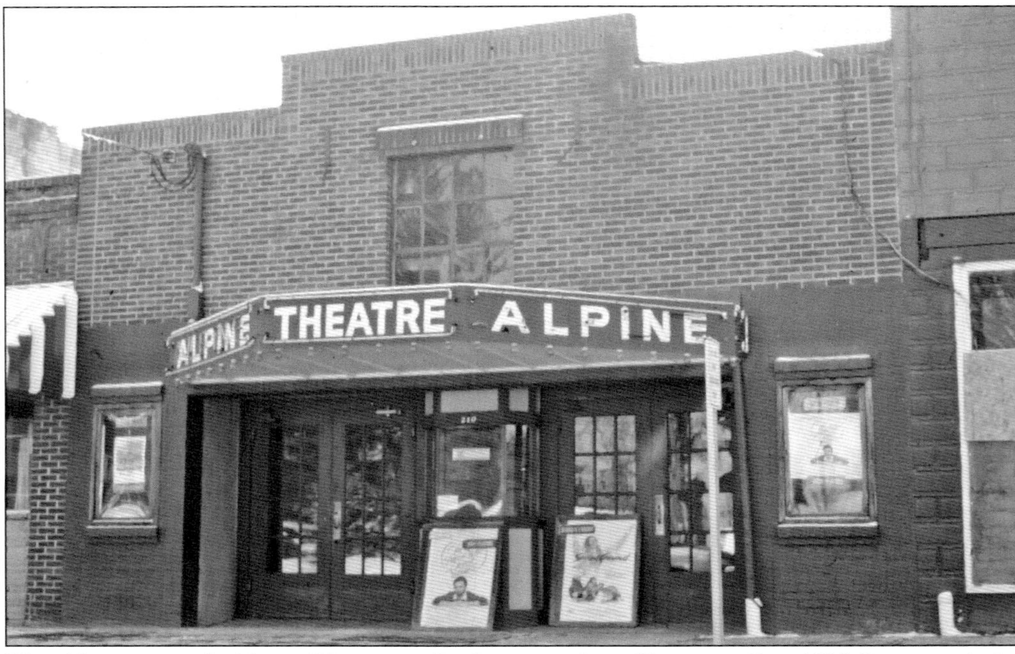

The Alpine circuit's Alpine Theatre in Ripley opened on Christmas Day 1936. Prices includec 15¢ children's admission, 10¢ popcorn, and 5¢ candy. The 408-seat brick movie house closed ir 1984. Downtown revitalization organization Main Street Ripley bought the intact theatre in 2003 following a restoration, it now hosts everything from plays and bands to free kids' films. (Courtesy of Theatre Historical Society of America, Edward T. Gibbs Collection.)

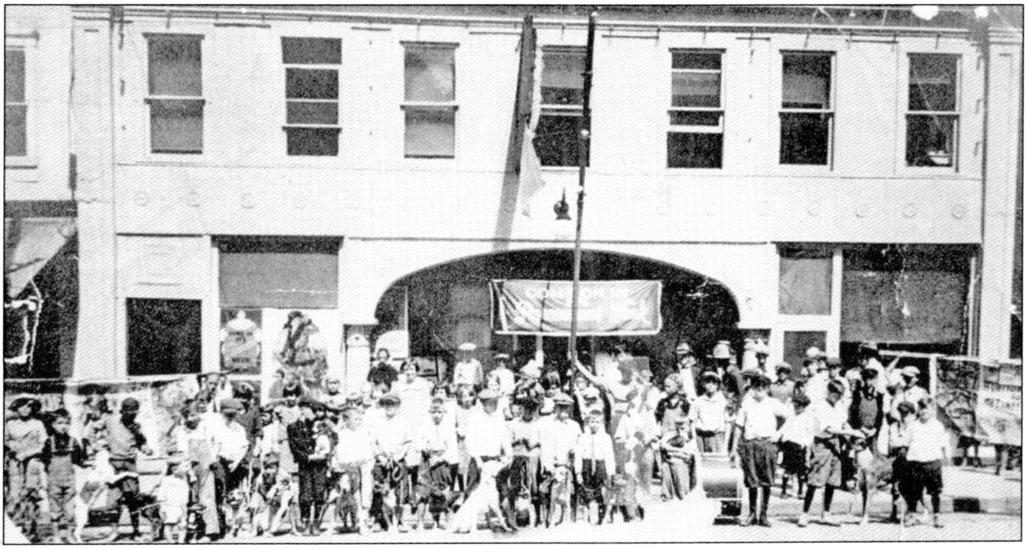

In 1907, Hamond H. Robey opened Dreamland, the first movie house in Spencer. He moved the nickelodeon to a new structure in 1911 and renamed it the Auditorium. Along with films, the Auditorium hosted events like the children's dog show in the above photograph. In 1926, a name change to the Robey Theatre accompanied a $100,000 remodel and expansion by Columbus, Ohio, architects Carmichael and Millspaugh. The Robey family owned the Italian Renaissance–neoclassical–style 425-seat theatre until 1978. Individually listed in the National Register of Historic Places since 1989, the Robey relit its neon blade sign in 2007 and still has its antique ticket machine. Believed to be America's oldest continuously operating movie theatre, the Robey shows first-run films nightly, year-round. (Above, courtesy of West Virginia State Archives, Historic Preservation Collection; below, courtesy of Theatre Historical Society of America, Editor's Collection.)

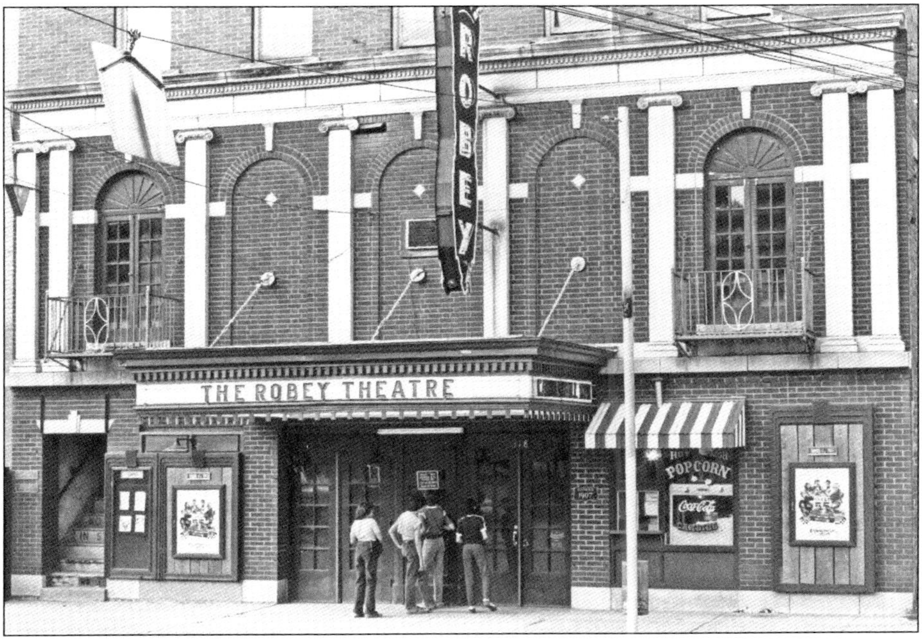

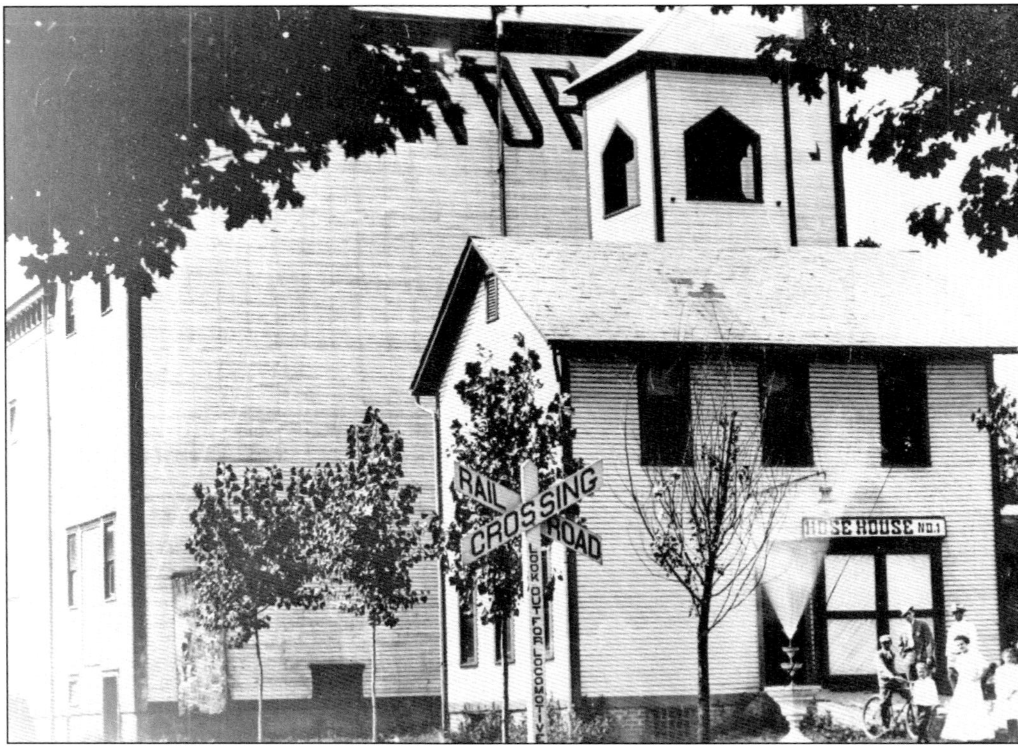

The Auditorium opened in 1902 in St. Marys. By 1922, Hamond H. Robey had purchased it, making it a 400-seat movie venue; it was later renamed the Robey Theatre. In 1948, then owner Alex Illar built St. Marys' Center Theatre, promptly closing the Robey. It reopened, operating until at least 1957. After years of reuse as apartments, it was razed in 1980. (Courtesy of West Virginia State Archives, Pleasants County Historical Society Collection.)

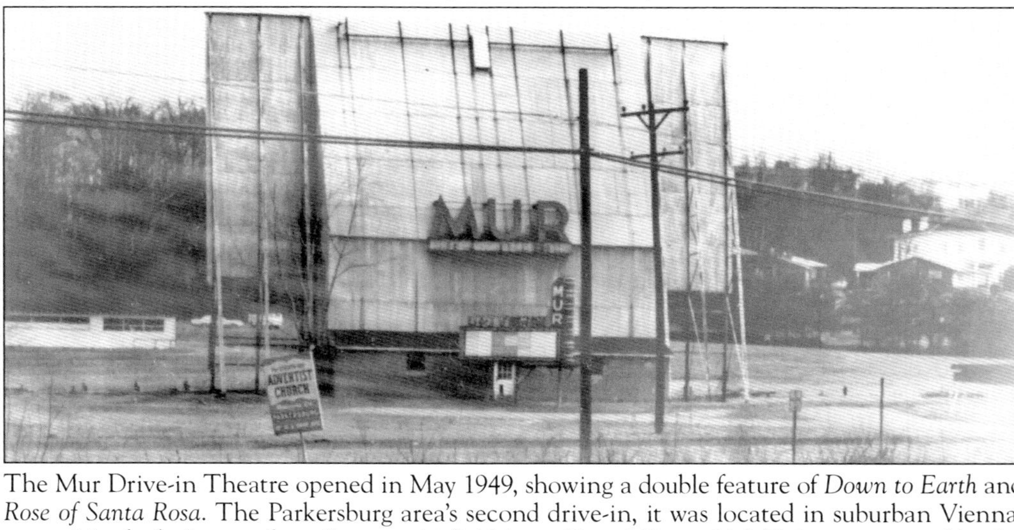

The Mur Drive-in Theatre opened in May 1949, showing a double feature of *Down to Earth* an *Rose of Santa Rosa*. The Parkersburg area's second drive-in, it was located in suburban Vienna across Murdoch Avenue from Stewart Airfield (now Grand Central Mall). Later operated by th Jur circuit, the 550-car Mur closed in 1969 or 1970 and was quickly demolished for a 1971 retai development. (Courtesy of Artcraft Studio.)

Five

Mountain Lakes

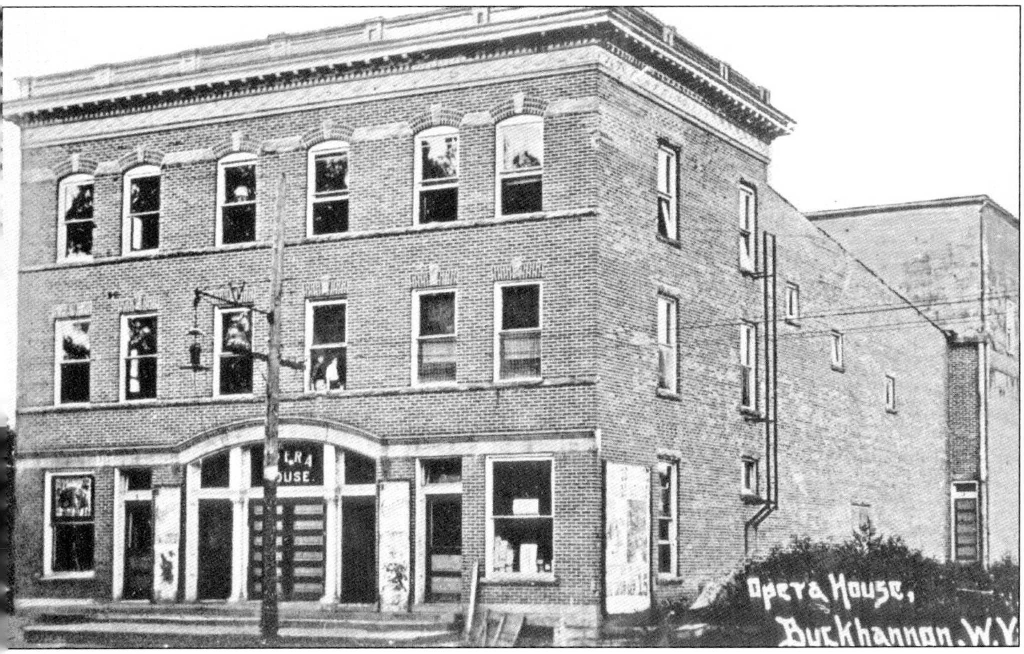

Buckhannon's 800-seat Grand Opera House, designed by Draper C. Hughes, opened in 1903. Manager M.E. Hymes played films there as early as 1917; he sold it in 1930. In 1950, its last West Virginia Wesleyan College yearbook advertisement claimed, "From vaudeville to motion pictures, the best of entertainment is at Grand Opera House." The venue closed during the 1950s and burned down in 1960. (Courtesy of Upshur County Historical Society.)

BENEFIT *Boy Scouts*

ONE ADMISSION TO THE

Princess or Wonderland *Theatre*

FRIDAY NIGHT, APRIL TWENTY-FOURTH, '14

The Princess and Wonderland were two early nickelodeons in Buckhannon. Wonderland, opened by Grant Hunter, was located in a now-gone building at 31 West Main Street (next door to what is currently the Upshur County Historical Society's research center). Both movie houses were operating by 1912, when M.E. Hymes managed them. In October 1914, Hymes bought them (and another theatre, the Hippodrome) from W.E. Phillips for $3,916.61. Hymes's advertisement for both theatres in a West Virginia Wesleyan College yearbook assured students, "Nothing of an objectionable nature is ever permitted in either of these houses, the object being to instruct and entertain at a nominal price." Later, Hymes installed a stage inside Wonderland in order to host vaudeville along with films while keeping the Princess solely focused on movies. Both closed before 1926. (Both, courtesy of Upshur County Historical Society.)

THE MIDNIGHT RIDE OF PAUL REVERE OR THE SPIRIT OF '76.

History repeated in motion pictures at the WONDERLAND THEATRE, Monday Night, March 3, 1913. The Midnight Ride of Paul Revere is famous in history and every man, woman and child has read about it.

We now produce it with the same realistic truthfulness as did your forefathers over one hundred years ago. See it today as you may never have another opportunity. I have secured this picture at an enormous expense and your patronage is earnestly solicited.

M. E. HYMES, Manager.

Admission, 10c.

[OVER]

The back text on this promotional hand fan states, "Compliments of Hippodrome Theatre, Buckhannon, W. Va." The Hippodrome, a nickelodeon, became part of M.E. Hymes's local circuit in 1914. Hymes operated it until at least 1917. That year, the Hippodrome's advertisement in West Virginia Wesleyan College's yearbook encouraged, "We invite the students to visit our theatre," claiming, "We are only showing the latest attractions." (Courtesy of Upshur County Historical Society.)

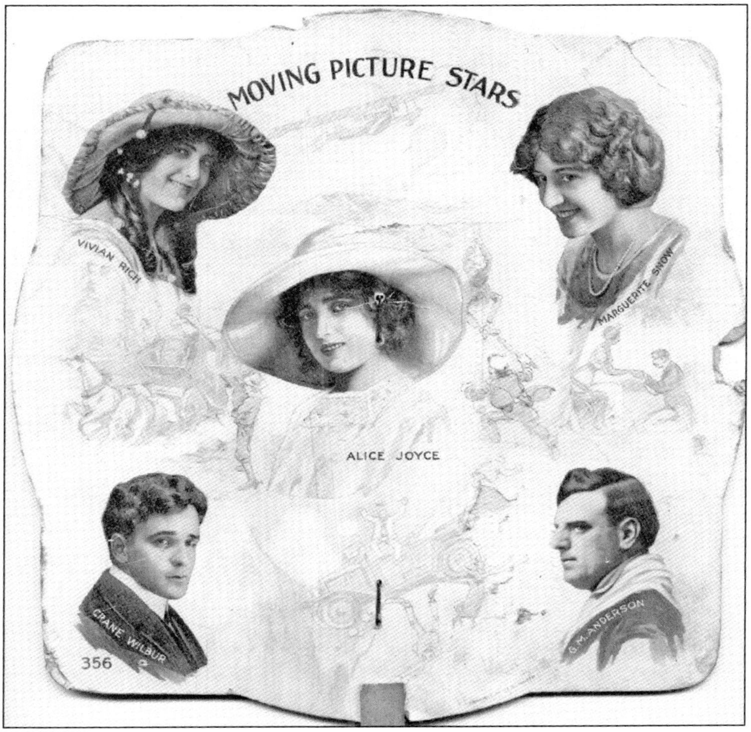

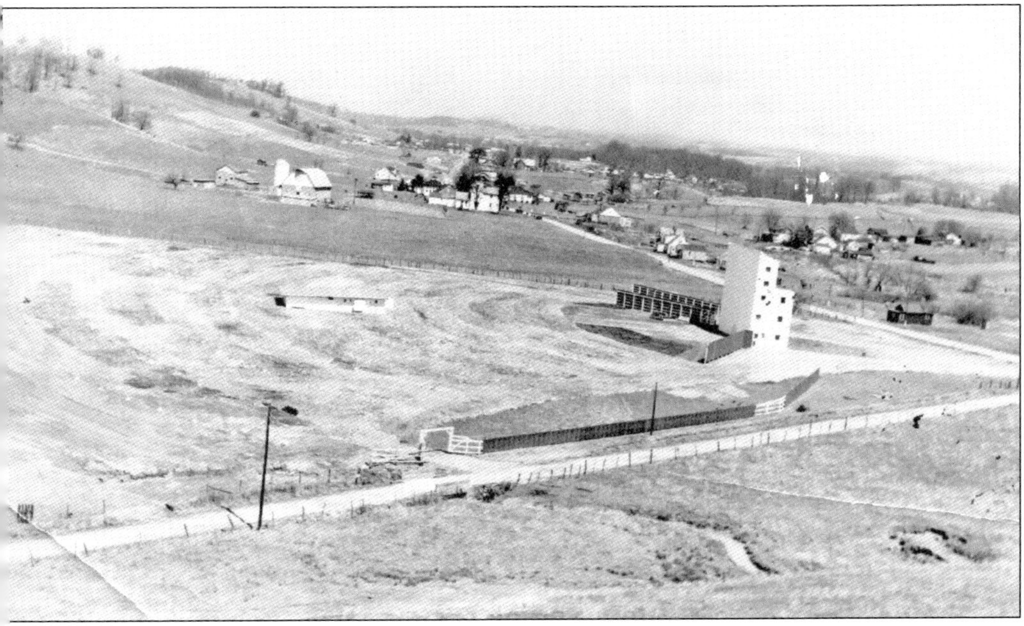

Garland West and his wife, Ota, opened Buckhannon's West Drive-in Theatre in 1949 or 1950. The seasonal venue, located on Stony Run Road at Route 20, received upgrades before its spring 1953 reopening. It offered 50¢ admission in the spring of 1964, when it was mostly playing second-run 1963 movies. After Garland's death, Ota operated the 350-car theatre until at least 1975. Nothing survives on-site. (Courtesy of Upshur County Historical Society.)

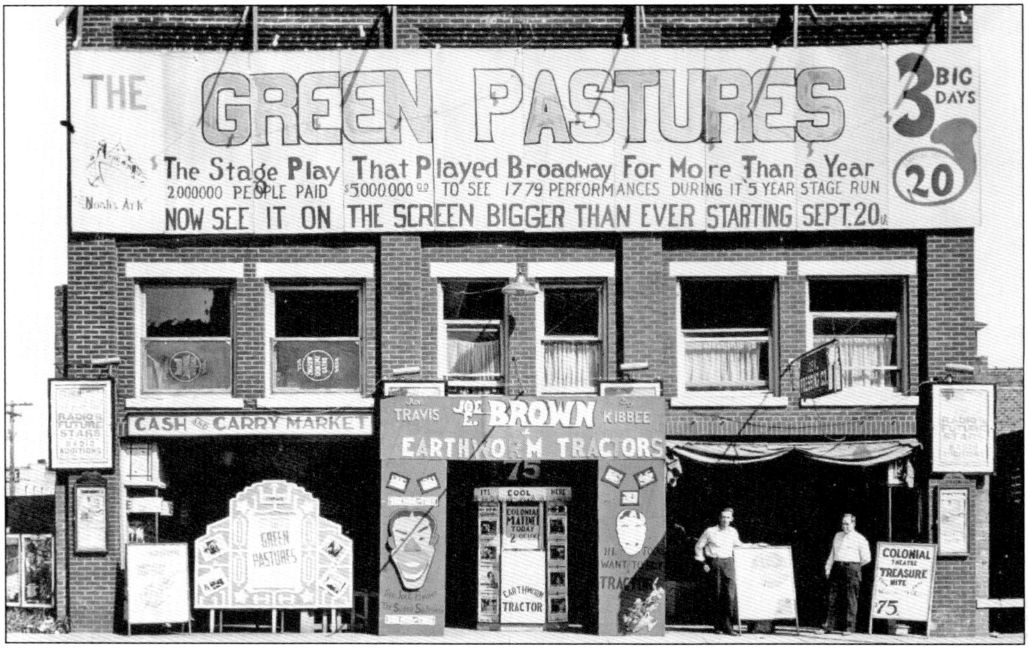

In 1924, O.M. White opened a Buckhannon movie house called the Euphemian Theatre. Before 1931, it underwent a series of name changes, including the White (around 1927), the Hippodrome (approximately 1928–1930), and the Colonial Theatre. The above 1937 photograph shows operator Garland West (right) outside the 400-seat Colonial; his family owned it from 1943 to 1979. West later remodeled it with a Vitrolite facade, a marquee, and other features. In 1973, writer Gray Barker leased the Colonial, renaming it Cinema V (below). He later twinned it, making the balcony a separate screening area. Cinema V closed in 1980. From 1982 until the 2010s, the building was used as a nightclub. The city purchased the vacant theatre in 2017 and is rehabilitating it into a community arts center. (Above, courtesy of West Virginia State Archives, Upshur County Historical Society/Tenney Collection; below, courtesy of American Classic Images.)

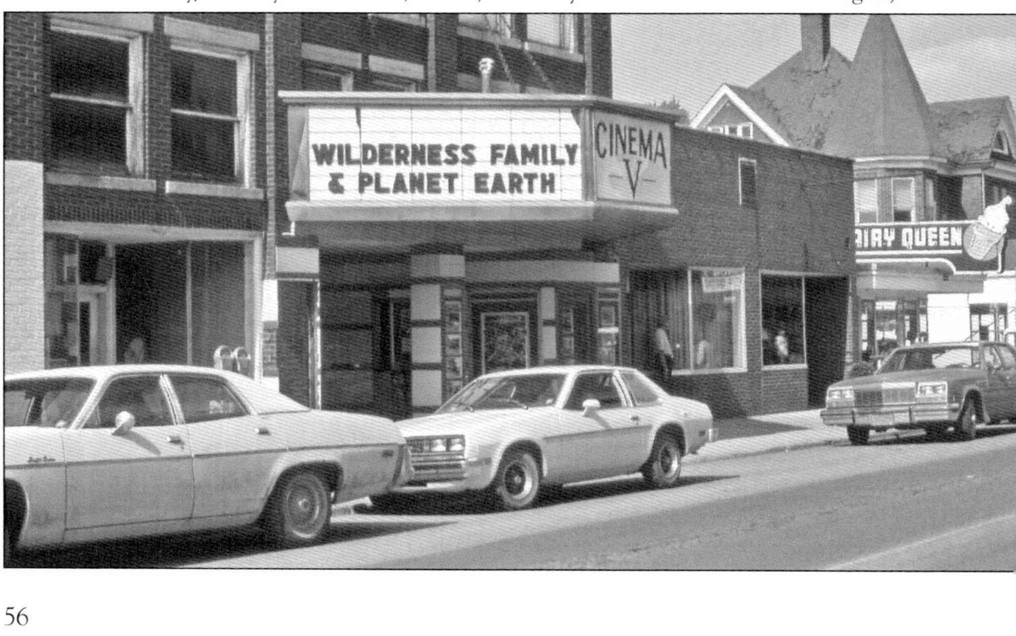

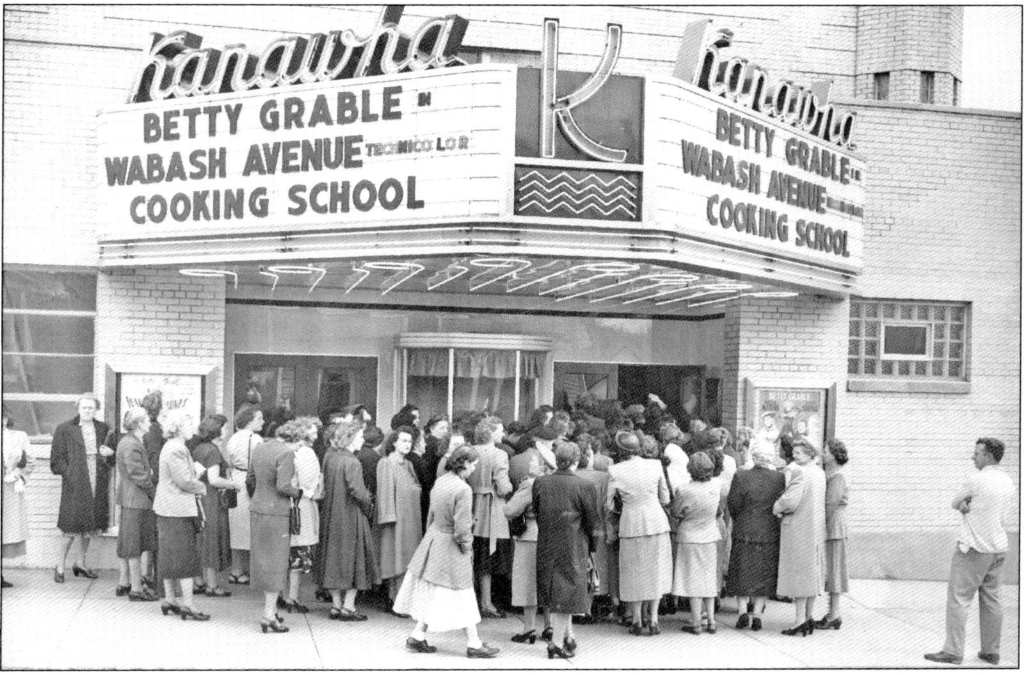

Buckhannon's Kanawha Theatre, originally owned and operated by Dale and Betty Colerider and Bud and Margaret Smallridge, opened in 1949 or 1950. While a 1950 yearbook advertisement at West Virginia Wesleyan College claimed that it was the "most beautiful theatre in West Virginia," the 1951 version simply called it "Buckhannon's largest and only air conditioned theatre." Along with playing films, the 680-seat venue held community events, such as the pictured 1950 cooking school that showcased electric kitchen appliances. The streamline moderne–Art Deco movie house survived a 1967 flood and was operated during the 1970s by Don Leigh McCulty, former partner of Cinema V's Gray Barker. It continued showing movies until at least 1987. Although the building is now a bar, its exterior still looks much like it did during the Kanawha Theatre's heyday. (Both, courtesy of Upshur County Historical Society.)

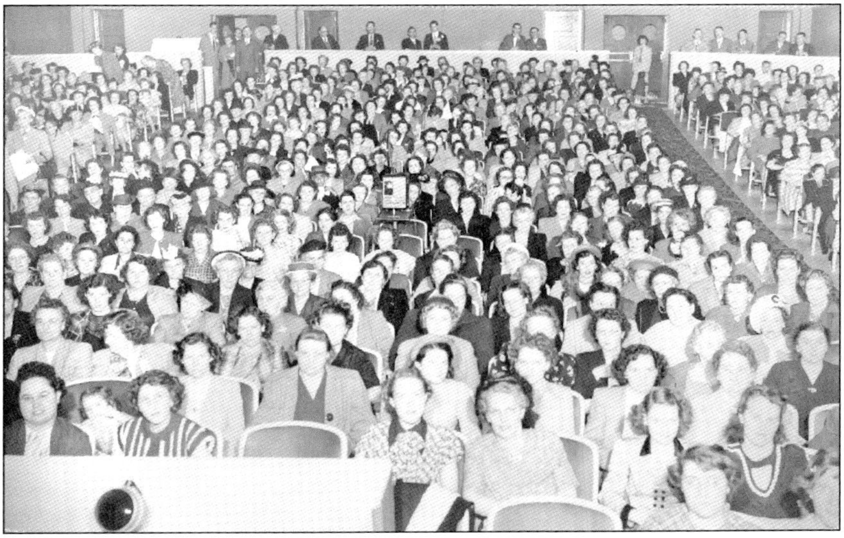

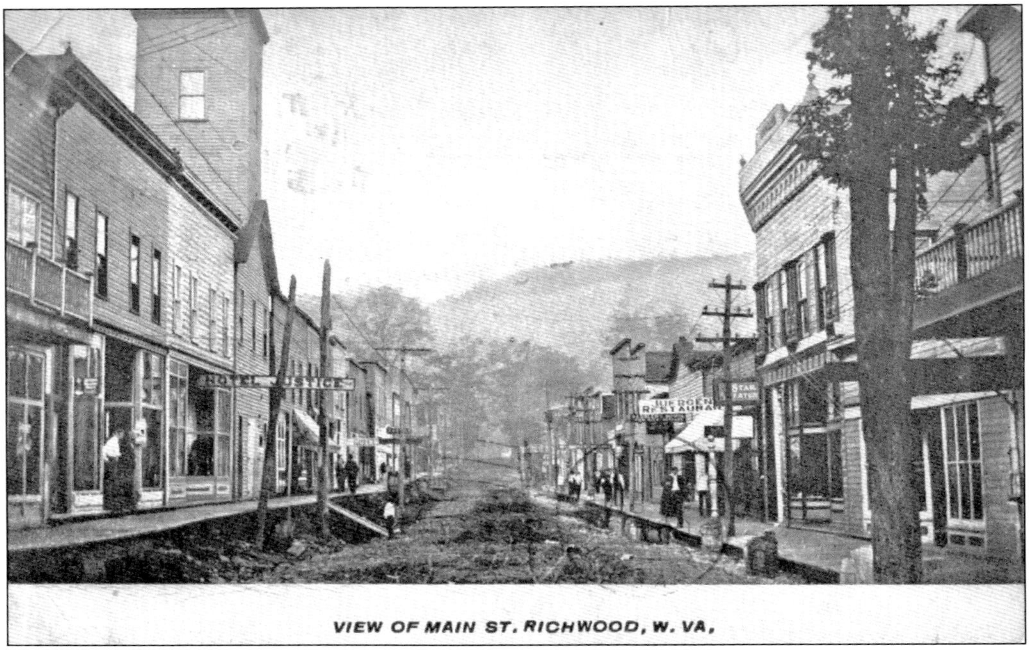

In the postcard above, the Star Theatre's sign is on the right, sticking out from a building on Richwood's dirt Main Street. On August 15, 1921, a massive fire destroyed 33 downtown structures, including the early nickelodeon. Charles and John Holt opened its replacement, the 562-seat New Star Theatre, in 1926. The New Star, made of steel, cinder block, and brick, was designed by architect Levi J. Dean to be fireproof. By 1952, its original rectangular marquee had been replaced by a triangular version covered in bulb lights. In February 1962, the New Star closed—with its marquee simply stating "The End." The building has since hosted commercial uses, as seen in the photograph below from 1991. The theatre's name still rests above the storefront today. (Above, courtesy of West Virginia & Regional History Center, WVU Libraries; below, courtesy of Michael Gioulis.)

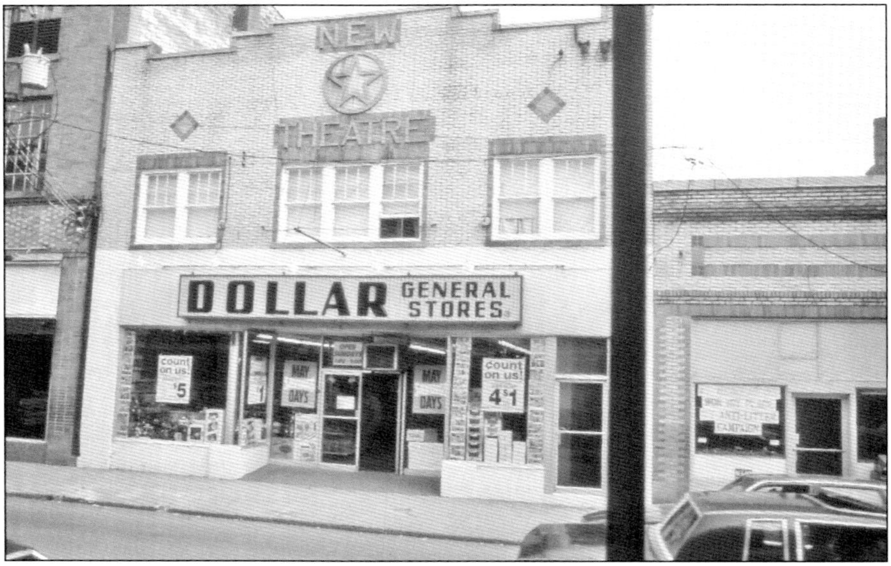

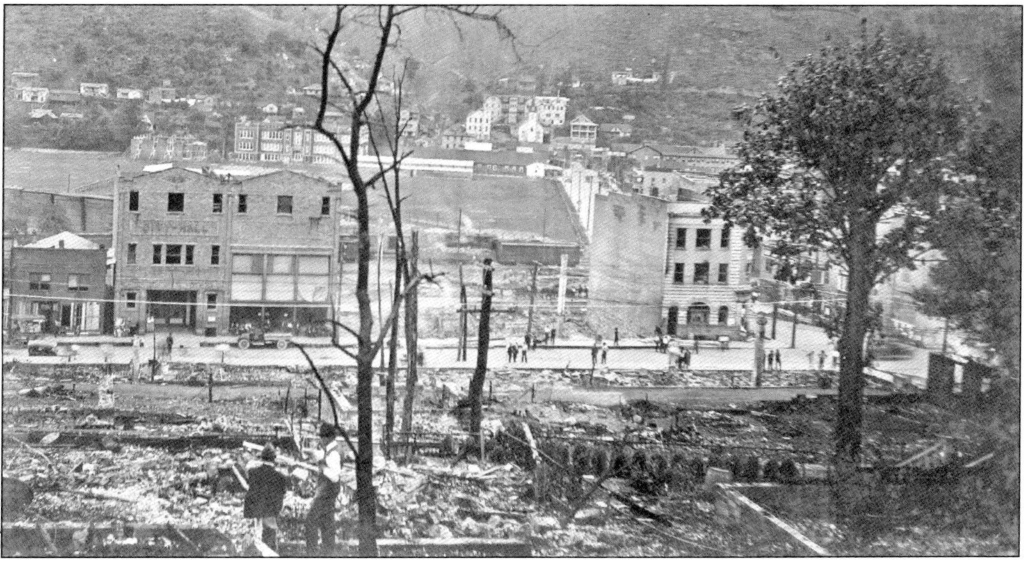

This photograph shows Richwood's Main Street after its devastating 1921 fire. The 1915 city hall (second from left), designed by J.A. Tincher, had an upstairs performance facility. In 1938, that became the Alpine circuit's City Auditorium movie theatre. Alpine operated the 400-seat venue until around 1954; the Jur circuit then briefly ran it. In 2006, the structure was razed. (Courtesy of West Virginia & Regional History Center, WVU Libraries.)

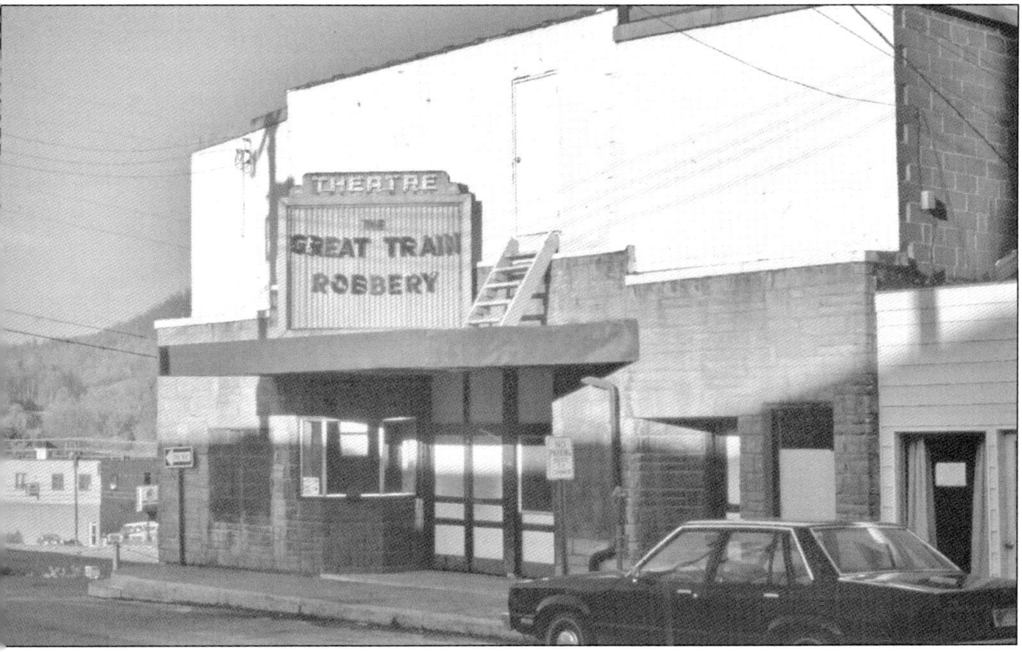

Harrison Groves opened Summersville's Groves Theatre on Court Street in December 1947. His son John ran the projector. The movie house originally had a neon blade sign and a marquee with streamline moderne speed lines; this photograph was taken around 1979, after a facade remodel. The Groves closed sometime between 1983 and 1991. Remodeled again, the building now holds a law firm. (Courtesy of Theatre Historical Society of America, Slide Collection.)

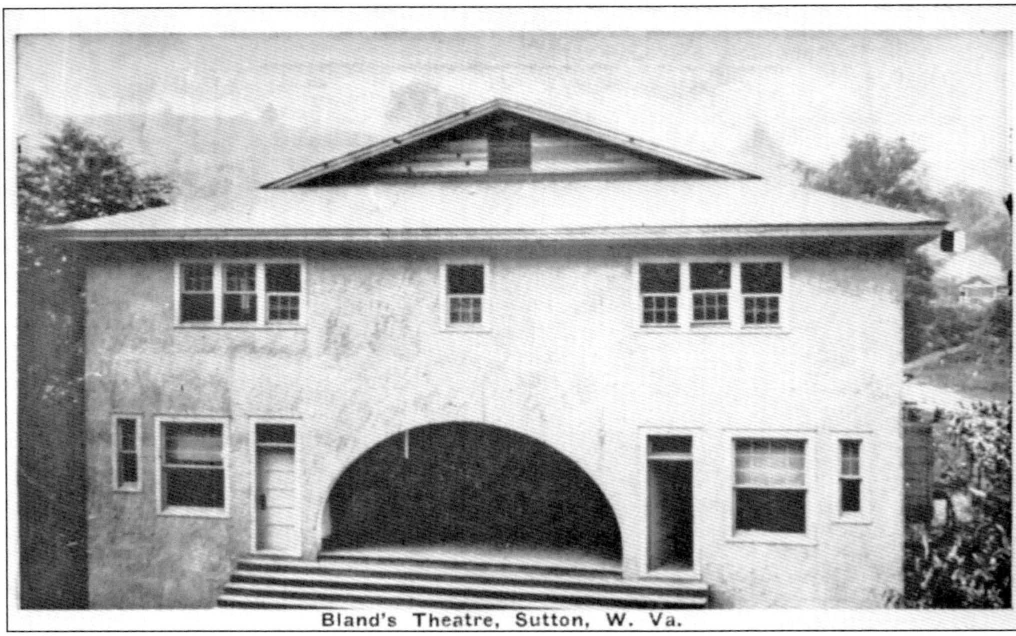

E.L. Bland opened the Bland Theatre in Sutton in 1920. The venue attracted attention for its unusual design as a combination movie house and dance hall, with a dance floor between its 400 seats and its screen and stage. In 1926, the Bland—noted as the city's only movie theatre at the time—was sold. Its name then disappeared from theatre listings. (Courtesy of West Virginia and Regional History Center, WVU Libraries.)

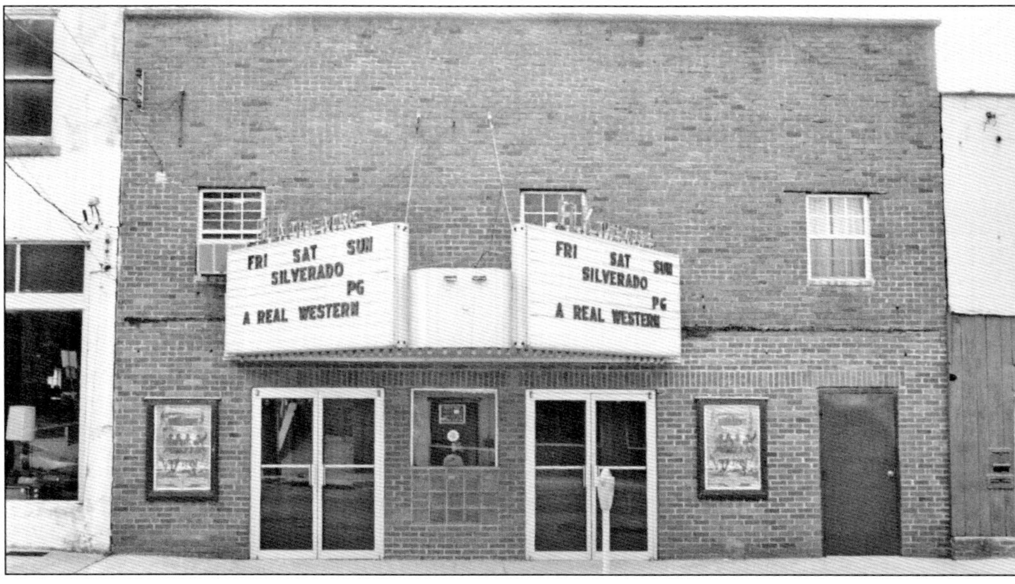

The Alpine circuit purchased Sutton's Victory Theatre in 1937, renaming it the Alpine. In 1945 the chain announced it was constructing a new Alpine in Sutton. The air-conditioned, fireproo building opened in 1946 with new equipment. Sometime between 1960 and 1977, the secon Alpine was renamed the Elk Theatre (as seen in this 1985 photograph). The 250-seat Elk stil shows first-run movies on weekends. (Courtesy of Michael Gioulis.)

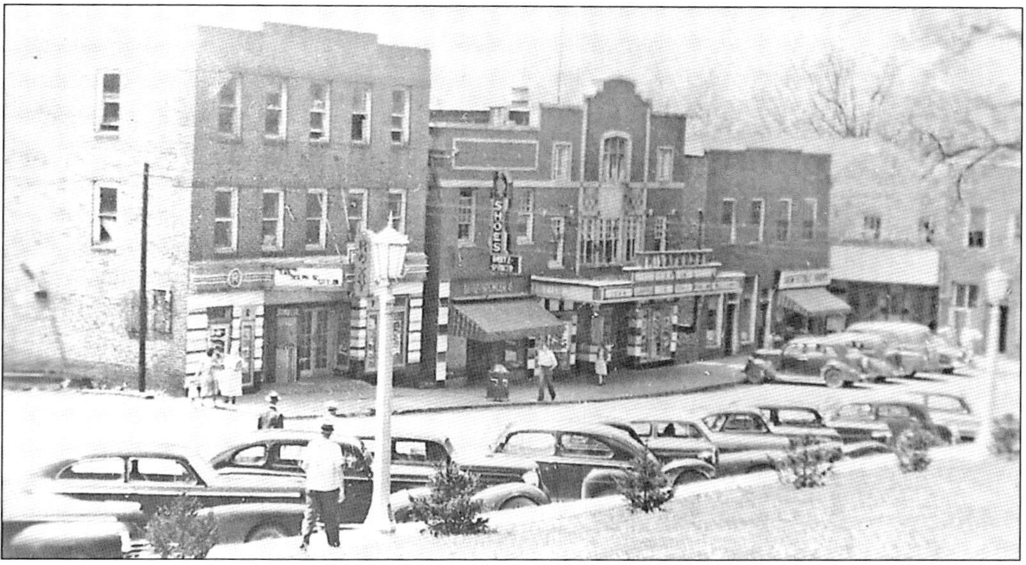

Two movie houses sat on Webster Springs' courthouse square. The 500-seat Art Deco–style Roxy Theatre (left) opened in 1939 and operated until at least 1957. To its right was the 400-seat Mill-Vance Theatre, which opened around 1930. Richard "Dick" Palmer bought it in 1932. By 1947, he also owned the Roxy. In 1973, a fire gutted the Mill-Vance and killed Palmer. (Courtesy of West Virginia & Regional History Center, WVU Libraries.)

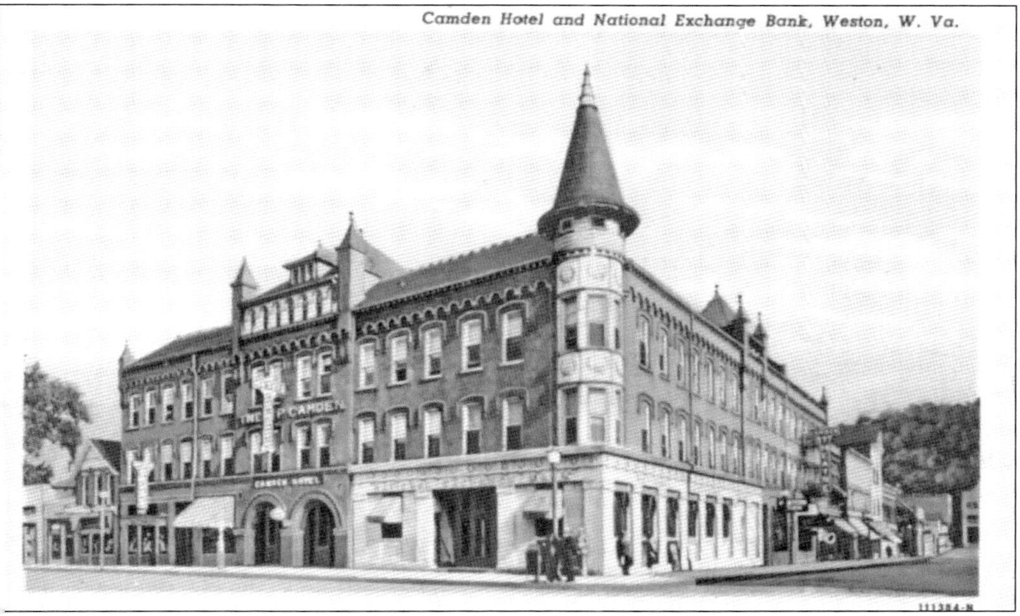

The Camden Opera House was part of Weston's 1896–1897 Camden Building (designed by Columbus, Ohio, architects Yost and Packard) from the beginning. Later known as the Camden Theatre, the 600-seat, ground-floor auditorium was presenting films by 1926. In 1938, the Fayton Amusement Company circuit bought it, keeping it open until 1958. Although the side-entrance theatre is gone, the Camden Building is part of the Weston Downtown Historic District. (Author's collection.)

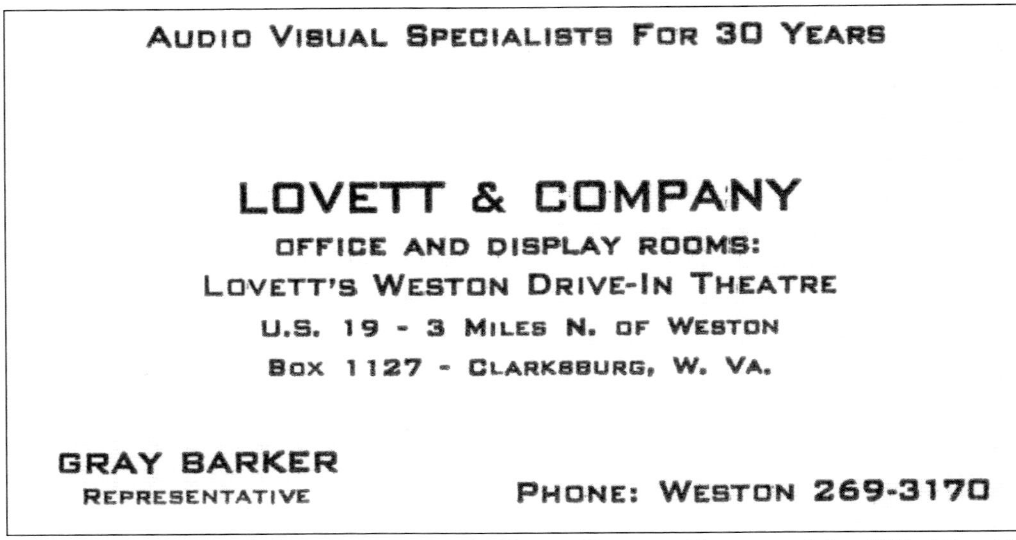

Delbert Lovett opened the 150-car Lovett's Weston Drive-in Theatre in May 1952. His wife, Bernice, owned and operated it after his death. The Lovetts also ran Lovett & Company, a theatre equipment business, from the same Weston property. This business card is for Gray Barker, who did sales for the company and advertising for the drive-in. The drive-in closed in the 1980s and was destroyed. (Courtesy of Clarksburg-Harrison Public Library.)

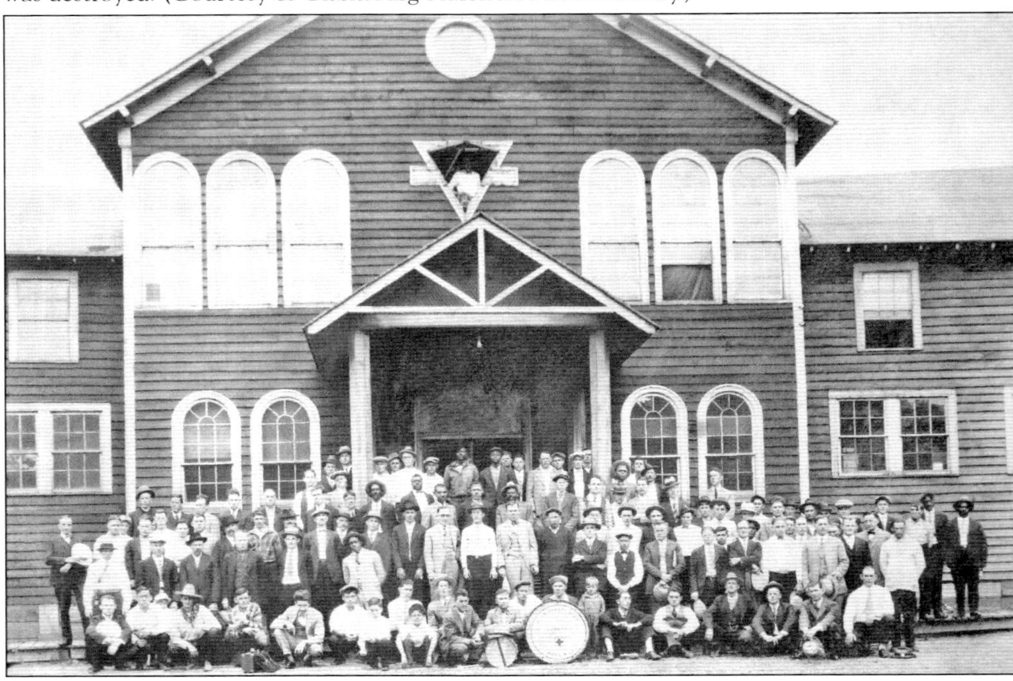

In Widen, a coal company town, the since destroyed YMCA building opened in 1920. It contained a gym, bowling alley, billiard hall, and 250-seat auditorium. Later known as the Widen Theatre and the YMCA Theatre, it showed films between approximately 1929 and 1956. This photograph shows Widen Safety Club members posing outside with Westerns actor Tom Mix (first row, third from left). (Courtesy of West Virginia State Archives, Dennis Griffith Collection.)

Six

Mountaineer Country

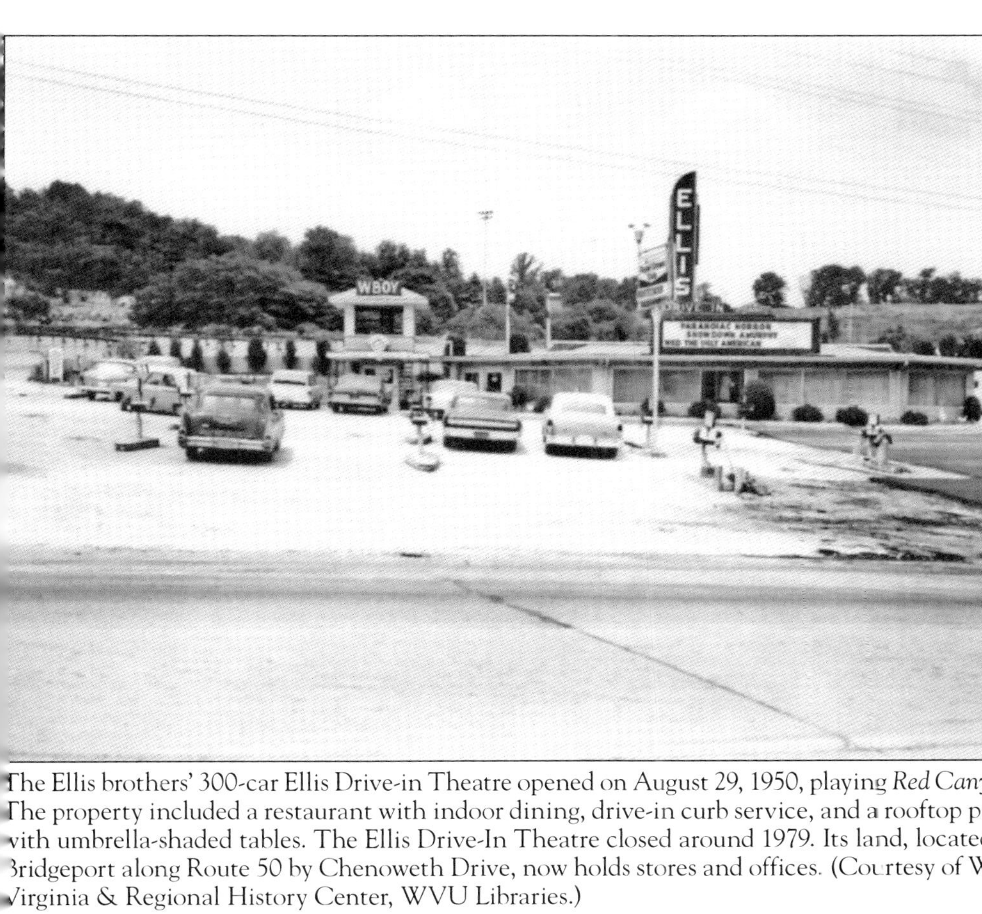

The Ellis brothers' 300-car Ellis Drive-in Theatre opened on August 29, 1950, playing *Red Canyon*. The property included a restaurant with indoor dining, drive-in curb service, and a rooftop patio with umbrella-shaded tables. The Ellis Drive-In Theatre closed around 1979. Its land, located in Bridgeport along Route 50 by Chenoweth Drive, now holds stores and offices. (Courtesy of West Virginia & Regional History Center, WVU Libraries.)

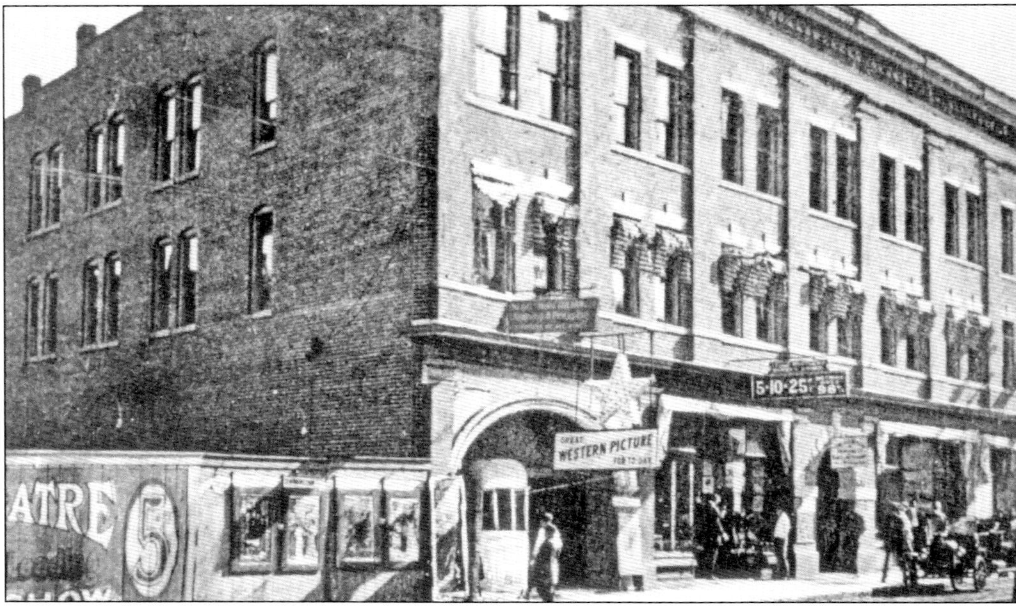

Jack Marks, an early film exhibitor who established and then sold nickelodeons in multiple states, opened the Star Theatre in 1902. Unable to locate a buyer for Clarksburg's first movie house, Marks stayed and operated the 230-seat Star until at least 1915. Located in the Greaney Building on South Fourth Street, near Traders' Alley, the Star was soon destroyed for retail development. (Courtesy of Theatre Historical Society of America, Editor's Collection.)

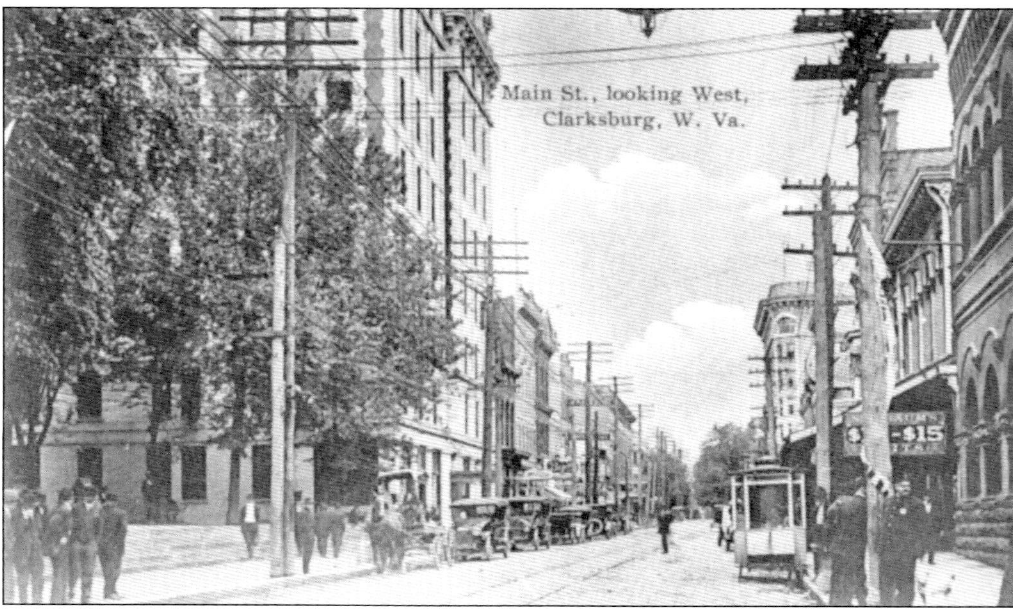

Operating as early as 1908 in Clarksburg's Independent Order of Odd Fellows building, the Bijou Theatre featured a sign that can be glimpsed in the middle of the left side of the block in this postcard. The nickelodeon advertised itself as a 5¢ "family theatre" where "all the nice people go." In 1923, Jack Marks took over the first-run movie house's operation. It closed around 1925 but its building still stands. (Author's collection.)

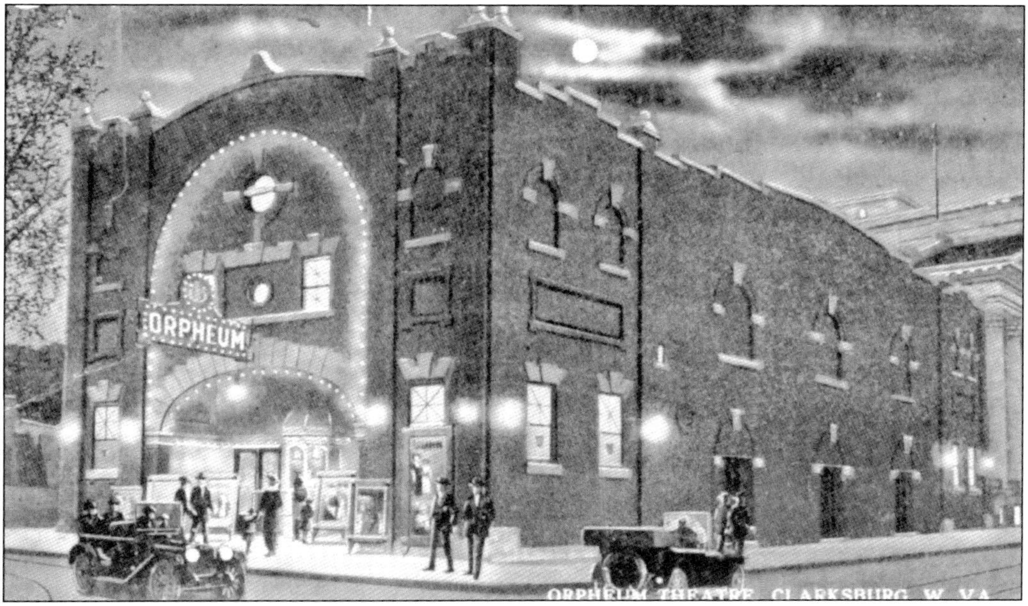

Frank Moore's Orpheum Theatre opened in 1913 on Fourth Street in Clarksburg. A 1914 *Clarksburg Daily Telegram* article about the "photoplay theatre" lauds its system of fans, noting, "Many people actually go there to escape the heat." The 350-seat Orpheum added a Moller pipe organ in 1915 and closed in 1929. By 1931, the since destroyed building housed Monongahela Power Company's offices. (Courtesy of Harrison County Historical Society.)

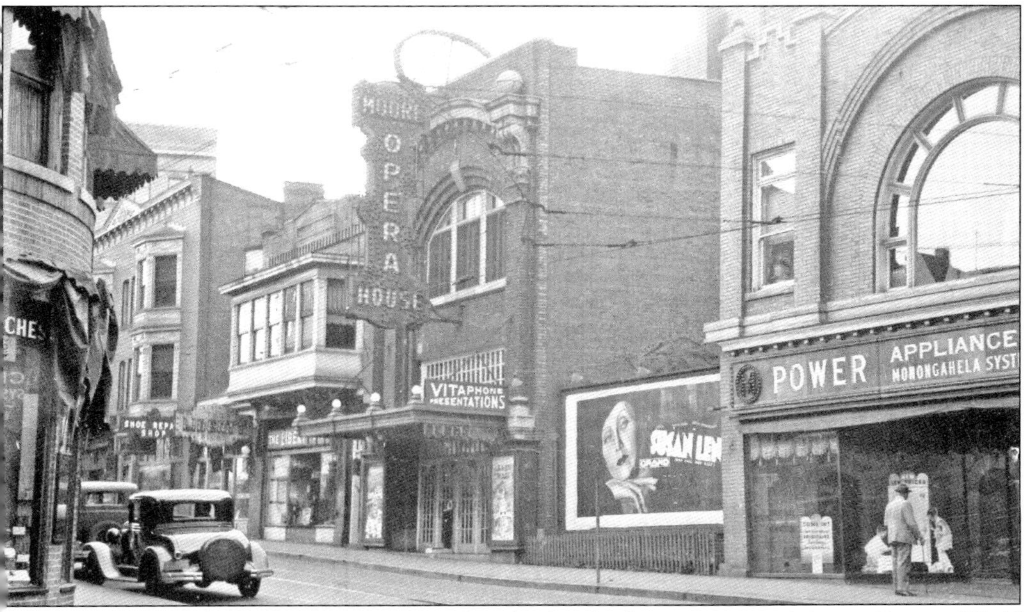

Jack Marks opened Moore's Opera House beside the Orpheum in 1918. *Moving Picture World* reported that the Frank Moore–owned venue, costing $150,000, featured a marble lobby and 1,400 leather seats. In 1931, it hosted Harry Powers's infamous trial for murdering two wealthy widows and one's three children. The theatre closed in 1956. A bank bought the building in 1994 and razed it. (Courtesy of West Virginia State Archives, Clarksburg Exponent Collection.)

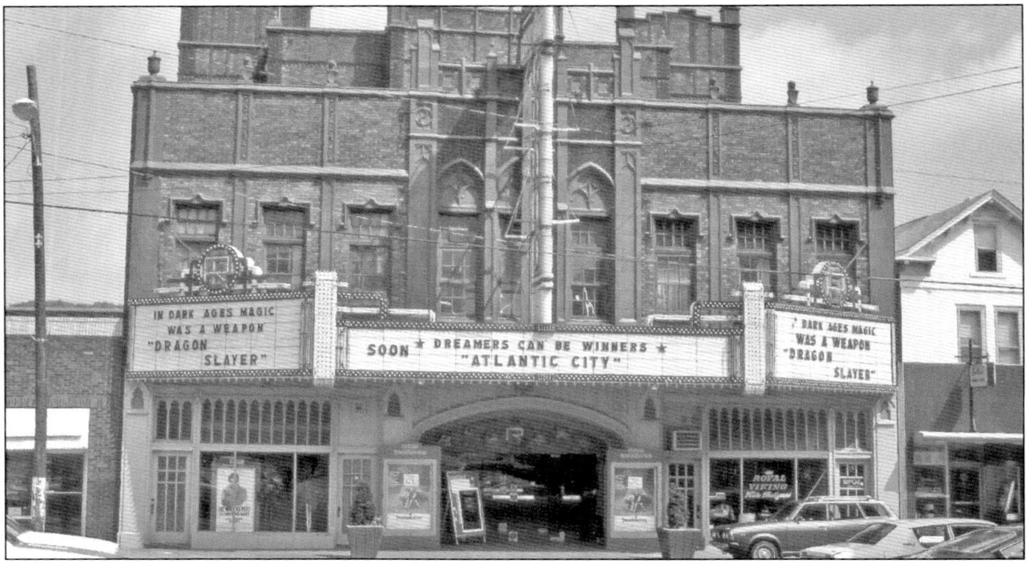

Clarksburg's Robinson Grand Theatre opened in 1913. In 1927, Claude Robinson's theatre became America's 13th with sound, part of a remodel and expansion that made it a 1,500-seat neo-Gothic picture palace. After a 1939 fire, its interior gained streamline moderne style. It closed in 1984. After a few years as the Rose Garden playhouse, it sat vacant. The city bought it in 2014 and has been renovating it into a performing arts center. (Courtesy of American Classic Images.)

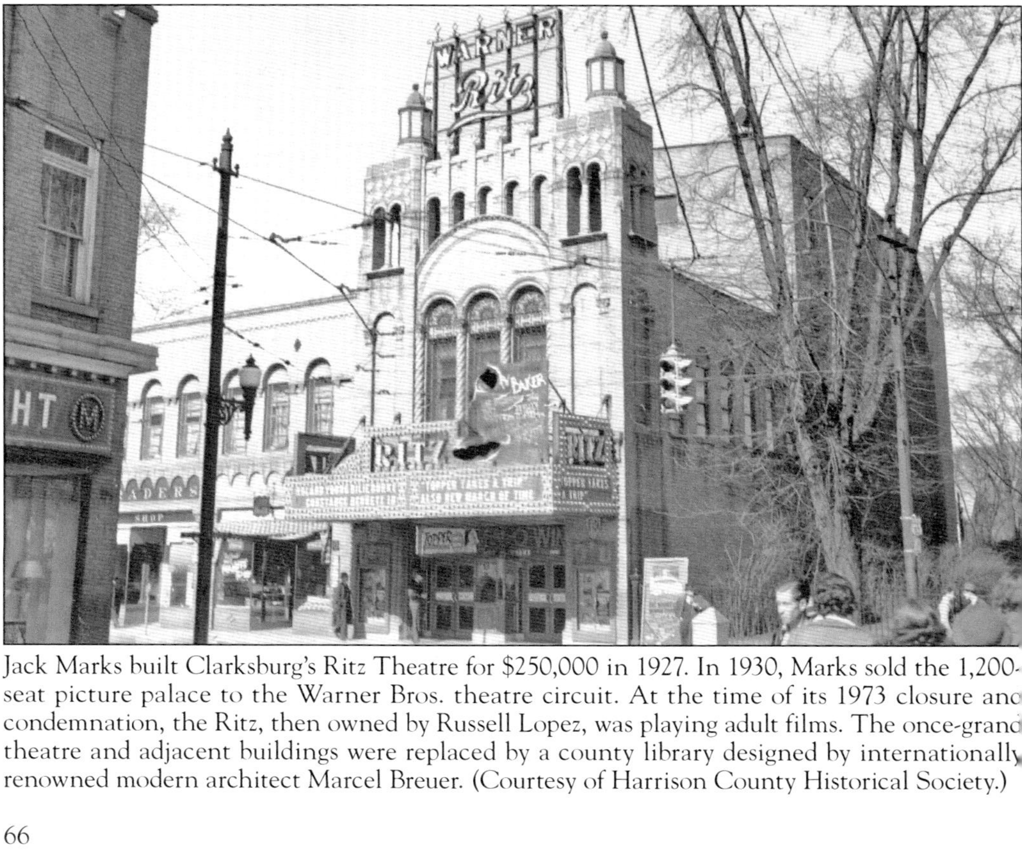

Jack Marks built Clarksburg's Ritz Theatre for $250,000 in 1927. In 1930, Marks sold the 1,200-seat picture palace to the Warner Bros. theatre circuit. At the time of its 1973 closure and condemnation, the Ritz, then owned by Russell Lopez, was playing adult films. The once-grand theatre and adjacent buildings were replaced by a county library designed by internationally renowned modern architect Marcel Breuer. (Courtesy of Harrison County Historical Society.)

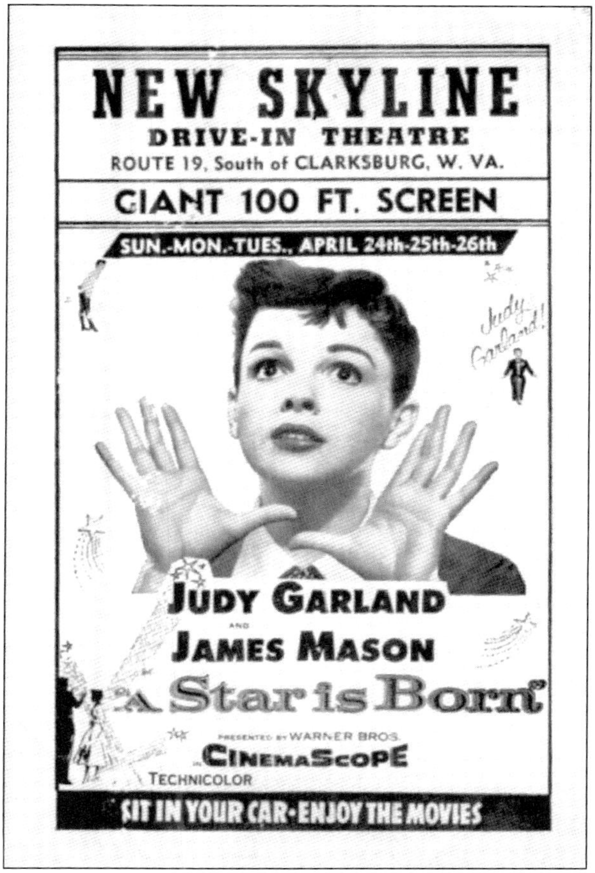

Clarksburg's Warner Skyline Drive-in Theatre, operated by Charles Warner, was open as early as 1948. Amenities included a playground and, by 1954, a 100-foot Cinemascope screen. Along with other sites in Clarksburg and Bridgeport, the drive-in is featured in Francis Ford Coppola's 1969 film *The Rain People*; the plot involves James Caan's character getting hired there. The Skyline closed in 1985; its marquee still stands. (Courtesy of Harrison County Historical Society.)

Fairmont's 1,260-seat Grand Opera House, designed by architect J.E. Allison, opened on the corner of Monroe and Jackson Streets in 1902. Renamed the Grand Theatre in 1915, it played films from then until 1920. That year, the building was purchased for reuse as an Odd Fellows lodge and commercial space. The heavily remodeled structure was demolished in the early 1980s. (Courtesy of West Virginia & Regional History Center, WVU Libraries.)

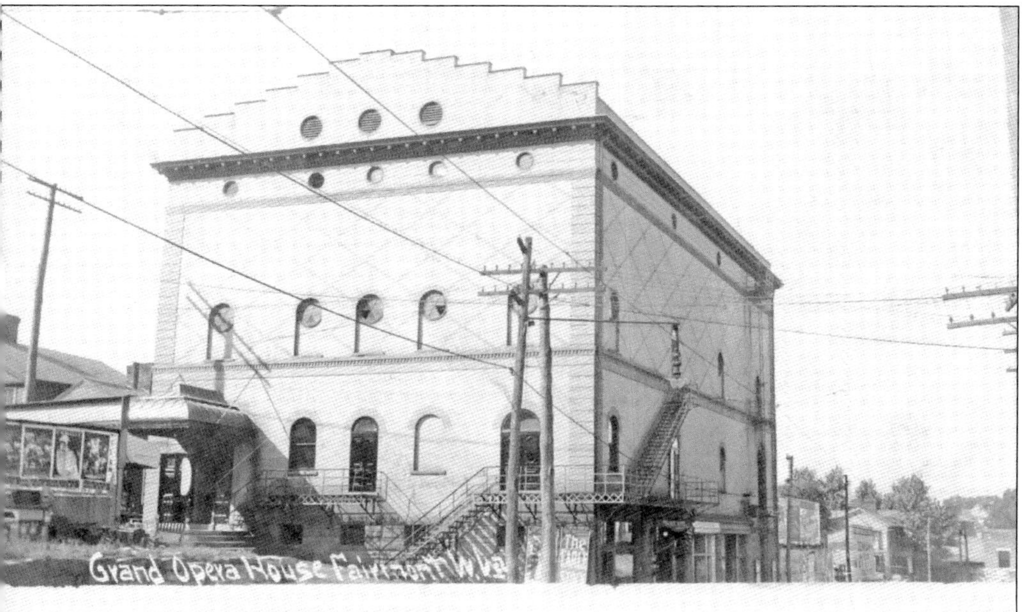

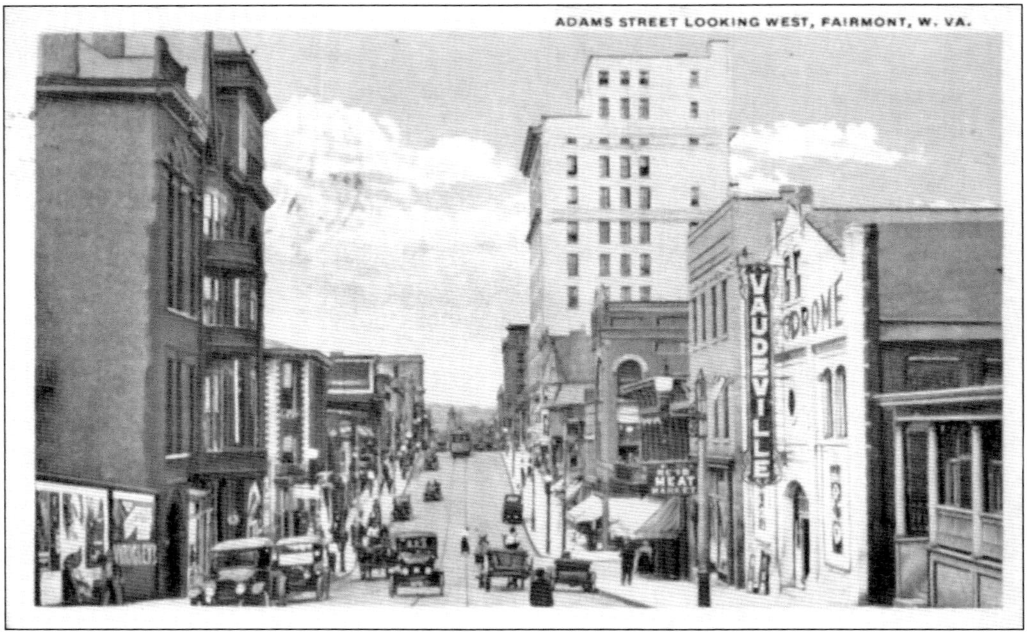

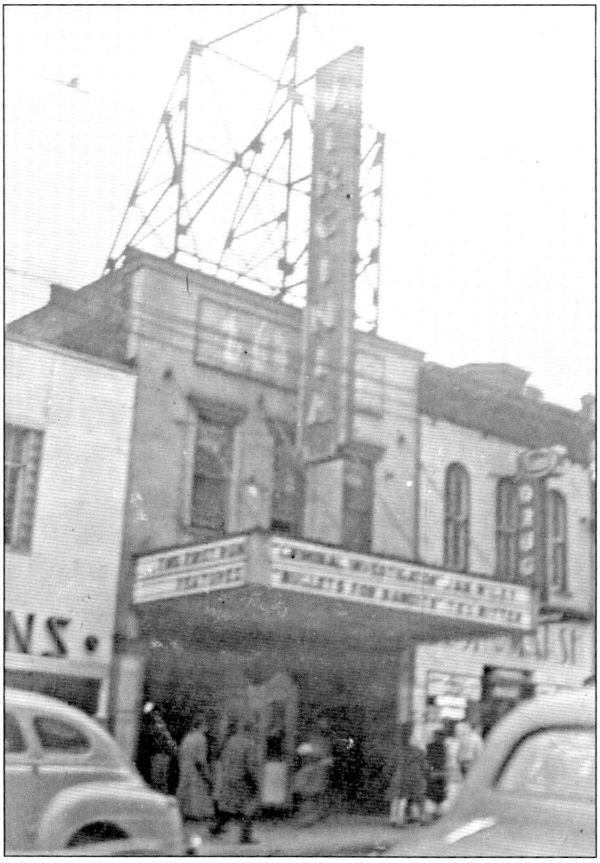

Although Fairmont's Hippodrome displayed a "Vaudeville" blade sign, the theatre was also advertising "two photoplays each day" in 1911. Manager Sol Burka began a $10,000 remodel in April 1922. That September, the venue became the Blue Ridge Theatre, its reopening including blackface minstrels and an unnamed "feature photoplay at popular prices." The venue closed in 1924, with its leased building (which no longer exists) changing to business usage. (Author's collection.)

The Virginia Theatre opened at 320 Adams Street in Fairmont in 1922, showing *Oliver Twist*. Its opening program claimed it offered "the choicest photoplays" in a "commodious, comfortable" setting. During the Great Depression, the movie house held food drives. The nearly 900-seat Virginia Theatre, owned by Warner Bros., shut down in the early 1950s. It was razed approximately a decade later. (Courtesy of Theatre Historical Society of America, Theatre File Collection.)

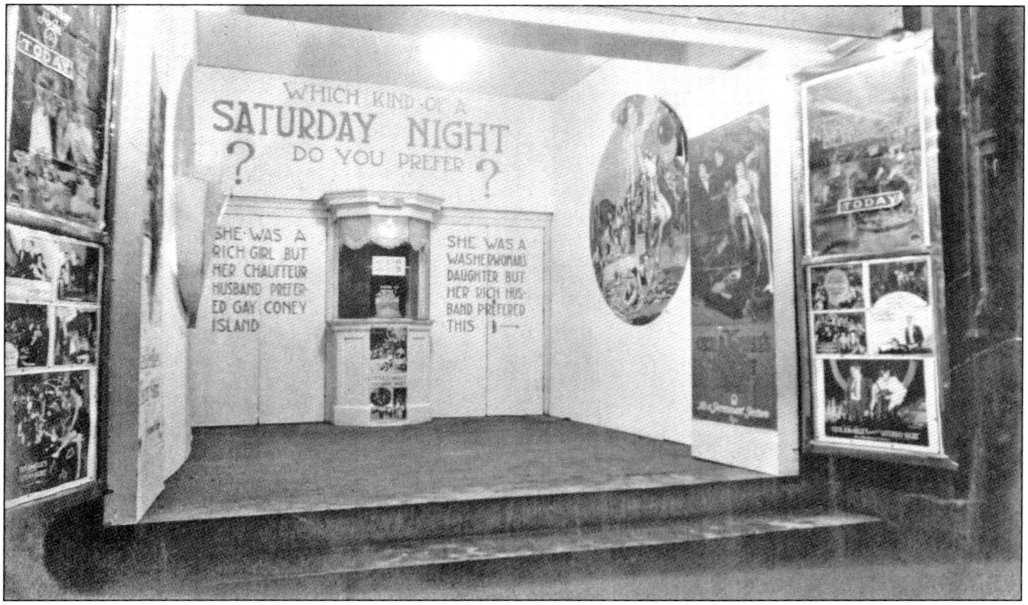

Film Daily Year Book's 1920 list of the state's primary, first-run film venues includes Fairmont's Nelson Theatre. The movie house gained attention in other national exhibition journals for the impressive exterior promotional displays that manager Floyd D. Morrow designed for specific films (such as Cecil B. DeMille's comedy *Saturday Night*, as shown by this 1922 photograph). The 400-seat Nelson closed by 1945. (Courtesy of West Virginia State Archives, Elizabeth Windsor Collection.)

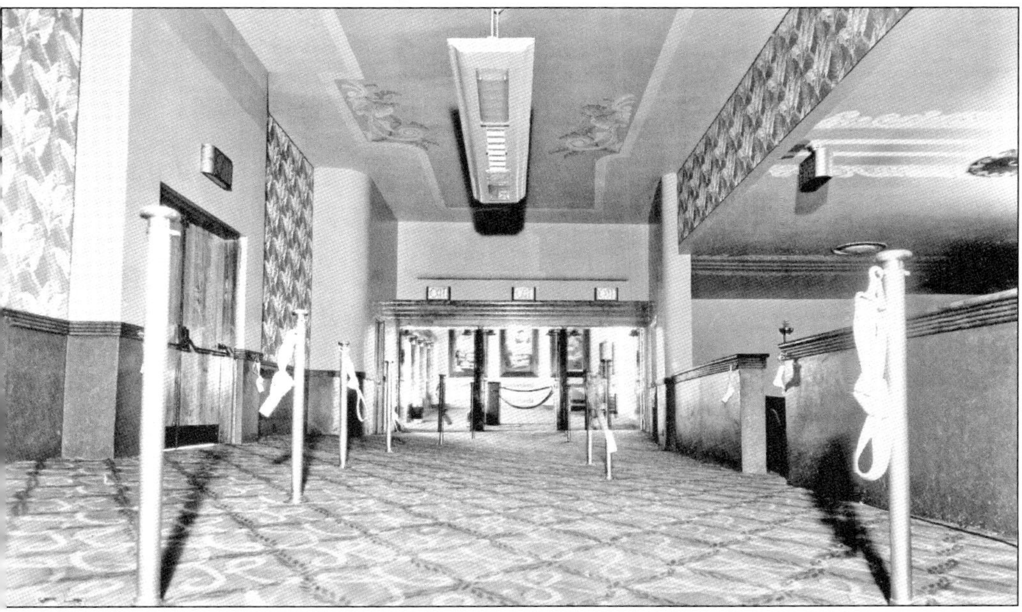

Designed by Ohio architect Peter M. Hulskin, Fairmont's Lee Theatre was built in 1939 at 321 Adams Street. The 600-seat, air-conditioned movie house, managed by co-owner Columbus Harr, cost $75,000. This photograph shows the Art Deco theatre's lobby; its exterior featured a speed-lined marquee and glass brick rows. The Lee closed in the 1960s. Its site became a bank's parking lot. (Courtesy of West Virginia State Archives, Elizabeth Windsor Collection.)

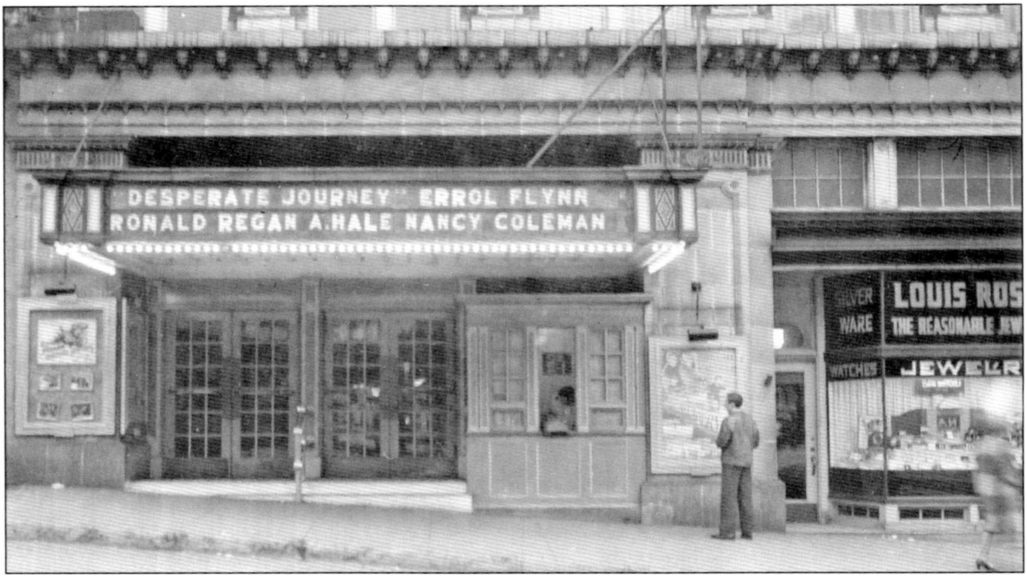

The original 1923 Fairmont Theatre, designed by Columbus architect Fred W. Elliott, was a $400,000 picture palace. It featured 1,272 seats, arched windows, a marble-floored lobby, and a light dome in the balcony's foyer. This elegant building on the 400 block of Adams Street fell into receivership in 1929 and was auctioned off. New owners remodeled, added sound, and reopened it. In 1944, fire destroyed the theatre, then owned by Warner Bros. Its 1946 replacement was a 1,567-seat, Vitrolite-covered Art Deco creation by Pittsburgh architect Victor A. Rigaumont. In 1973, owner Joe Carunchia triplexed it, dividing the auditorium and enclosing the balcony. In 2005, the theatre's marquee proclaimed, "Always 3 great movies." Despite preservation efforts, it was demolished in 2012 for a state office building. (Above, courtesy of Theatre Historical Society of America, Theatre File Collection; below, courtesy of American Classic Images.)

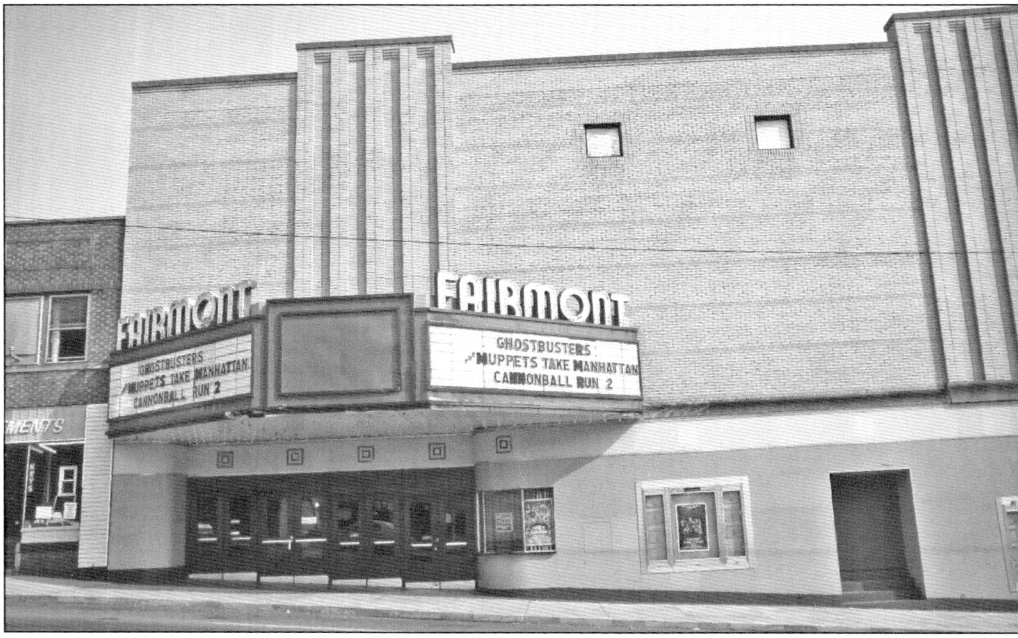

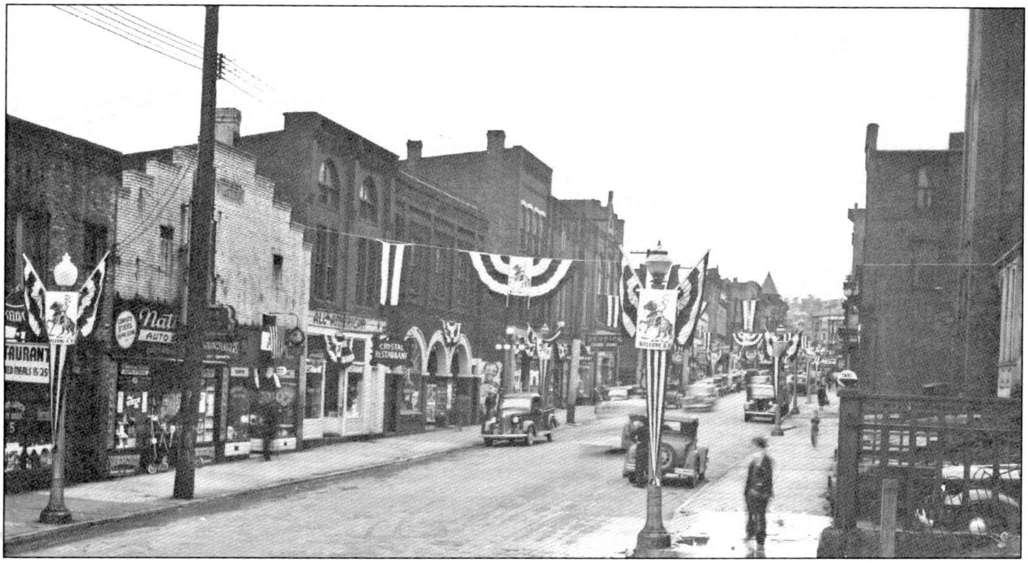

Grafton's Hippodrome, specializing in vaudeville and film, opened in 1912. Prior to 1918, J. Lester Bush bought it, renaming it the Strand Theatre. The building's three large arches are visible in the above streetscape. In 1948, Bush sold the 500-seat Strand to Michael Manos. Architect Victor A. Rigaumont then remodeled the building to its current appearance. Its reopening as the Manos Theatre in July 1949 featured the film *The Life of Riley*, a parade, and a radio broadcast. Seen below around 1979, the Manos last showed movies in 1998. Since then, it has sat vacant, aside from opening for occasional special events. In 2018, the city acquired the Manos with the plan of turning it into a community event space. (Above, courtesy of West Virginia & Regional History Center, WVU Libraries; below, courtesy of Theatre Historical Society of America, Slide Collection.)

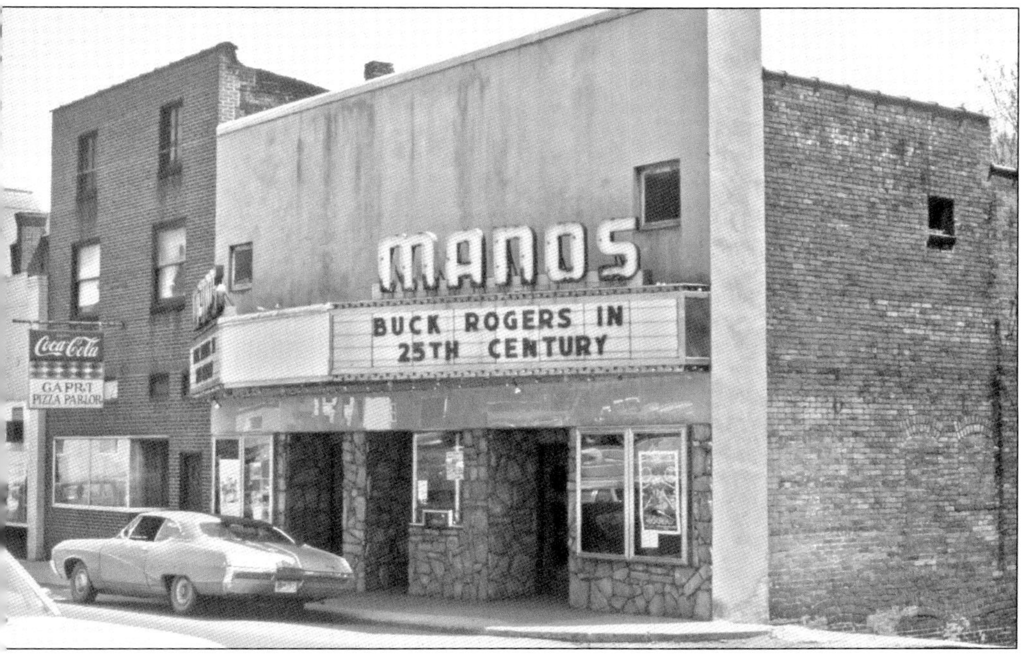

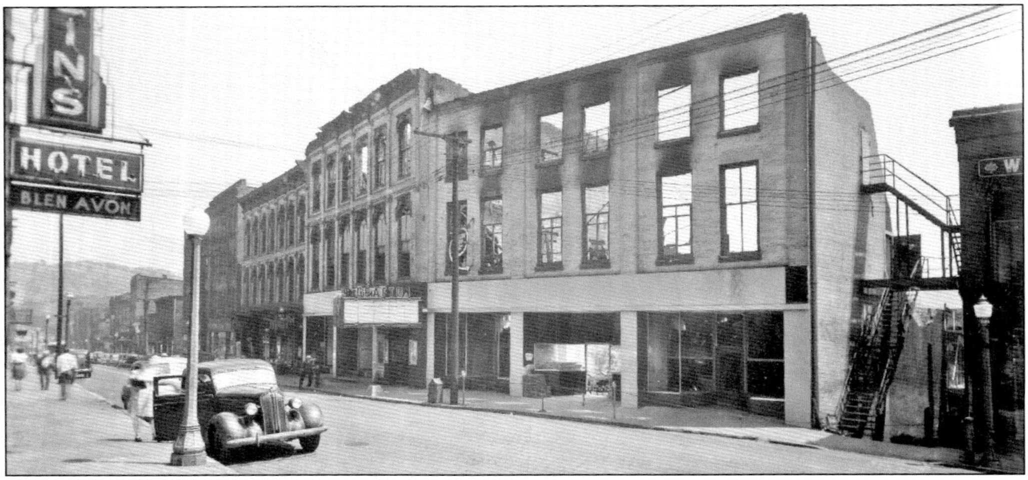

John George Brinkman's Brinkman Opera House opened in Grafton before 1897. Located on the Brinkman Building's second floor, it started showing films for 5¢ in 1909. Its name changed to the Grafton Theatre around 1946, shortly before its 1947 projector fire damaged the block (as seen here). Although the theatre did not reopen, the Italianate-style Brinkman Building survives. (Courtesy of West Virginia & Regional History Center, WVU Libraries.)

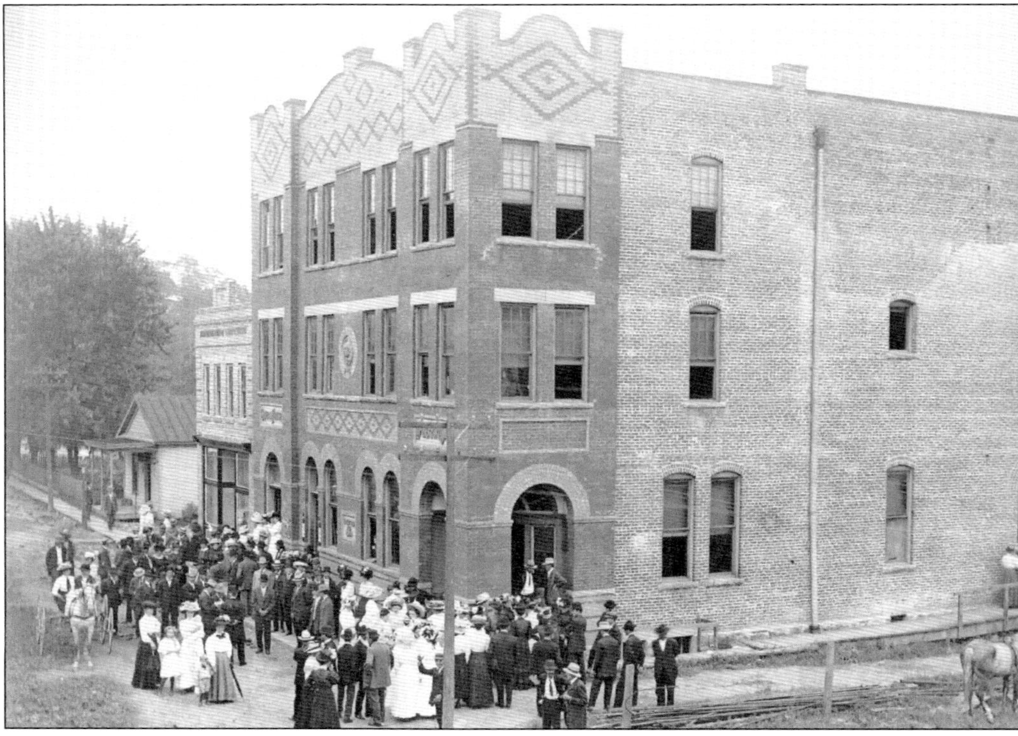

Lumberport's 600-seat Opera House opened on January 10, 1906, managed by Dr. L.C. Oyster The auditorium was on the first floor of this elaborate brick building. It was showing films by 1930. The Opera House was sold in 1935 and again in 1937, shortly before it stopped appearing in film exhibition listings. By that time, it only sat 250 people. It later burned down. (Courtesy of Harrison County Historical Society.)

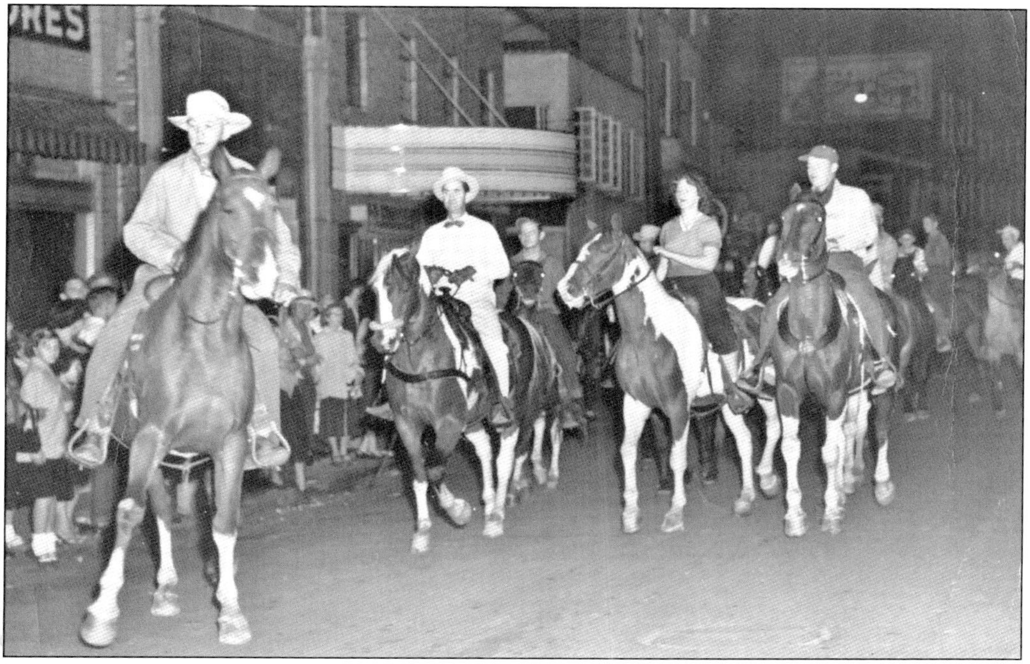

The Mannington Theatre, designed by prolific theatre architect Victor A. Rigaumont for Dr. C.P. Church, opened in 1936 in Mannington. This photograph shows the 1953 Mannington Fair Parade passing the 430-seat theatre. It survived until at least 1984, when it added a popular theatre attraction: a game room. The theatre's streamline moderne marquee still stands today, with the building reused as a bar. (Courtesy of West Augusta Historical Society.)

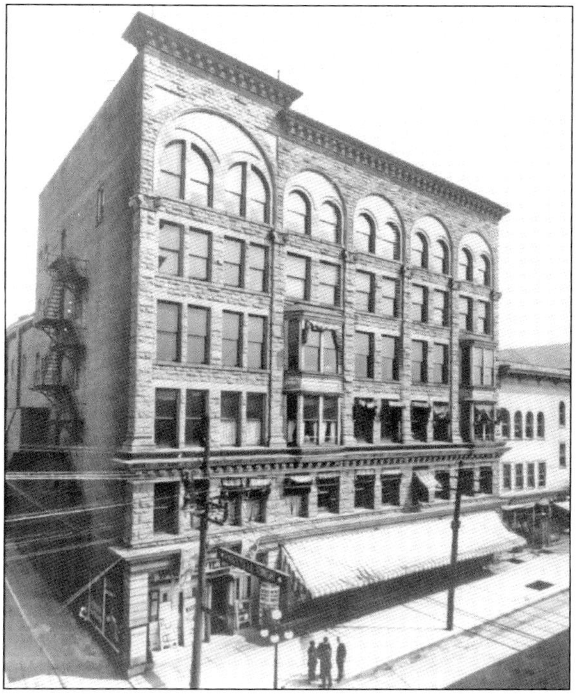

Morgantown's 700-seat Swisher Theatre opened before 1901 in prominent businessman Harold Llewellyn Swisher's seven-story office building. The performance hall was remodeled in 1914 into a film venue called the Strand Theatre. In 1927, Morgantown's worst fire ever destroyed the 400-seat Strand's building and all other structures on the east side of High Street's 300 block, causing $2 million in damages. (Courtesy of West Virginia & Regional History Center, WVU Libraries.)

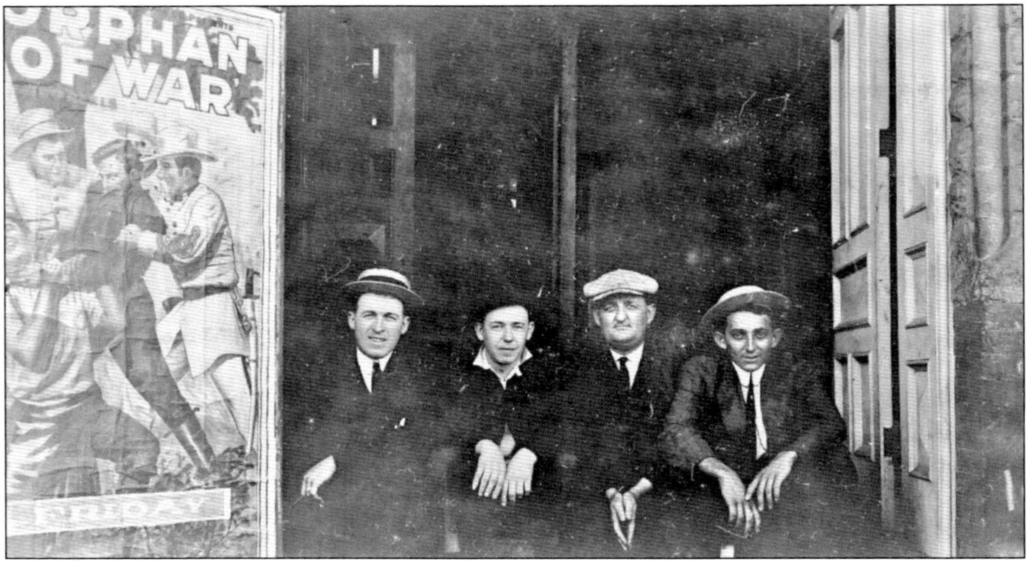

These men are seated in the Grand Theatre's doorway next to a poster for a 1913 film. The Grand was in a three-story Walnut Street building with multiple arches and fanlights. In 1906, H.A. Christy turned this traditional theatre into Morgantown's first movie house. The 500-seat Grand was a nickelodeon, still offering 5¢ admission in 1914. It closed around 1936. (Courtesy of West Virginia & Regional History Center, WVU Libraries.)

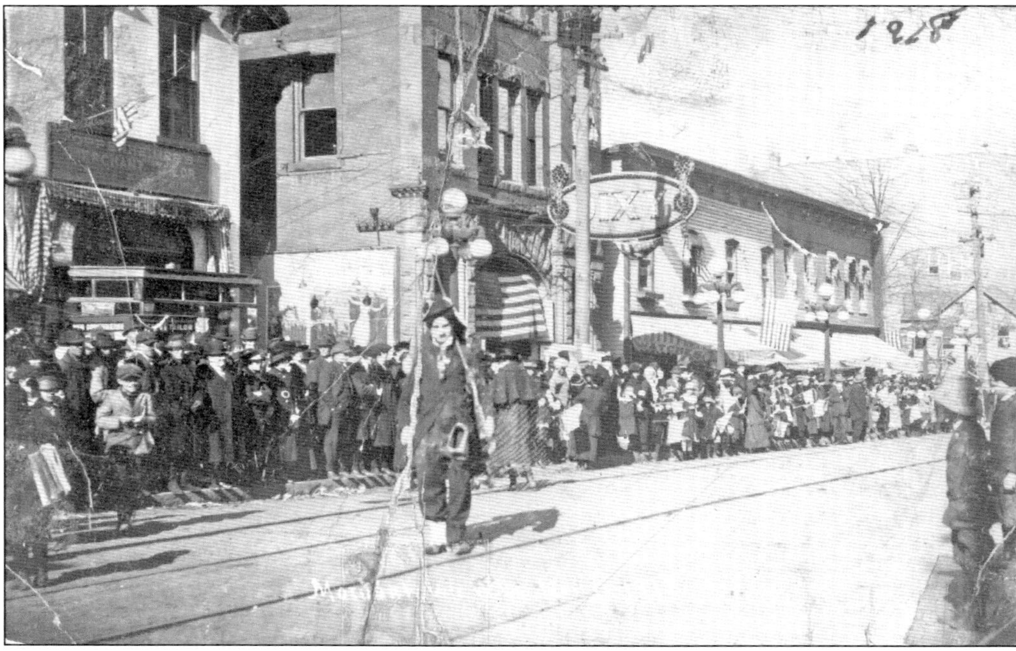

Morgantown's 420-seat Dixy Theatre opened in late 1914 or early 1915 in architect Elmer Jacobs's Richardsonian Romanesque Donley Building, built in 1895. (The building has changed little since this 1918 image.) In a 1920 West Virginia University yearbook, the Dixy marketed itself as "clean classy," offering "the best orchestra, with the best pictures." It closed that year for its space to become commercial. (Courtesy of West Virginia & Regional History Center, WVU Libraries.)

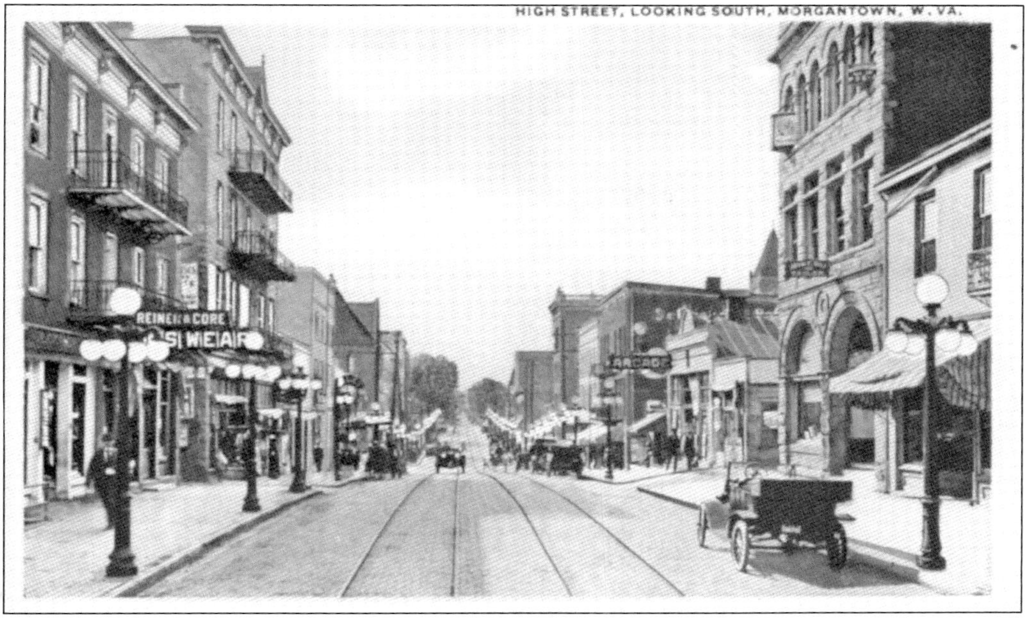

Morgantown's Arcade Theatre was operating as early as 1912 on the corner of High and Wall Streets. In 1914, the 500-seat nickelodeon still offered 5¢ admission. Its 1919 advertisement in West Virginia University's yearbook contained a poem that concluded, "There's laughter and mirth in this picture place, and as movies progress, we keep up the pace." Proprietor Frank W. Rodgers's 1923 yearbook advertisement is more specific, touting the movie house's orchestra, "big ventilating fan," and Simplex projectors, all providing "good, comfortable, and clean entertainment." In 1932, the Arcade was sold and renamed the Morgan Theatre. The Metropolitan Theatre's George Sallows bought the 400-seat Morgan in 1936, greatly remodeling it into the Art Deco building below. The second-run Morgan closed around 1976. Today, the heavily remodeled building hosts a store. (Above, author's collection; below, courtesy of Morgantown History Museum.)

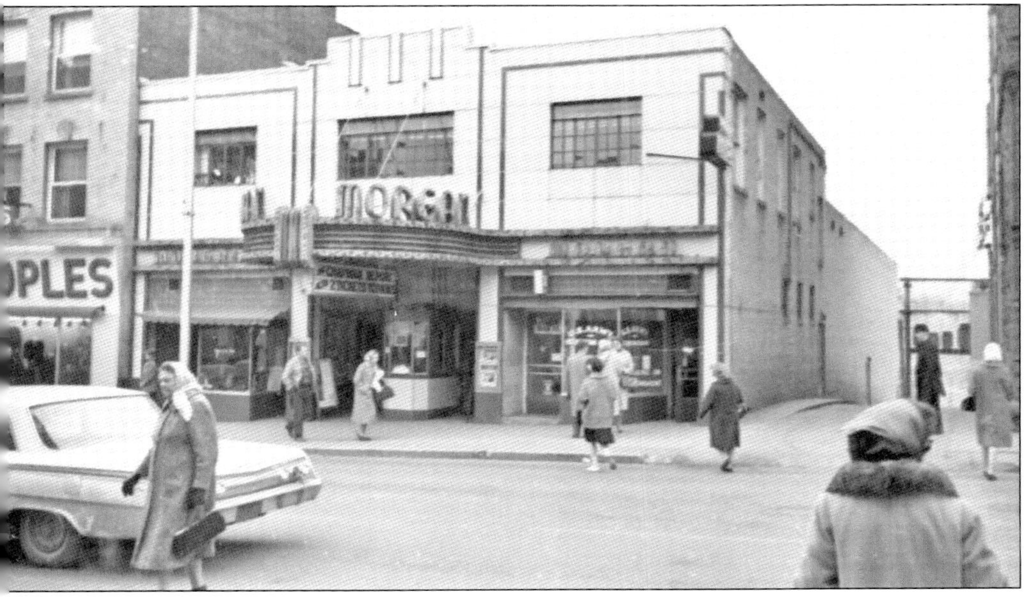

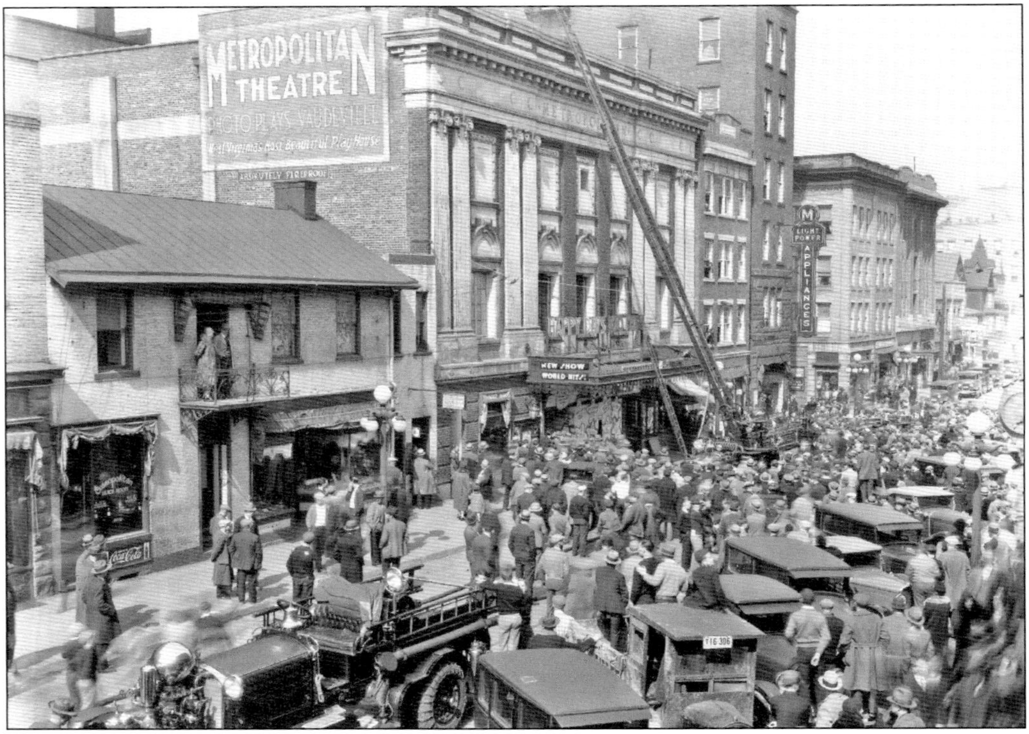

The Comuntzis family opened the 1,300-seat Metropolitan Theatre in 1924 in Morgantown. C.W. Bates designed the $500,000 neoclassical structure. A Mighty Wurlitzer came in 1928; the projection room expanded after a 1930 fire; air-conditioning arrived in 1933. Historically known for its touring shows and test screenings of upcoming Hollywood films, the Met is now a publicly owned performance venue. (Courtesy of West Virginia & Regional History Center, WVU Libraries.)

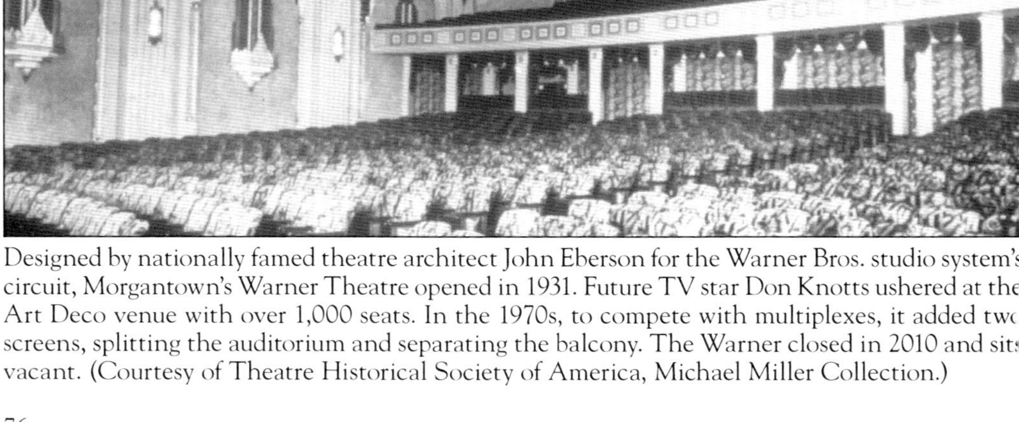

Designed by nationally famed theatre architect John Eberson for the Warner Bros. studio system's circuit, Morgantown's Warner Theatre opened in 1931. Future TV star Don Knotts ushered at the Art Deco venue with over 1,000 seats. In the 1970s, to compete with multiplexes, it added two screens, splitting the auditorium and separating the balcony. The Warner closed in 2010 and sits vacant. (Courtesy of Theatre Historical Society of America, Michael Miller Collection.)

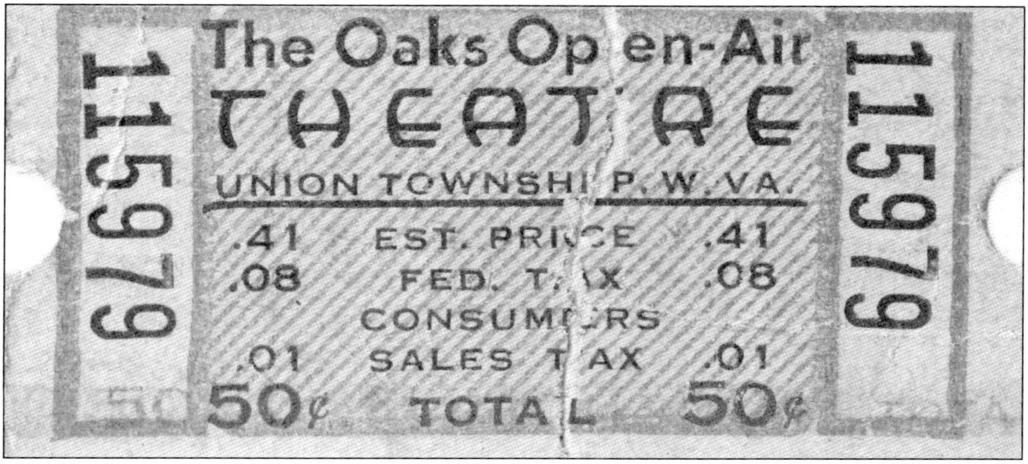

The Oaks Open-Air Theatre was located near Morgantown in Union District, by Cheat Lake. Jack Maple's 500-car drive-in opened in 1949 or 1950. It showed major films with free children's admission, plus late-night "Adults Only" movies. In 1953, drive-in church services started there on Sundays. John DeAngelis bought the Oaks' equipment in 1956, using it to open Morgantown's 1957 Blue Horizon Drive-in. (Courtesy of Morgantown History Museum.)

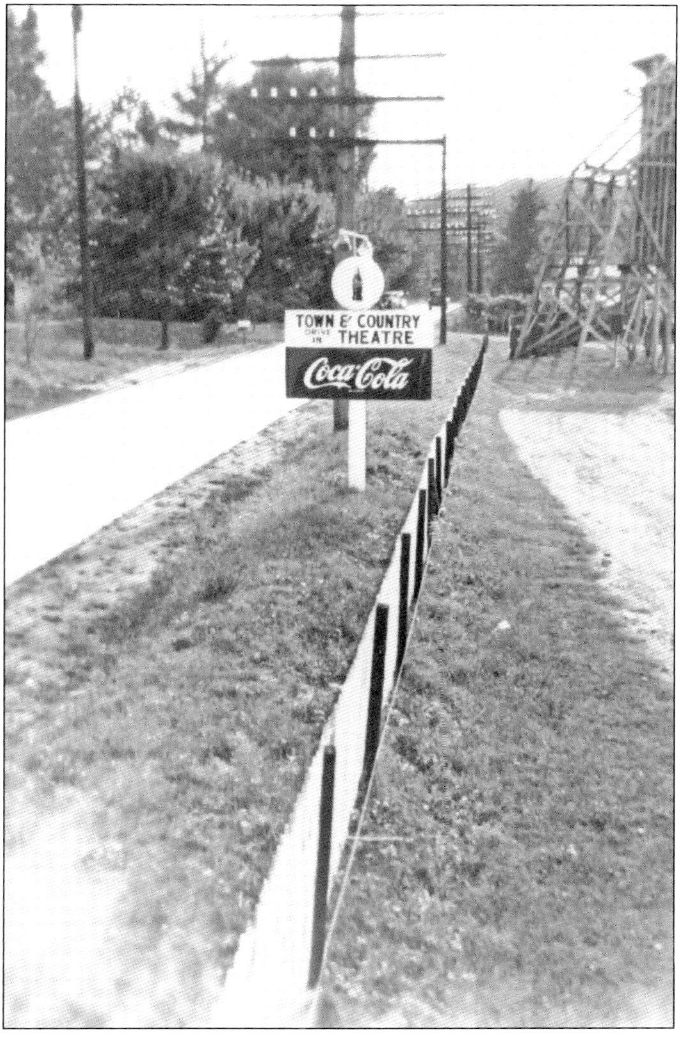

The Town & Country Drive-in Theatre held its grand opening on August 16, 1949, with a screening of *Northwest Passage*. Formerly the Cheat Drive-in, the renamed 200-car theatre's site was north of Morgantown along Fairchance Road. In 1950, it was overseen by William Cobun; by 1953, science fiction writer Gray Barker was also involved. The drive-in did not show up in exhibition journals after 1959. (Courtesy of Morgantown History Museum.)

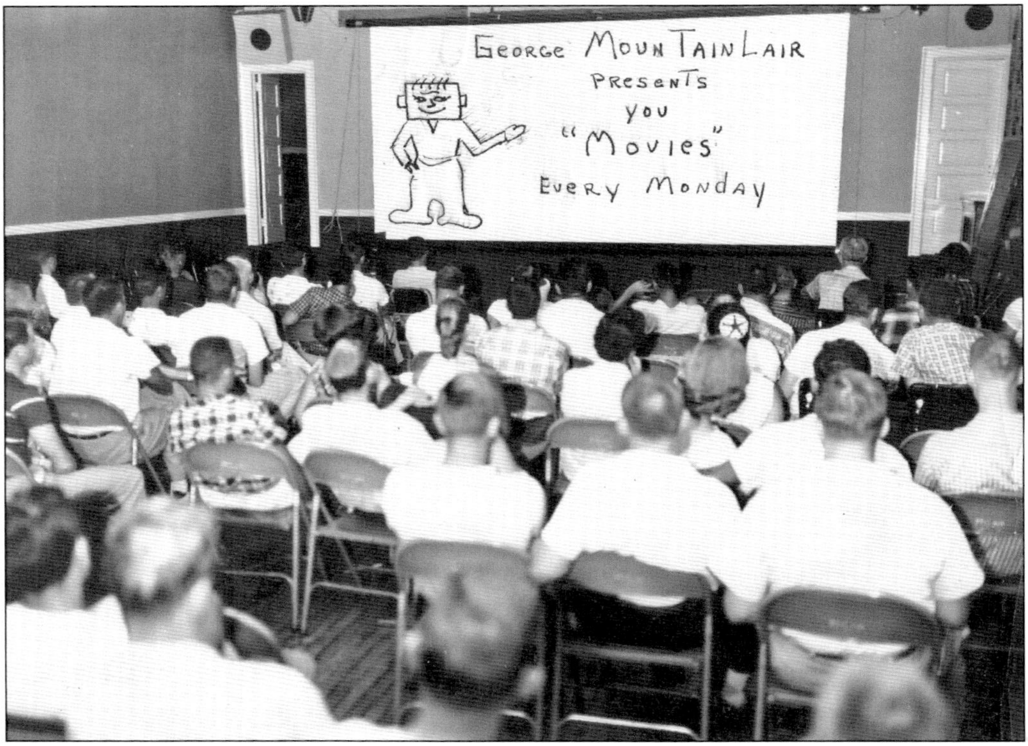

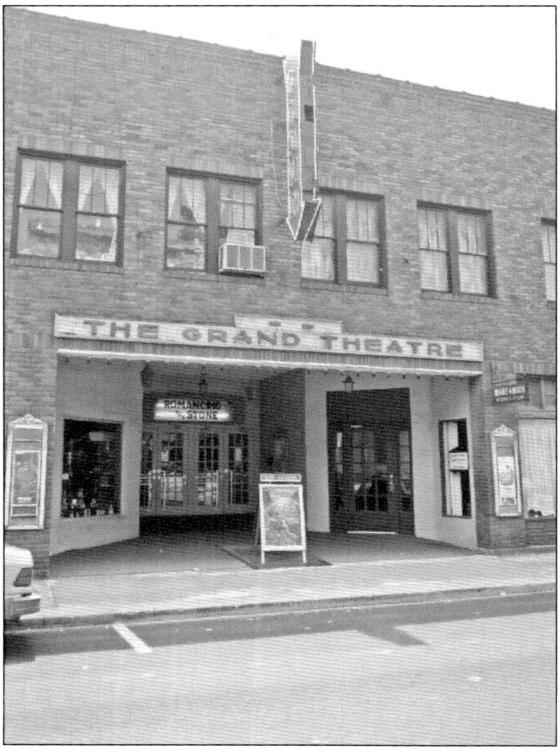

West Virginia University's Mountainlair student center, which opened in 1948, screened "movies every Monday" in its theatre (as this 1950s image shows). A student committee chose the films, which included major Hollywood features, travel documentaries, cartoons, and even filmed versions of the Mountaineers' away games. In 1968, a new Mountainlair was built; its Gluck Theatre still holds various free screenings. (Courtesy of West Virginia & Regional History Center, WVU Libraries.)

The 500-seat Grand Theatre opened in Philippi as a vaudeville and movie venue around 1927. In 1931, a woman, Elizabeth T. Phillips, purchased it—a fairly unusual situation in that era. The Grand closed in 1999. Local individuals announced plans in 2006 and 2013 to reopen it, but both attempts fell through financially. The marquee, blade sign, and poster cases visible in this 1984 photograph are gone. (Courtesy of American Classic Images.)

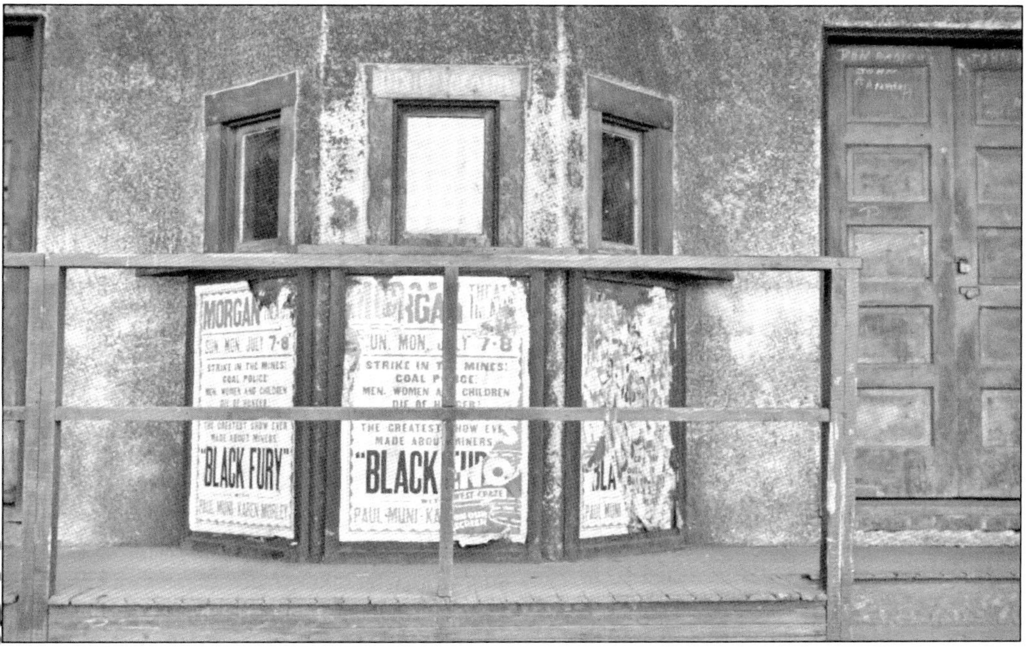

Nick Salvati and Joe Mascioli opened the 315-seat Dixie Theatre in 1923 in the Pursglove community, part of the Scotts Run coal mining district. With the Great Depression devastating the mining area, the theatre shut down around 1933. In this 1935 photograph, the poster on the Dixie's decaying box office advertises a coal-strike movie playing at nearby Morgantown's Morgan Theatre. Little remains in Pursglove today. (Courtesy of Library of Congress.)

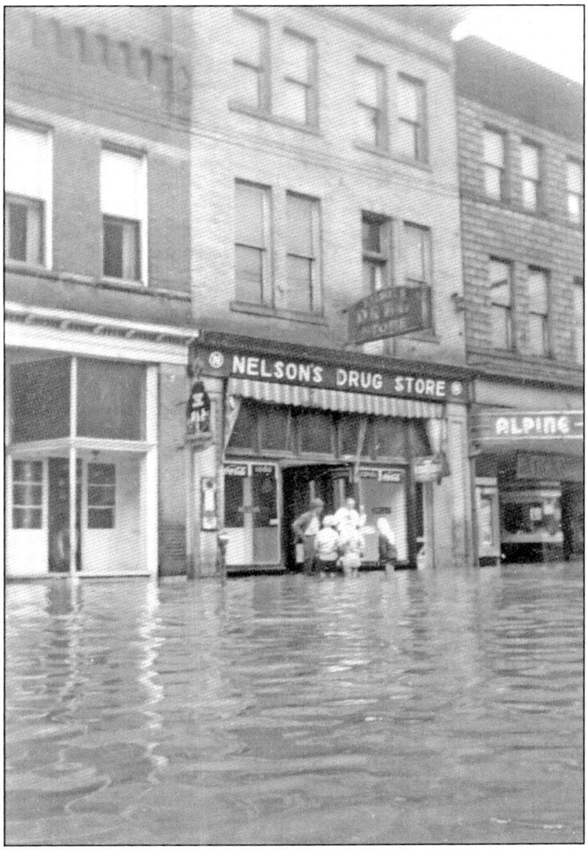

C.W. Perrine opened Salem's Strand Theatre on Main Street in 1916. In 1935, the Alpine circuit bought it. The 300-seat theatre, renamed the Alpine, received a full remodel in 1939. It survived floods in 1944 and 1950 (shown here). By 1962, Gray Barker owned it, installing Cinemascope equipment and a wide screen. The Alpine closed during the 1960s and got demolished before 1980. (Courtesy of West Virginia State Archives, Ancel Hutson Collection.)

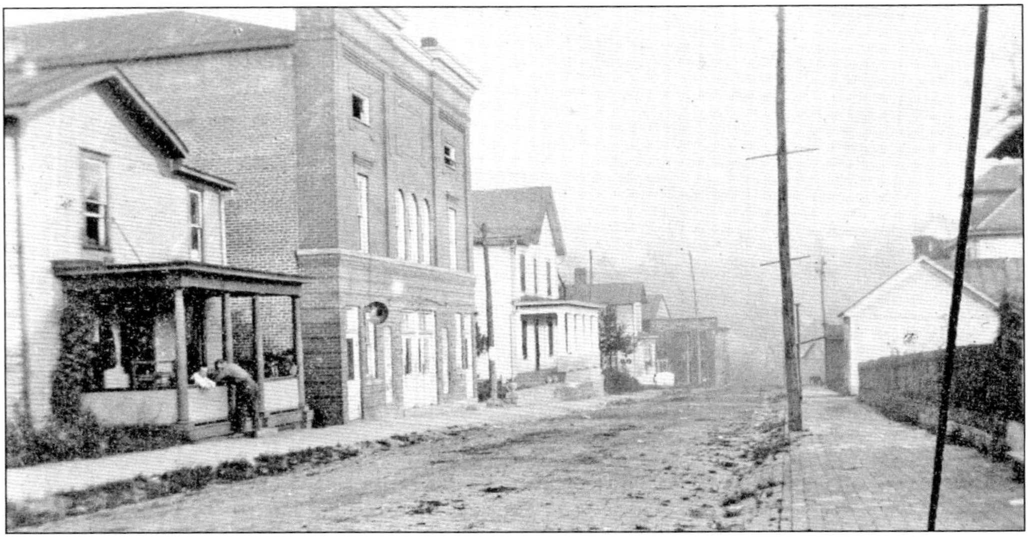

Shinnston's 670-seat Opera House (second from left in this 1912 photograph) opened in 1909 and closed in 1915. In 1920, it reopened as the Rex Theatre, a movie venue. After a 1940 fire destroyed the theatre's back end, including the stage, owner Frank DePace converted it into the Rex Skating Rink. The building, now gone, stood until at least 1977. (Courtesy of West Virginia State Archives, Jack Sandy Anderson Collection.)

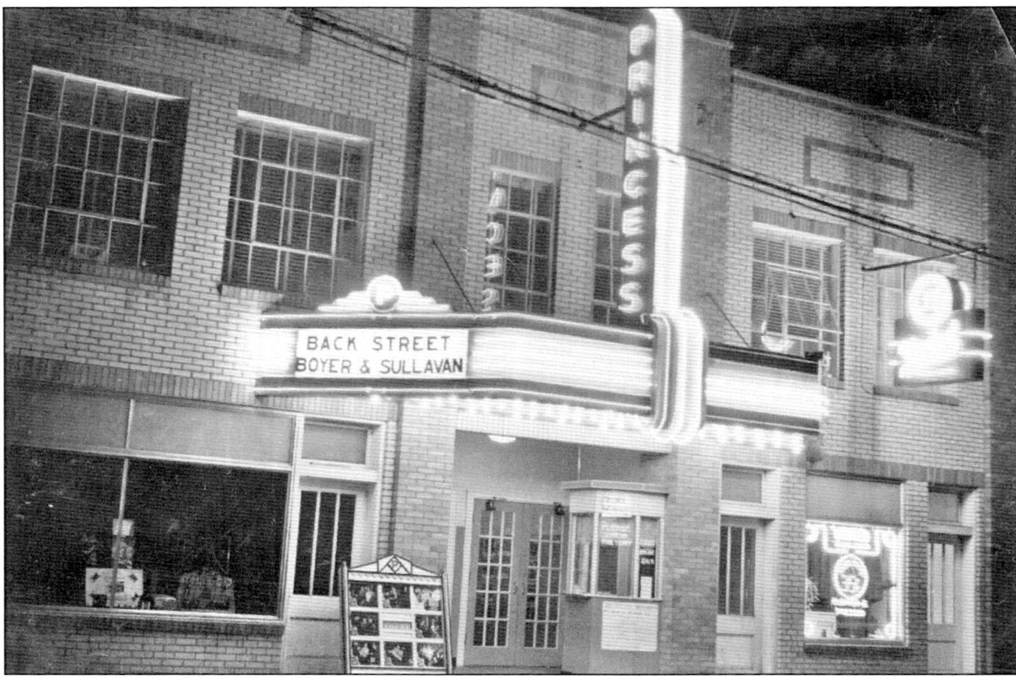

The Princess-Rex Theatre opened in 1915 on the 300 block of Shinnston's Pike Street. In 1940, it moved across the street, shortening its name to the Princess. The new movie house had over 500 seats, including a balcony for African Americans. Since it closed in 1961, its building has been reused by various businesses (as has the Princess-Rex's building). The Princess's marquee, projection booth, and projector survive. (Courtesy of Lowe Public Library.)

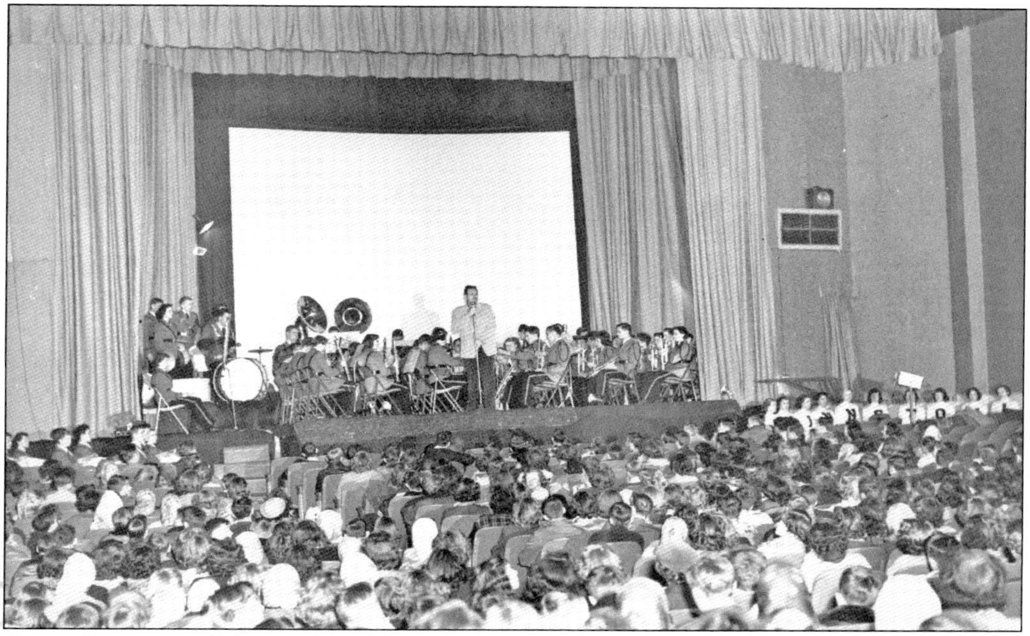

George Rice opened Shinnston's 850-seat Rice Theatre in 1948. Frank "Buck" Shaffer, Shinnston High School's band director, soon asked if his students could give concerts there. Thus, after a stage enlargement, it not only showed films but also hosted many band performances. Shaffer is seen here directing a 1952 show in front of the movie screen. The Rice closed in 1957 and was demolished in 2012. (Courtesy of Bice-Ferguson Memorial Museum.)

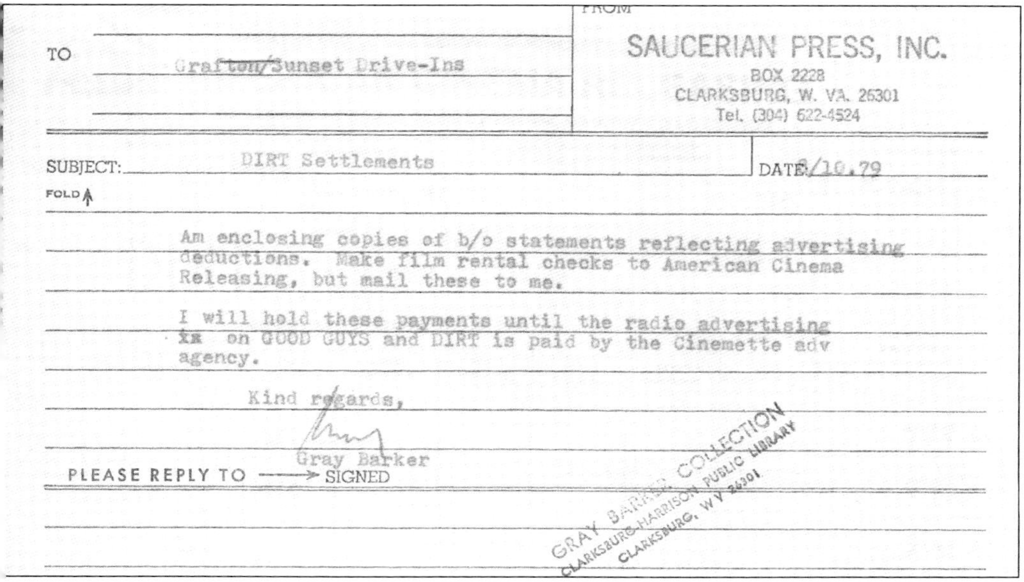

TO Grafton/Sunset Drive-Ins

FROM
SAUCERIAN PRESS, INC.
BOX 2228
CLARKSBURG, W. VA. 26301
Tel. (304) 622-4524

SUBJECT: DIRT Settlements DATE 8/10.79

FOLD

Am enclosing copies of b/o statements reflecting advertising deductions. Make film rental checks to American Cinema Releasing, but mail these to me.

I will hold these payments until the radio advertising xx on GOOD GUYS and DIRT is paid by the Cinemette adv agency.

Kind regards,

Gray Barker

PLEASE REPLY TO → SIGNED

West Virginia's oldest operational drive-in, the 400-car Sunset Drive-in Theatre in Shinnston, opened in 1947. The Ellis family has owned it since 1955. Upgrades have included FM stereo sound and digital projection. Originally open year-round (through using in-car heaters), it now operates on weekends in season. The drive-in features double bills of first-run films on its massive screen, as well as a daytime flea market. (Courtesy of Clarksburg-Harrison Public Library.)

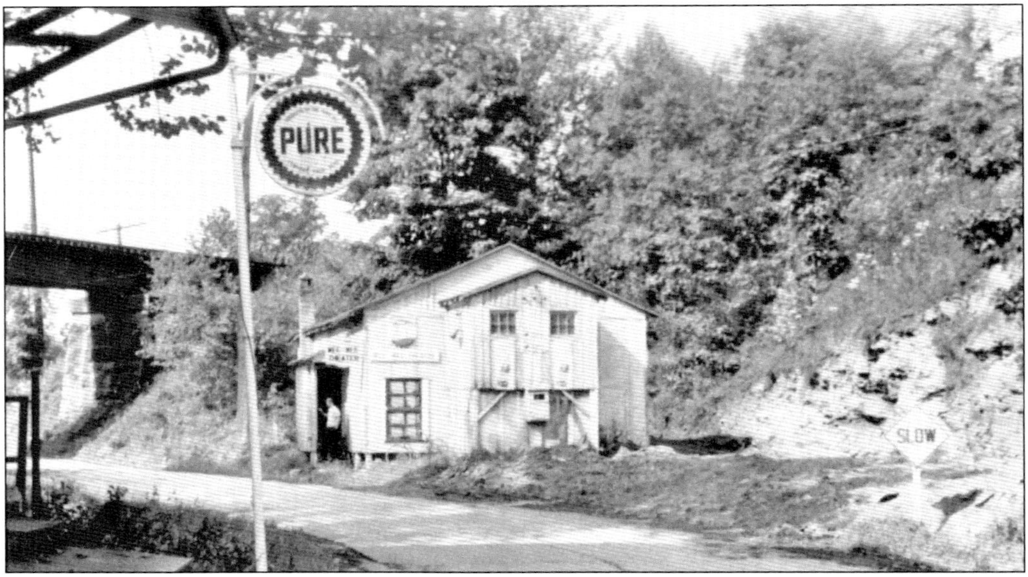

In the small Harrison County community of Wallace, the Wee Wee Theatre was a short-lived film venue. It operated during the 1950s, with locals remembering seeing Westerns there as kids. It also held community events like a children's Bible school. One resident recalls that the theatre's last showing was of the 1957 movie *Old Yeller*. The building no longer exists. (Courtesy of West Virginia State Archives, Sylvia Lyon/Albert Hussell Collection.)

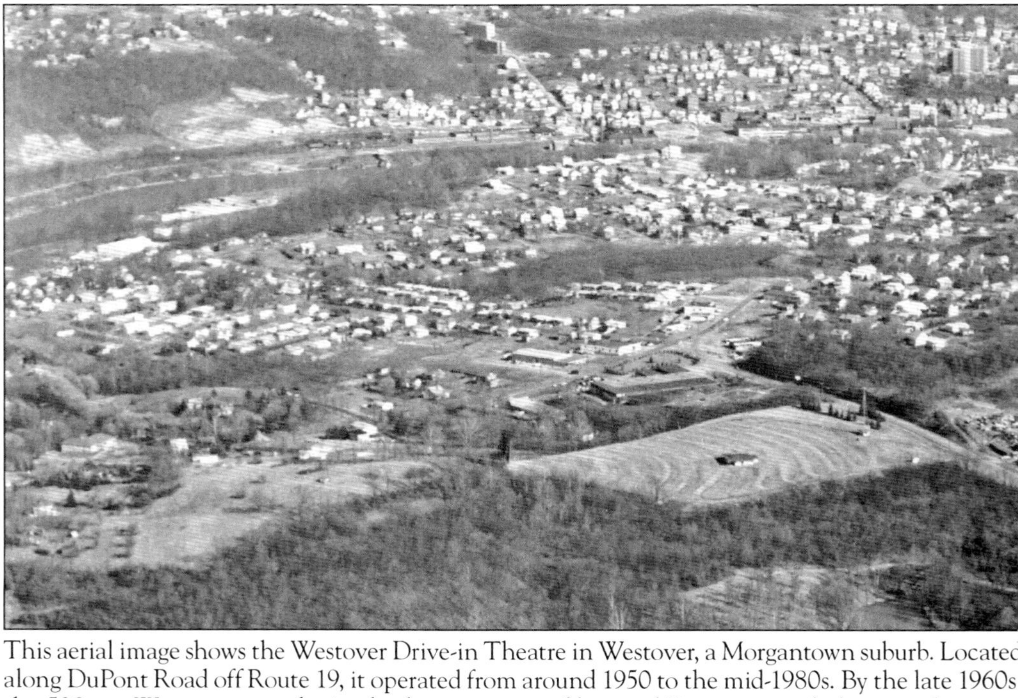
This aerial image shows the Westover Drive-in Theatre in Westover, a Morgantown suburb. Locatec along DuPont Road off Route 19, it operated from around 1950 to the mid-1980s. By the late 1960s the 500-car Westover was playing both mainstream films and B movies, including sexploitatior and biker flicks. It also held a weekly swap meet advertised as "West Virginia's largest." Houses later replaced the drive-in. (Courtesy of Morgantown History Museum.)

Seven

New River–Greenbrier Valley

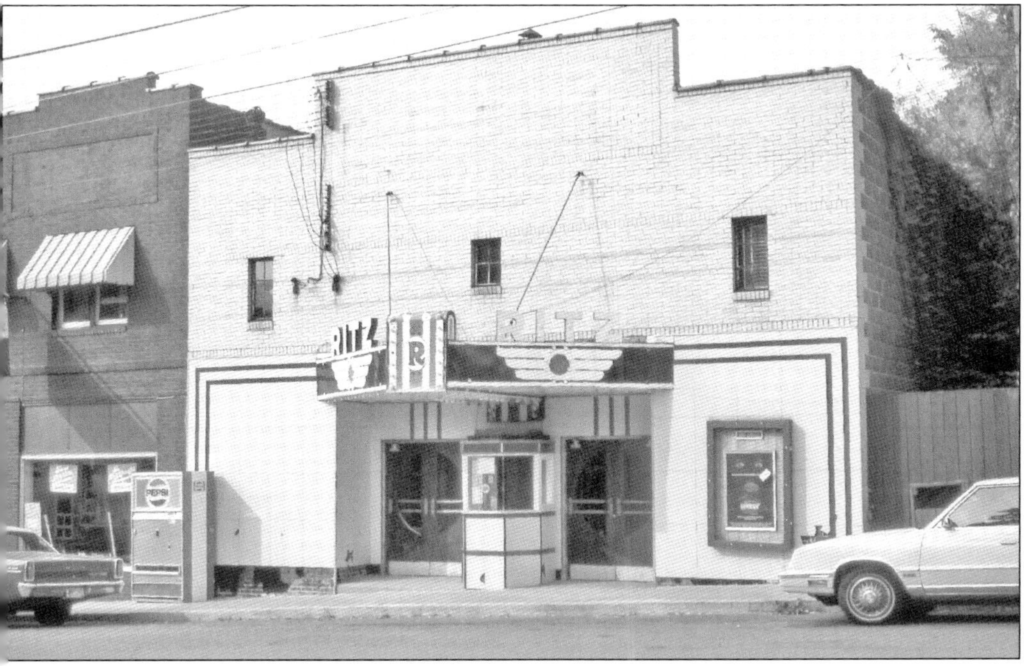

Ansted's Lyric Theatre showed films as early as 1915. In 1933, Morton O'Neal bought the 245-seat Lyric from Garland Skaggs, reopening it as the Ritz Theatre. From 1978 to 1979, new operators briefly called it Cinema 63. Later regaining its Ritz name, the movie house was still operating as of this 1987 image. Missing its marquee, Vitrolite facade, and ticket booth, the building is now a VFW post. (Courtesy of American Classic Images.)

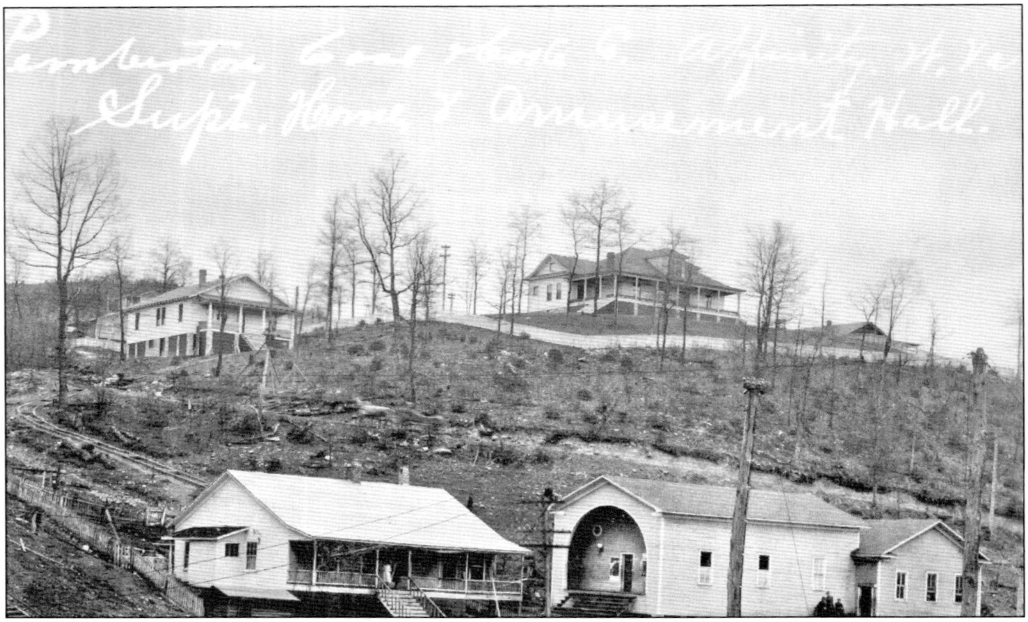

The Affinity coal camp's Amusement Hall (lower right), also called the Affinity Theatre, was presenting movies by 1919. That year, it joined the new Winding Gulf Exhibitors Association, which booked films for members. The 150-seat movie house closed in 1930, reopened, and closed again by 1932. The building was still hosting plays, meetings, and other events as of 1936. Little remains in Affinity today. (Courtesy of West Virginia State Archives, Coal Town Collection.)

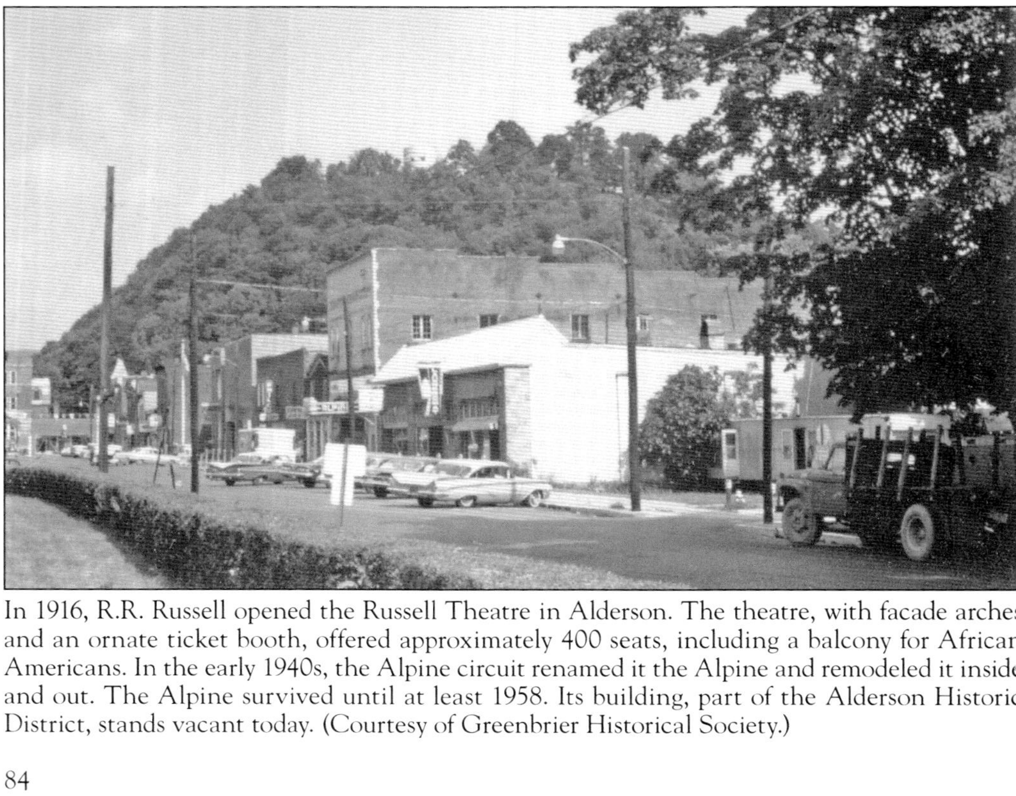

In 1916, R.R. Russell opened the Russell Theatre in Alderson. The theatre, with facade arches and an ornate ticket booth, offered approximately 400 seats, including a balcony for African Americans. In the early 1940s, the Alpine circuit renamed it the Alpine and remodeled it inside and out. The Alpine survived until at least 1958. Its building, part of the Alderson Historic District, stands vacant today. (Courtesy of Greenbrier Historical Society.)

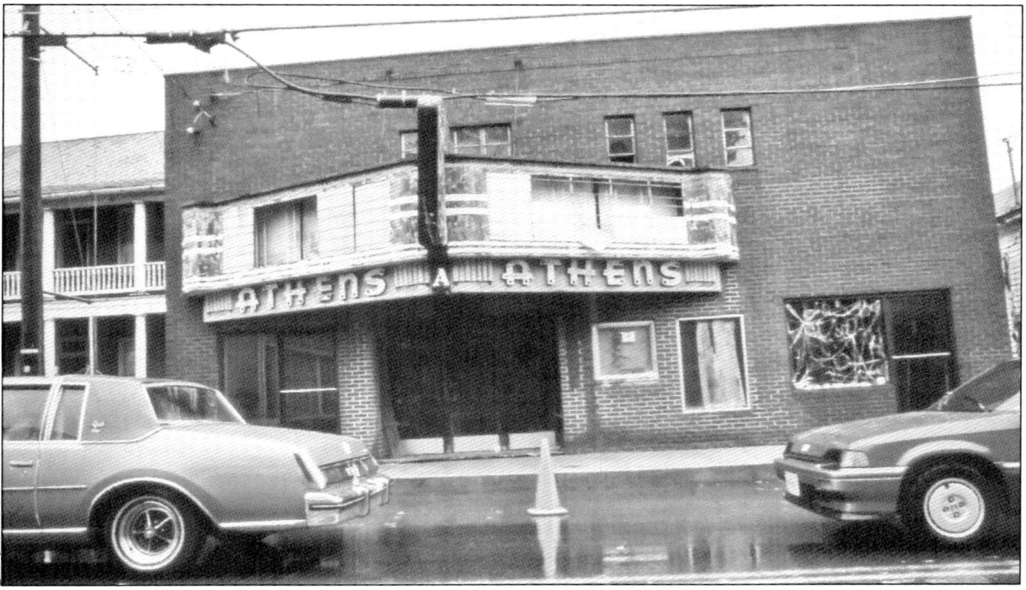

In the college town of Athens, Concord College alum J. Woodrow Thomas opened the Athens Theatre in 1947. Concord's head coach–athletic director, Robert Kyle, managed the Athens for years. The movie house was part of the Thomas family's local circuit until at least 1975. The arched, metal building (hidden behind a brick front) then sat vacant, as this 1990 photograph shows. It was later demolished. (Courtesy of Michael Gioulis.)

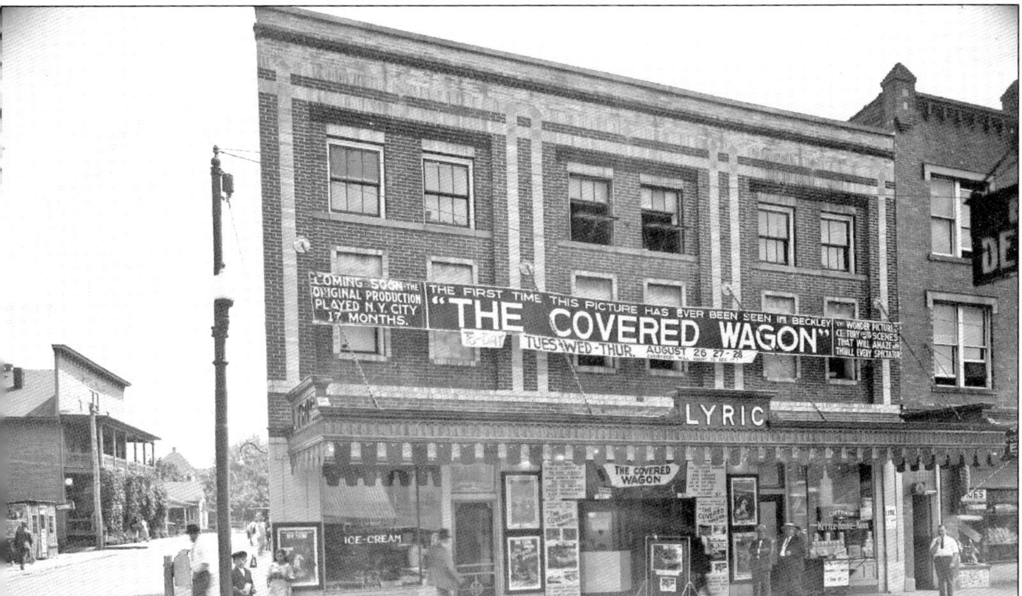

Beckley's 1920 Lyric Theatre (the second by that name) was on the corner of Neville and Heber Streets. Fire destroyed it in January 1924. Its 750-seat replacement, pictured here, closed in April 1967 with the movie *Riot on Sunset Strip*. The Lyric was immediately remodeled for retail; that use continued until it collapsed during a massive blizzard in March 1993. (Courtesy of West Virginia & Regional History Center, WVU Libraries.)

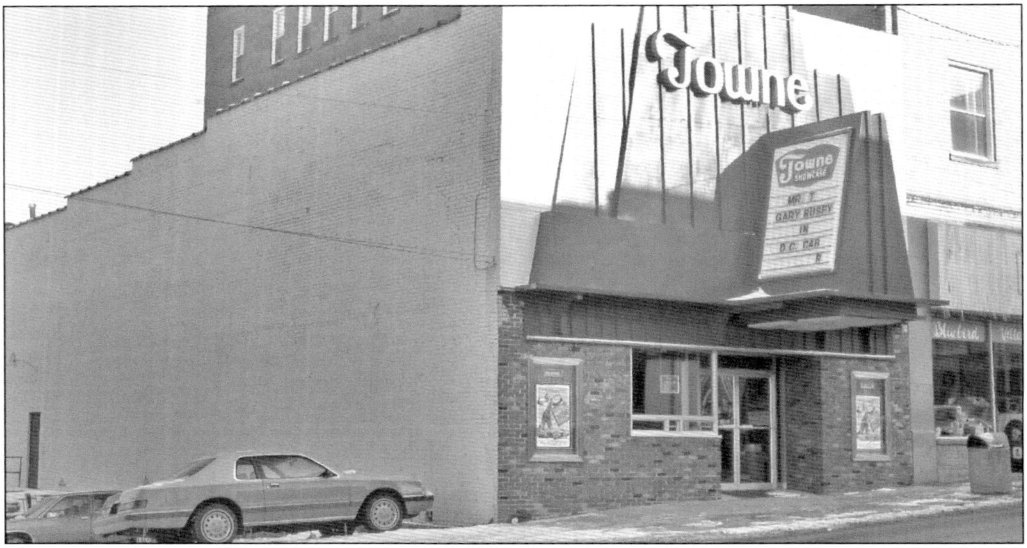

The Palace Theatre opened on North Kanawha Street in Beckley in December 1923. An April 1924 fire (by the same arsonist who set the Lyric's fire) caused $50,000 in damage. The 500-seat Palace was rebuilt. It closed around 1959, becoming the Curtain Callers Playhouse by 1961. The Thomas family remodeled and reopened it as the first-run Towne Cinema in 1973. Closing in 1986, it was later demolished. (Courtesy of American Classic Images.)

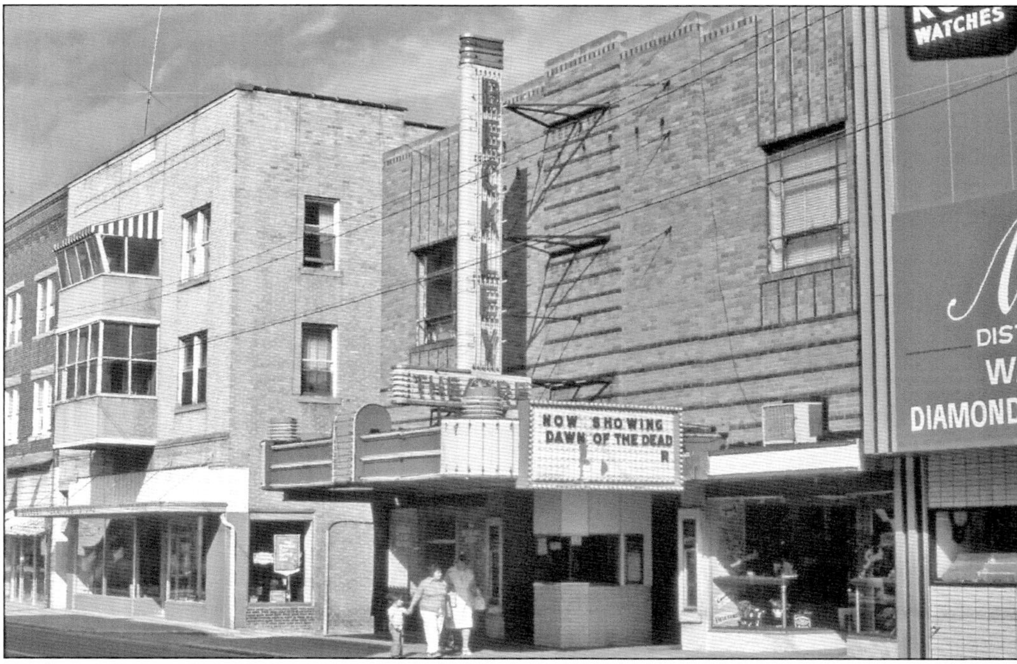

Ferd Midelburg opened the $100,000 New Beckley Theatre on the 400 block of Beckley's West Neville Street in 1936. Meanor and Handloser designed the 900-seat Art Deco movie house (featuring a white marble lobby), generally just called the Beckley Theatre. The Thomas family's local circuit owned it by the 1970s. It closed in 1982. The long-vacant building, destroyed in 1997 was replaced by a parking lot. (Courtesy of American Classic Images.)

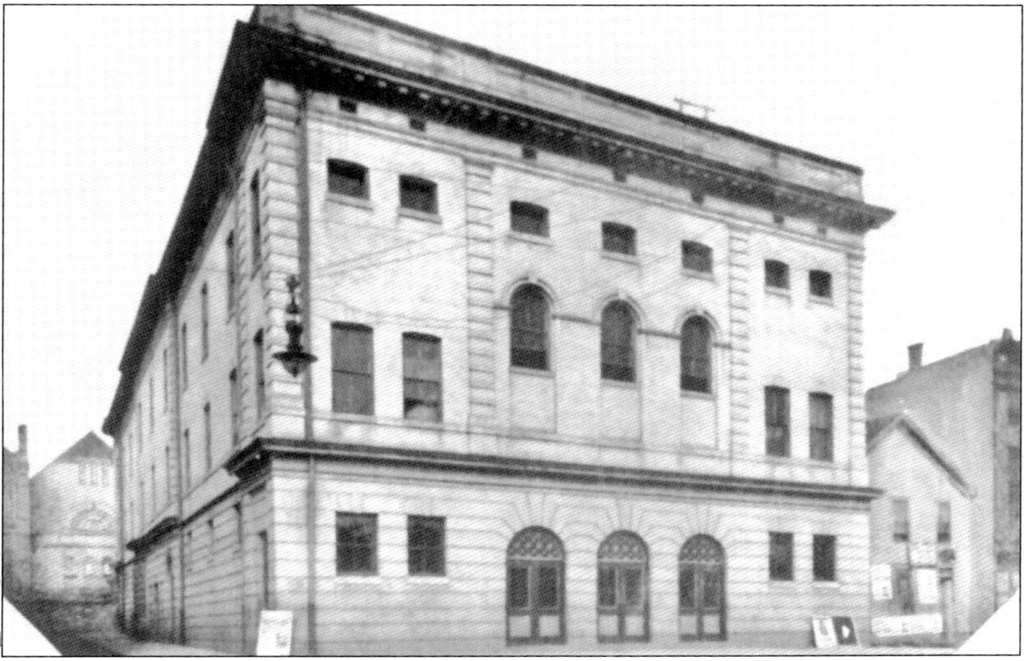

The Elks Opera House opened in 1902 in Bluefield, beside the still-standing Elks Building. It was showing films by 1912. Along with movies, the 500-seat auditorium was known for hosting touring Broadway shows. Architects Holmboe and Lafferty's Renaissance Revival structure was converted into the A.W. Cox department store in 1927. Part of the Bluefield Downtown Commercial Historic District, it now holds apartments and offices. (Courtesy of Eastern Regional Coal Archives.)

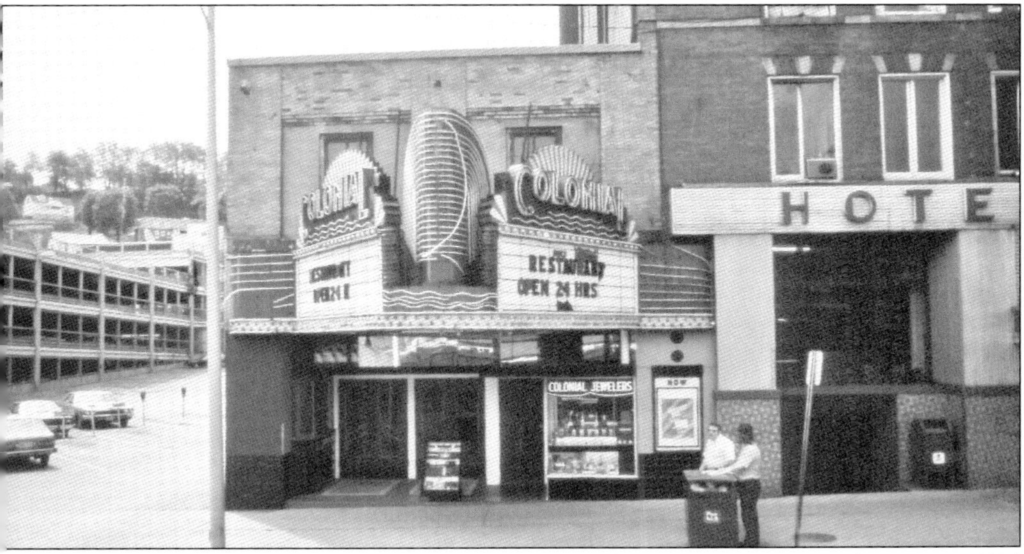

Samuel L. Matz opened Bluefield's 350-seat Colonial Theatre on Princeton Avenue in 1916 beside his 1911 Hotel Matz (right). In 1940, Max Matz gave the Colonial an Art Deco remodel. Later part of the Newbold-Keesling circuit, it closed in 1979. The Colonial then sat vacant (with a storefront in use when this 1985 photograph was taken). In 2009, the hotel collapsed onto it; both were lost. (Courtesy of Michael Gioulis.)

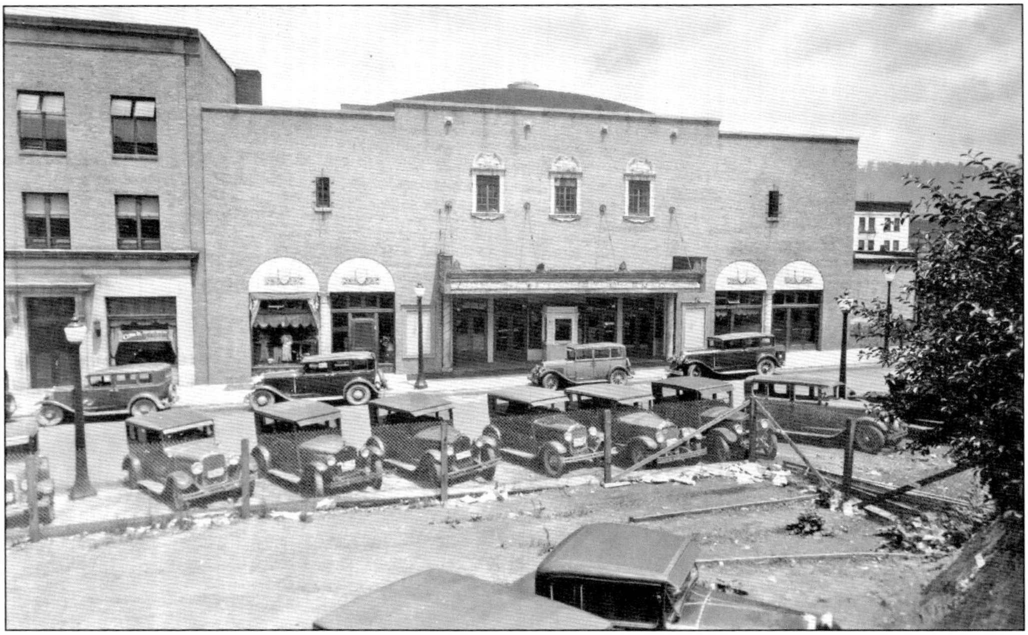

Alex Mahood designed the Moorish-style Granada Theatre, built in 1927 in Bluefield. The 1,500-seat picture palace offered air-conditioning and a balcony for African Americans. In 1930, it received what it advertised as "the largest picture in the state." After its 1980s closure, a nightclub came in. In 2013, the local development authority purchased the empty Granada. The Bluefield Preservation Society is fundraising for its rehabilitation. (Courtesy of Eastern Regional Coal Archives.)

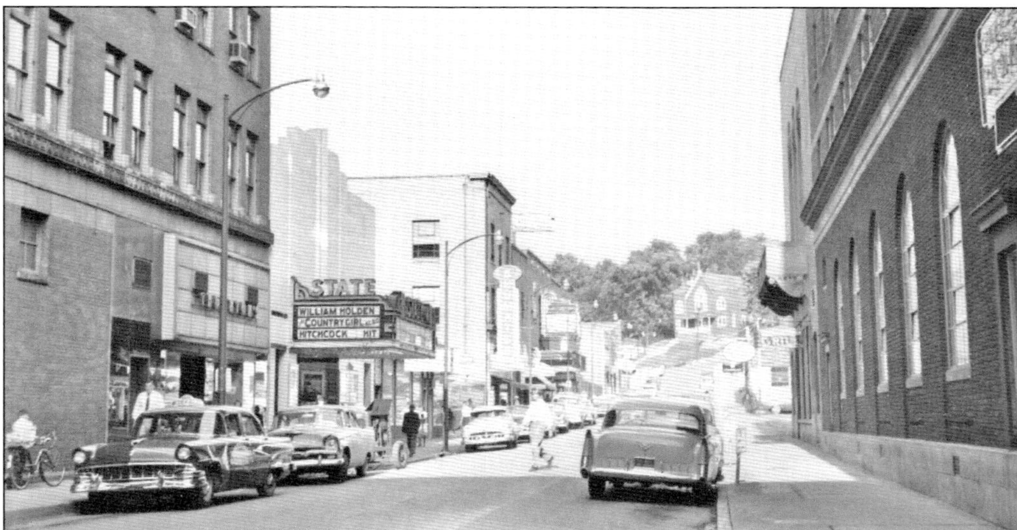

Bluefield's 766-seat Art Deco State Theatre opened in 1937. In 1942, Oscar-winning actress Greer Garson came on a national war bond tour. With the State's ticket booth decorated like a bomb shelter, she hammered a nail into "Hitler's Coffin" in front. The Paramount-owned movie house operated into the 1950s. Its building later served commercial uses. After a fire, only its lobby (now a café) survived. (Courtesy of Eastern Regional Coal Archives.)

The Bradshaw Theatre was operating before 1930 in the P.M. Hatfield Building in McDowell County's town of Bradshaw. In 1936, Absalom Buzlea bought it. He and his sister Florence then operated the 300-seat movie house. The Bradshaw was open until at least 1955, when Absalom shifted its booking policy, giving it two film changes per week. The structure was vacant when this 1983 photograph was taken. (Courtesy of American Classic Images.)

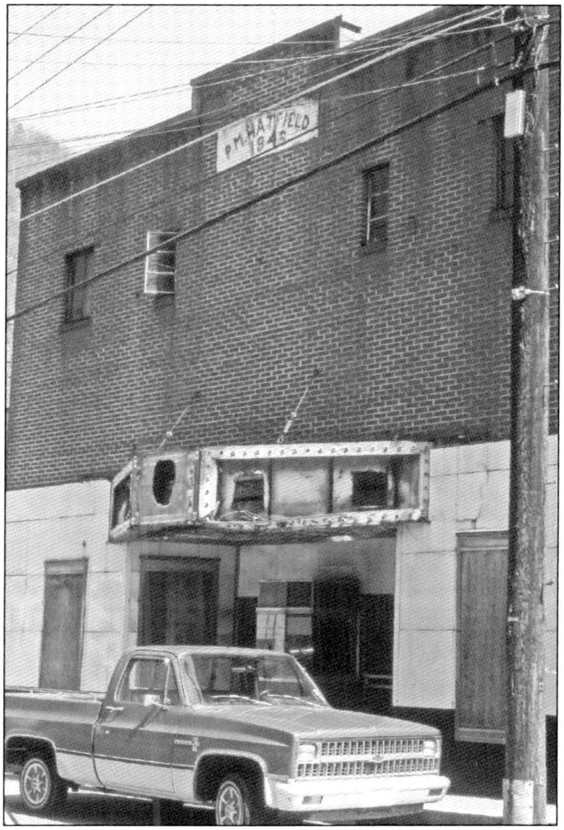

Elite Bramwell's Bramwell Theatre, designed by Alex Mahood, opened in 1921. It was known briefly as the Palace Theatre, but its original name returned in 1937. Open into the early 1960s, the 250-seat venue was then remodeled for other uses with auditorium partitions and a flattened floor. In 2012, the town announced plans to rehabilitate the theatre into an event center and playhouse. It is still vacant. (Courtesy of Eastern Regional Coal Archives.)

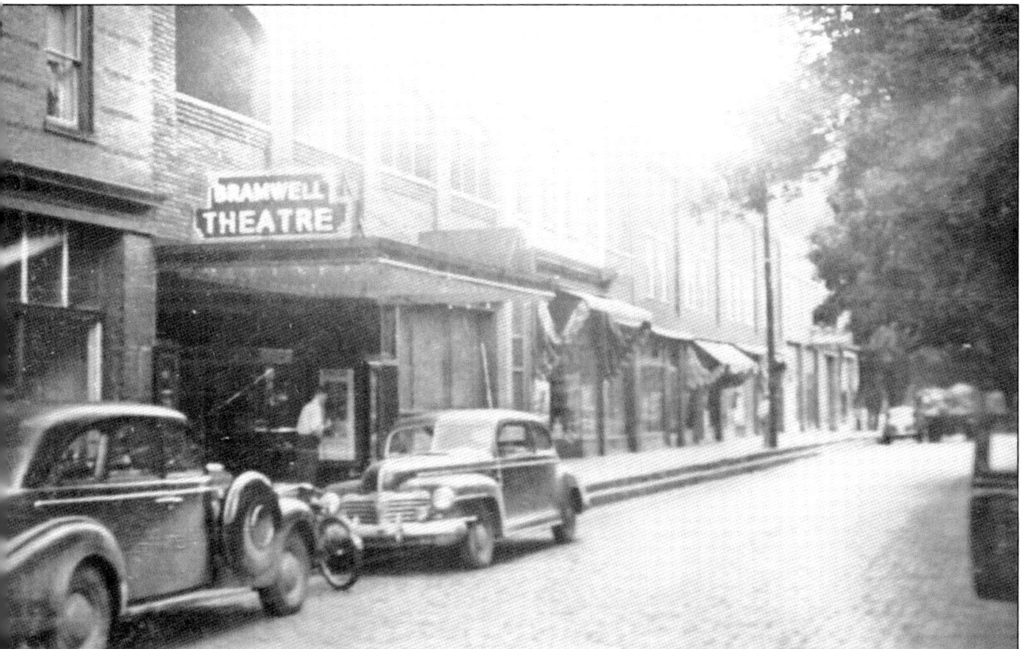

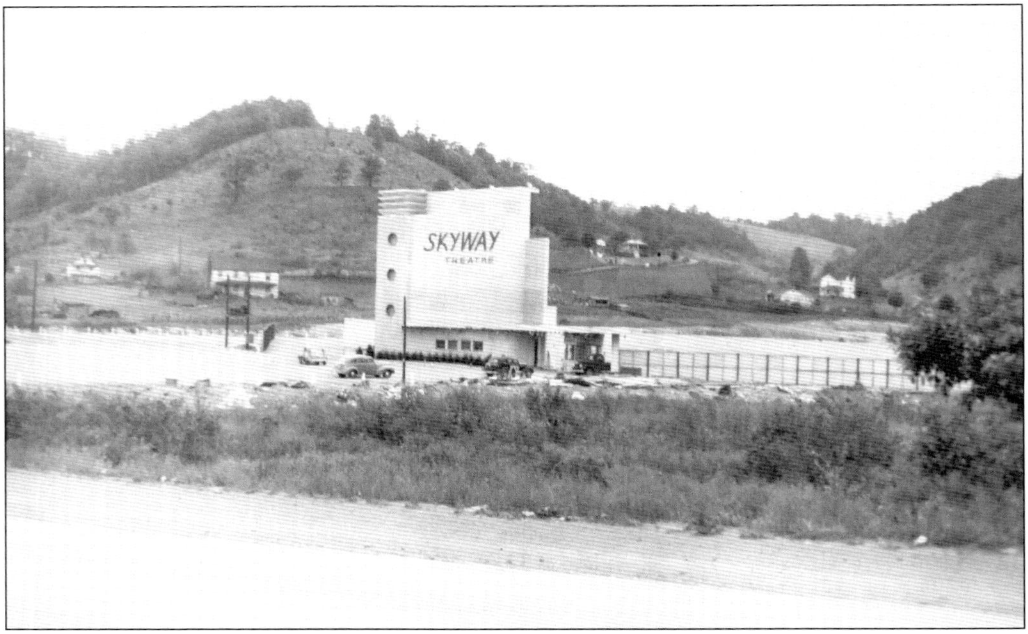

The $200,000 Skyway Outdoor Theatre opened along Route 52 at Airport Road in Brush Fork, near Bluefield, in September 1948—showing *Slave Girl*. Alex Mahood's streamline moderne design included portholes and neon stars on the massive screen tower. The 600-car drive-in, part of the Switow circuit, later joined Newbold-Keesling. The Skyway played major movies until its 1980 closure for replacement by a strip mall. (Courtesy of Eastern Regional Coal Archives.)

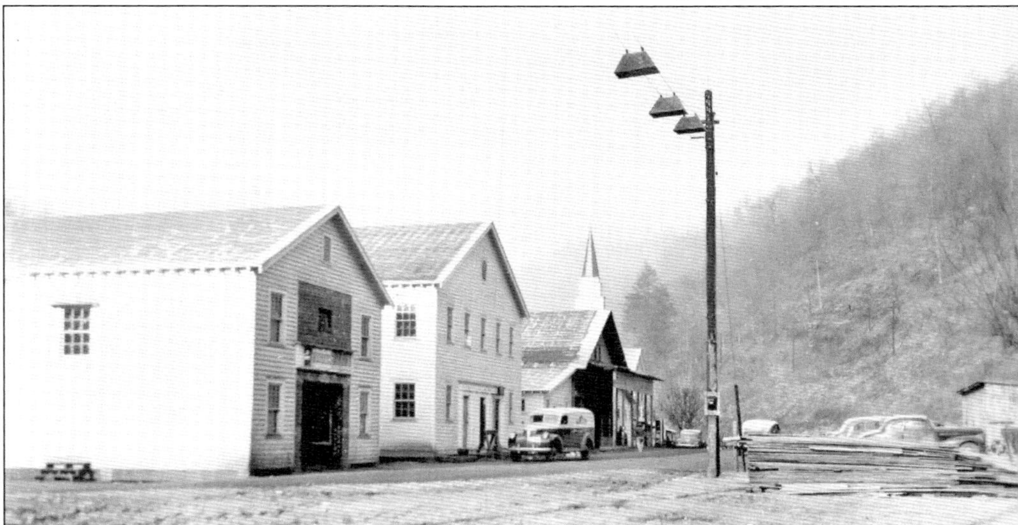

In Caretta, a McDowell County company town, the 200-seat Caretta Theatre (left) opened around 1943. That year, its owner, Carter Coal Company, filed a complaint against five movie studios claiming it was unfair that other (larger) local theatres got new films first. An arbitrator dismissed the charge, cementing the Caretta Theatre's second-run status. Operating until at least 1957, it later disappeared. (Courtesy of West Virginia State Archives, Woodrow Richardson Collection.)

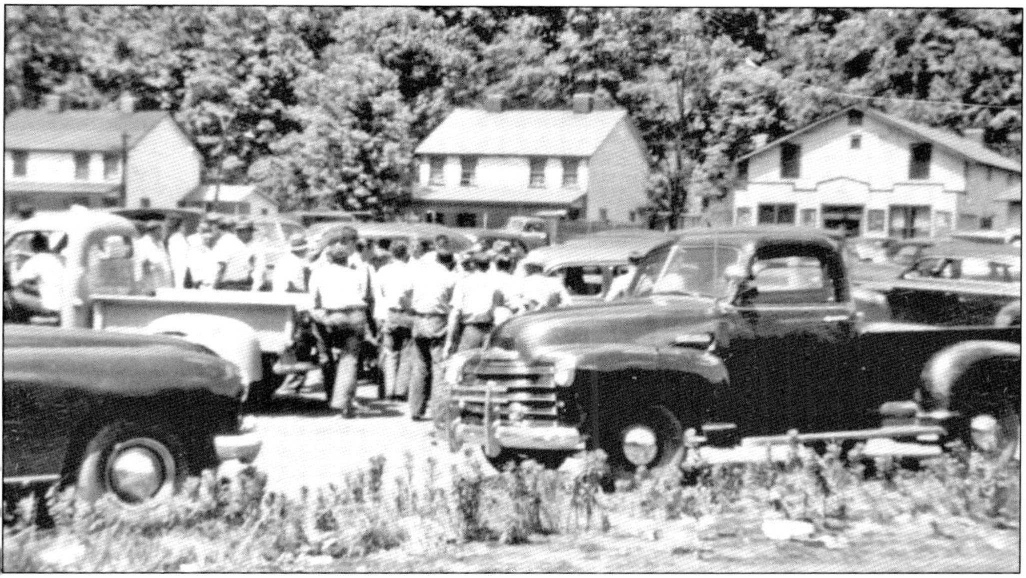

The Dorothy Theatre and a soda fountain are both located in the building on the right in this 1951 photograph. In front, miners line up for their final paychecks after the mine closed in Dorothy, a Raleigh County community. Open by 1918, the 200-seat movie house continued to operate until at least 1965, when it was part of the Moore circuit. (Courtesy of West Virginia State Archives, Coal Town Collection.)

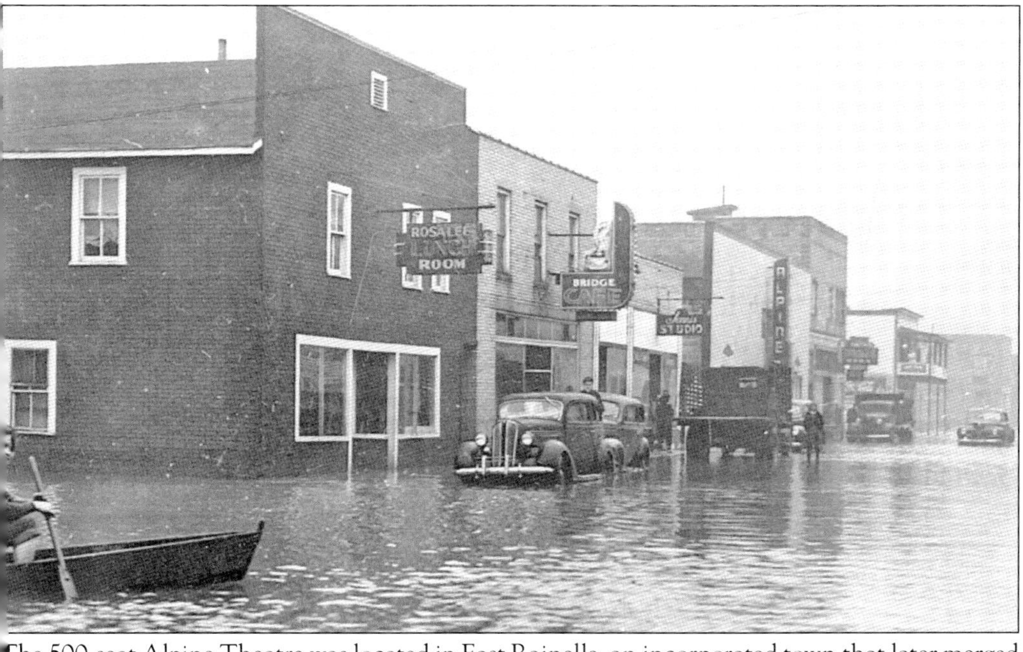

The 500-seat Alpine Theatre was located in East Rainelle, an incorporated town that later merged with Rainelle. Built in 1937 by Erwin Younkin as the Rainelle Theatre, it was renamed by the Alpine circuit in 1938. The first-run movie house survived the 1946 flood shown here. By 1956, it was operated by the Jur circuit. The Alpine was boarded up and decaying by 1984; it no longer exists. (Courtesy of Greenbrier Historical Society.)

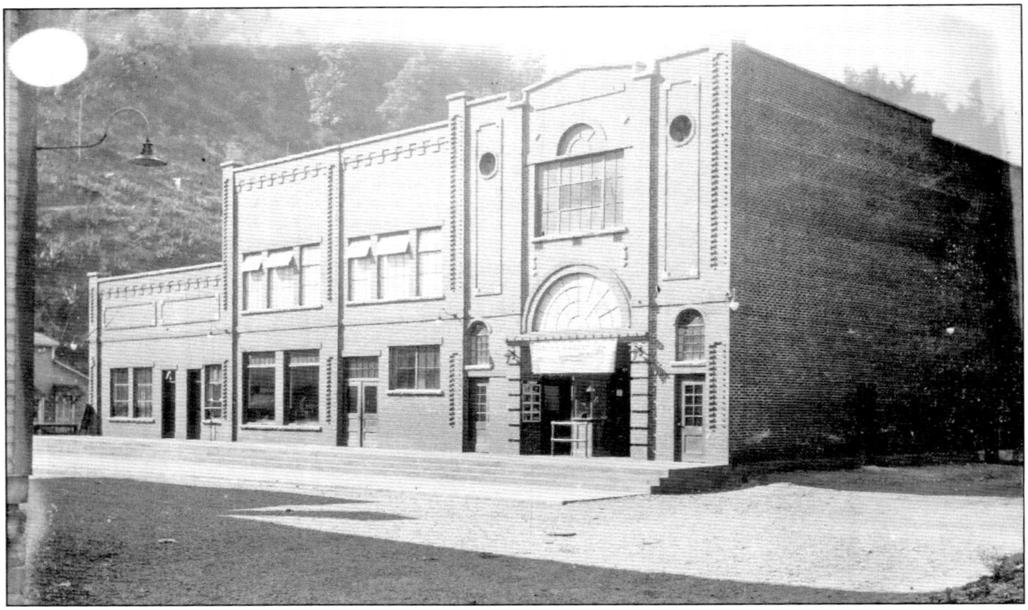

In McDowell County's Elbert coal camp, a fire destroyed the Elbert Theatre in 1923, causing $40,000 in damage. A year later, the multifunction Elbert Recreation Center rose on its site. The new Elbert Theatre's fanlight-covered, separate entry distinguished it from the rest of the structure. The 400-seat movie house, once part of the Rogers circuit, was still open as of 1957. (Courtesy of West Virginia State Archives, Coal Life–US Steel Collection.)

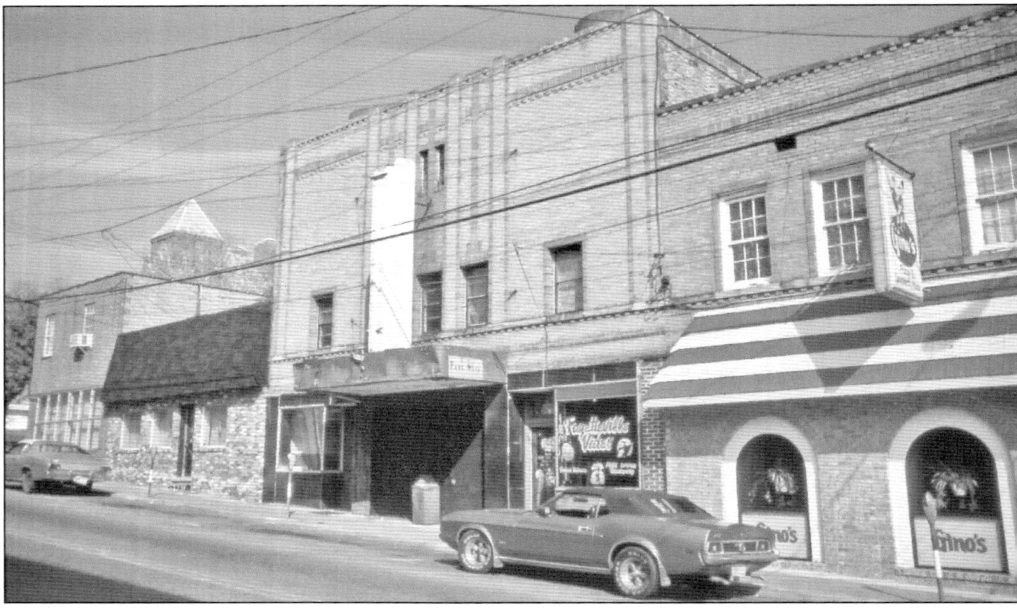

Fayetteville's 200-seat Fayette Theatre, operated by Grant Thomas, opened in 1935. The movie house closed in the 1960s and then sat vacant, as this 1985 photograph shows. In 1992, Congressman Tom Louisos leased the intact building to the Fayette County Historical Society for a dollar per year. After a renovation, the Fayette reopened in 1993 with plays. Now owned by a nonprofit organization, it continues to host performances. (Courtesy of American Classic Images.)

John C. Norman, West Virginia's first African American architect, designed the 1935 Gauley Theatre and the adjacent Conley Hotel in Gauley Bridge. Shown here during a 1940 flood, both were built for C.A. Conley, the Fayette County sheriff. By 1969, the 400-seat movie house was part of the Moore circuit. The Gauley Theatre is now gone, but the hotel still operates as the New River Lodge. (Courtesy of Fayette County Public Library.)

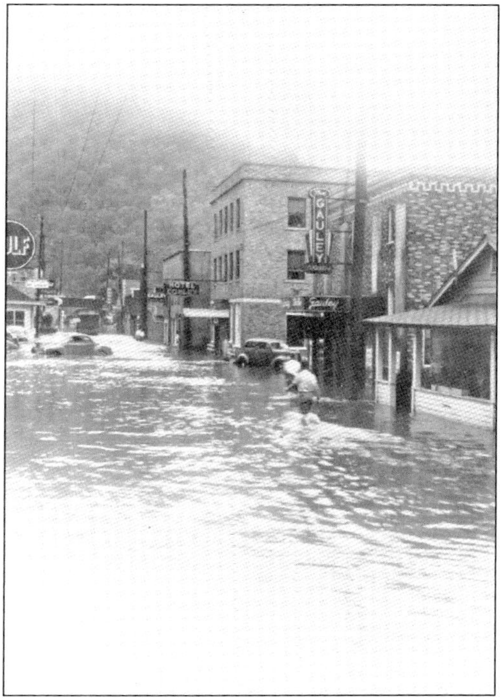

Designed by Columbus, Ohio, architect Frank L. Packard, the Opera House in Glen Jean opened in 1896. Films were shown there from as early as 1923 until its closure. E.L. Mackey purchased the 300-seat venue—with a unique, circular auditorium—in 1933. During World War II, the theatre closed and the building was taken apart, although its stone foundation remained. (Courtesy of West Virginia & Regional History Center, WVU Libraries.)

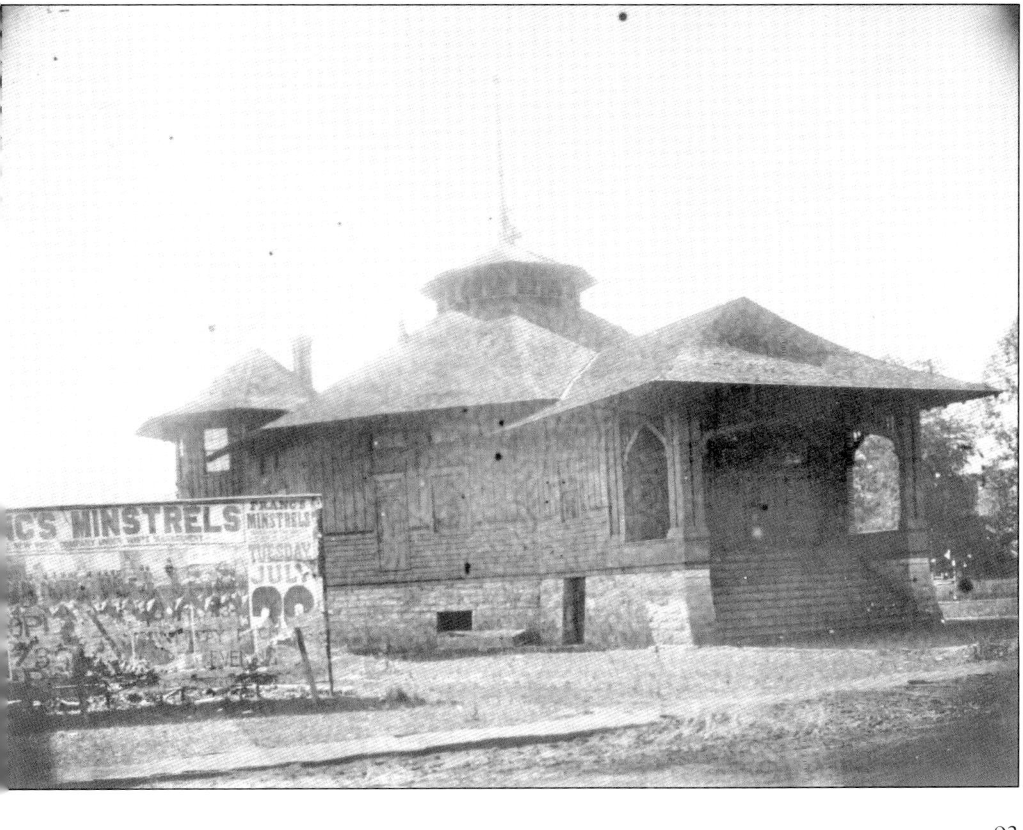

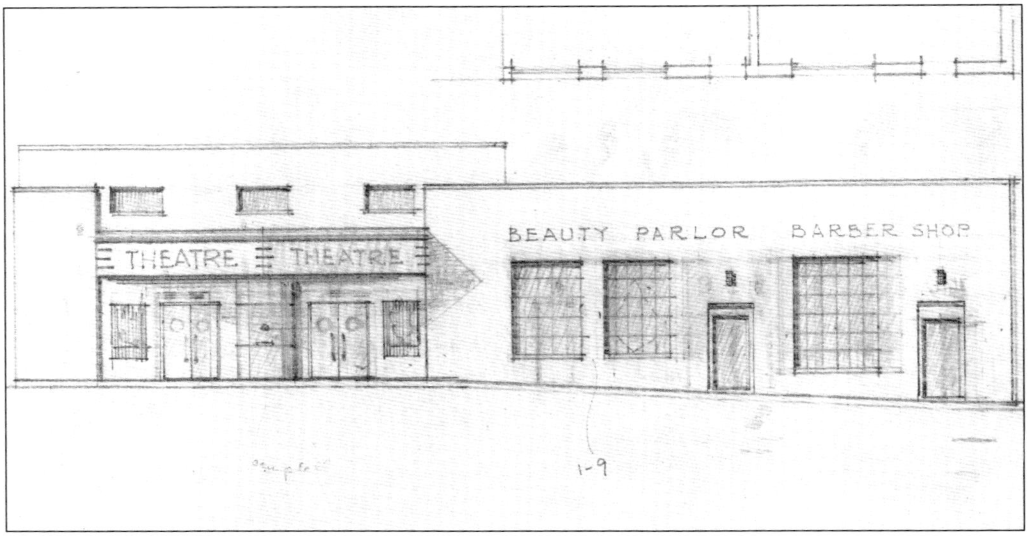

Alex Mahood designed this theatre blueprint in 1945 to replace a burned multiuse facility built in 1921 in the Wyoming County company town of Glen Rogers. The 250-seat venue, officially labeled the Amusement Hall but also called the Glen Rogers Theatre, showed films into the late 1950s. In 1960, the coal mine closed. Glen Rogers's main buildings then sat empty and decaying—still the Amusement Hall's situation. (Courtesy of Eastern Regional Coal Archives.)

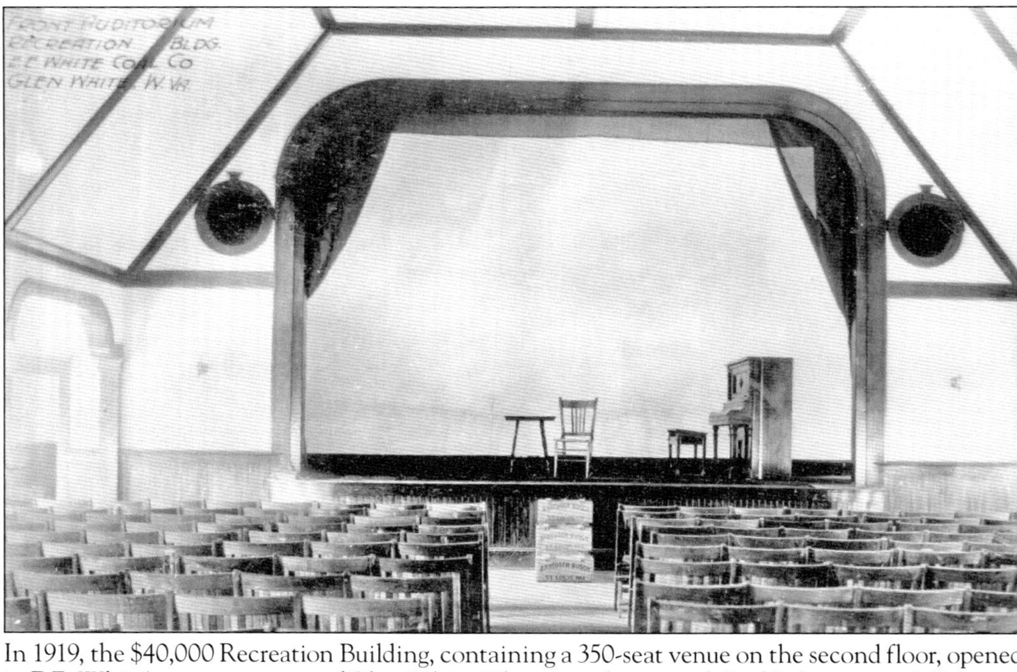

In 1919, the $40,000 Recreation Building, containing a 350-seat venue on the second floor, openec in E.E. White's company town of Glen White. That year, the journal *Coal Industry* noted, "Moving picture shows of the highest order are shown in the auditorium five nights of every week." Afte the mine's 1945 shutdown, the Glen White movie theatre closed in April 1948. (Courtesy of Wes Virginia State Archives, Coal Town Collection.)

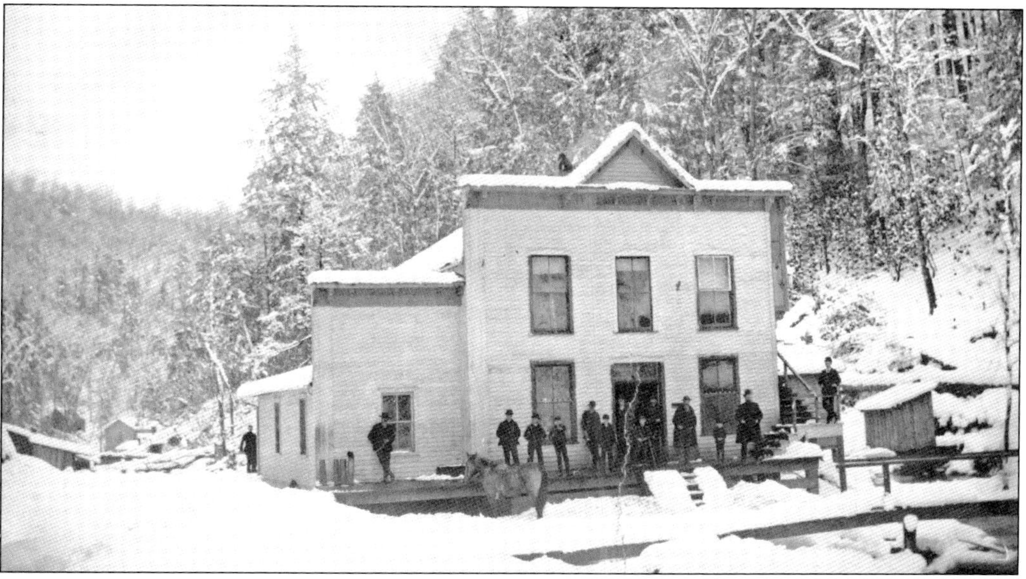

After Justus Collins bought the Goodwill Coal and Coke Company in 1905, the Goodwill coal camp's company store (pictured) became a recreation center. Its first floor held the Goodwill Theatre, which was showing movies by 1927 (when it was sold). A pool room and dance hall were above. The 100-seat venue featured sound equipment by 1931, the year it burned down. (Courtesy of West Virginia & Regional History Center, WVU Libraries.)

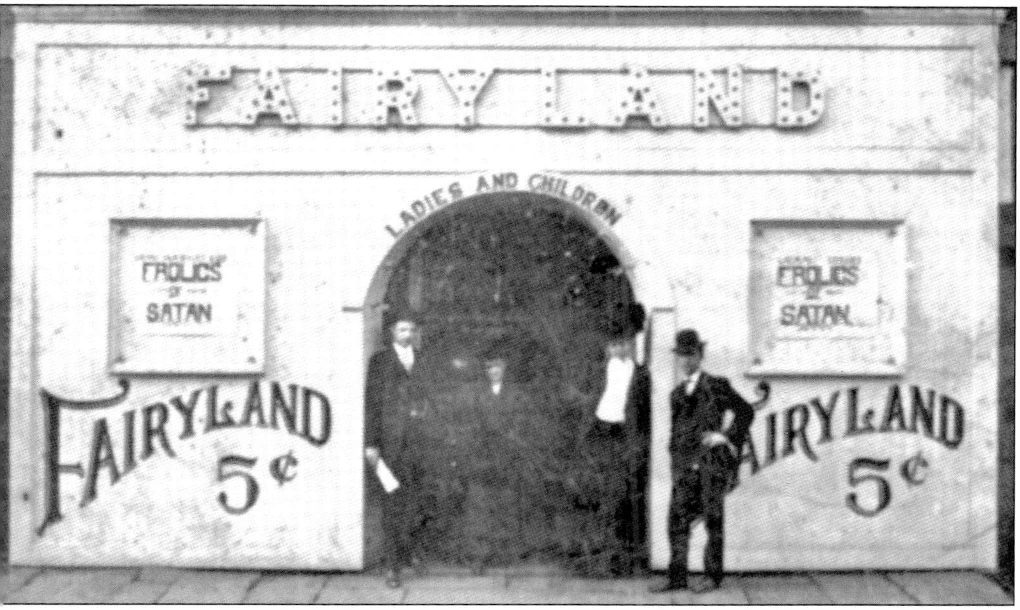

Fairyland, Hinton's first nickelodeon, opened in 1906 inside an 1893 bank building. A 1920 Hinton High School yearbook advertisement notes that Fairyland's "program changed daily," offering "high class motion pictures." Fairyland stopped appearing in local newspaper listings in January 1921. Its three-story structure on Third Avenue's 200 block, featuring a pressed-metal and cast-iron facade, is part of the Hinton Historic District. (Courtesy of West Virginia & Regional History Center, WVU Libraries.)

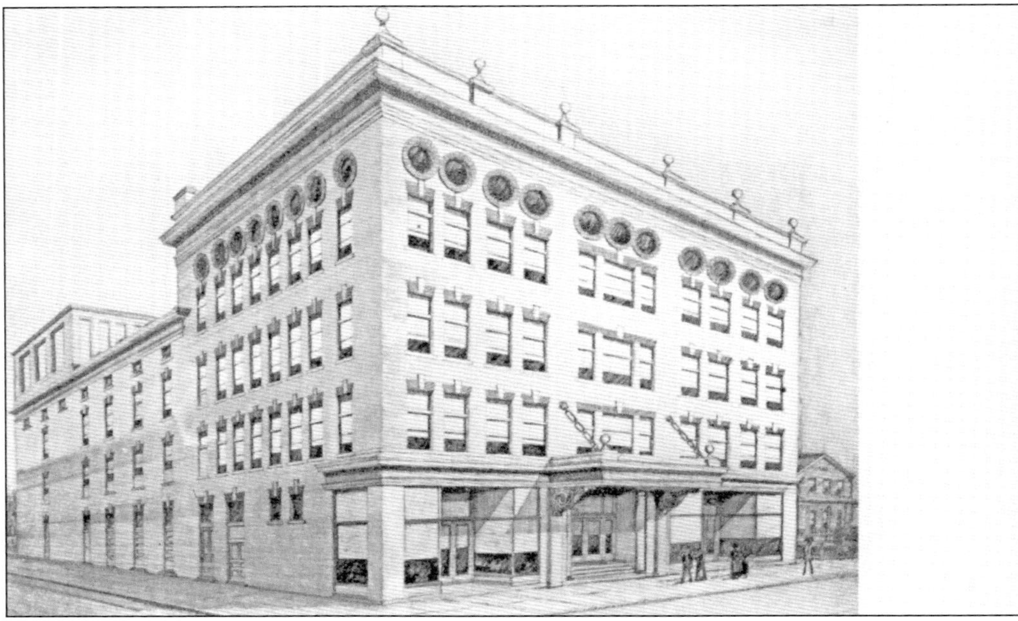

Hinton's 1907 Masonic building contained the Masons' meeting hall, apartments, commercial space, and a dual-balcony auditorium. The Masonic Opera House, later called the Masonic Theatre, showed movies by 1914. Damaging 1919 and 1946 fires caused remodels. Termed "Southern West Virginia's finest theatre" in a 1923 Hinton High School yearbook advertisement, the 600-seat Masonic operated at least until 1957. A 1972 tornado destroyed it. (Author's collection.)

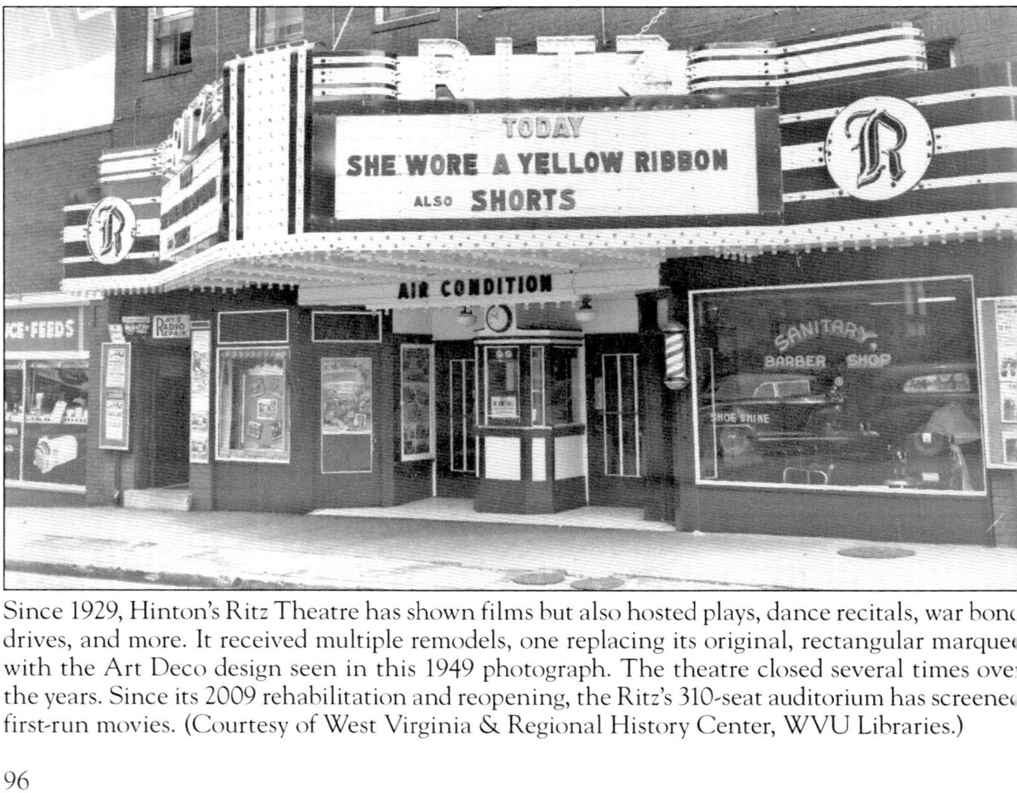

Since 1929, Hinton's Ritz Theatre has shown films but also hosted plays, dance recitals, war bond drives, and more. It received multiple remodels, one replacing its original, rectangular marquee with the Art Deco design seen in this 1949 photograph. The theatre closed several times over the years. Since its 2009 rehabilitation and reopening, the Ritz's 310-seat auditorium has screened first-run movies. (Courtesy of West Virginia & Regional History Center, WVU Libraries.)

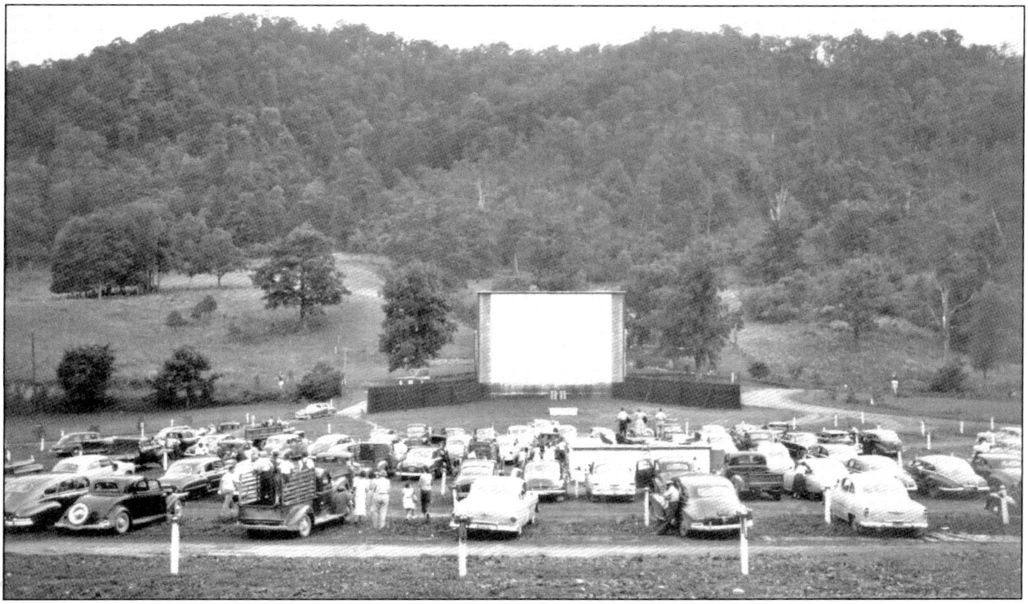

The Greenbrier Drive-in Theatre opened on June 30, 1950, on Route 12 in southeastern Hinton beside the Greenbrier River. Open nightly in summer, it touted "nature's own air conditioning." Along with playing movies, it held special events like a 1951 Independence Day festival and a 1966 Stanley Brothers concert. The drive-in closed by 1977. Its snack bar still stands. (Courtesy of West Virginia & Regional History Center, WVU Libraries.)

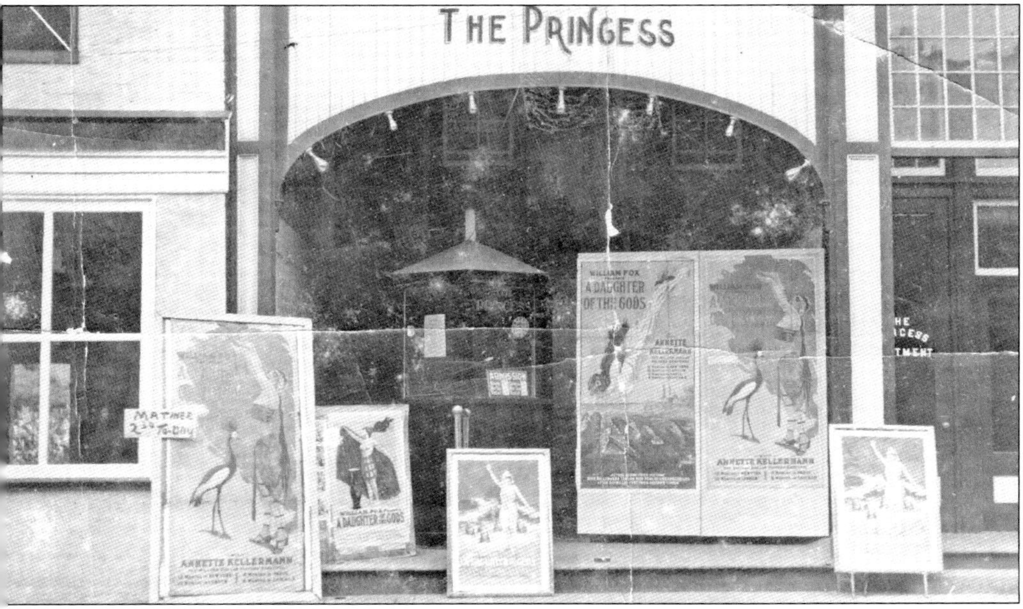

Located in Lewisburg, the Princess advertised itself as "Greenbrier's finest theatre." In this 1916 photograph, it was playing the racy, controversial film *A Daughter of the Gods*. The 200-seat movie house was purchased in 1939 by E.R. Custer and Floyd Price, who already owned the nearby Lewis Theatre. After the theatre's closing around 1942, the Princess's building went through multiple commercial uses; it is now an Irish pub. (Courtesy of Greenbrier Historical Society.)

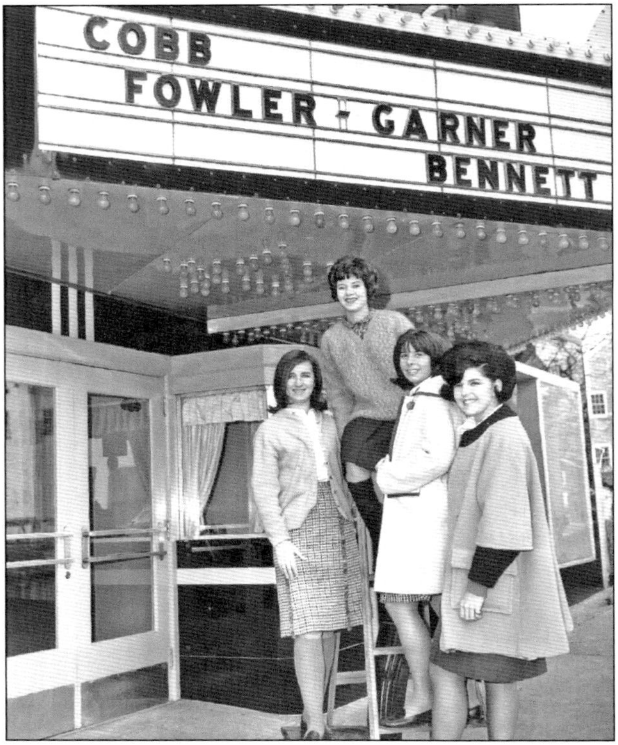

Designed by Charleston architect R.L. Whitten, the 1939 Lewis Theatre's Art Deco facade featured glazed terra-cotta blocks, black Vitrolite panels, and neon signage. Although it has since been remodeled, the continuously operated theatre with over 600 seats still fulfills its original function. The popular Lewisburg venue presents art house films as well as performances by its company in residence since 2009, Trillium Performing Arts Collective. (Courtesy of Greenbrier Historical Society.)

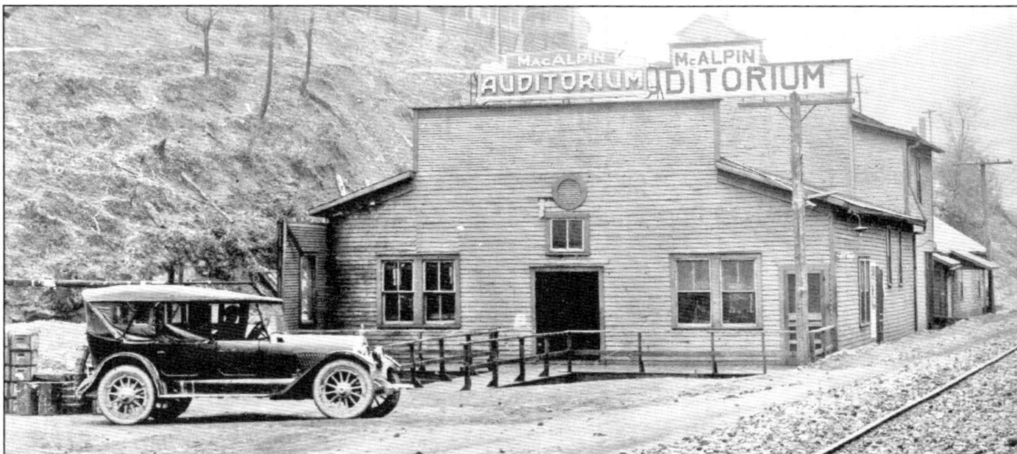

In Raleigh County's coal company town of McAlpin, the 1917 YMCA building contained the McAlpin Auditorium. (As the film venue's two conflicting signs show in this 1920s photograph, i and the town were originally called MacAlpin.) The theatre joined the Winding Gulf Exhibitor Association in 1919. It closed in 1927 after burning. By 1965, the YMCA's site was a parking lot (Courtesy of West Virginia State Archives, Coal Town Collection.)

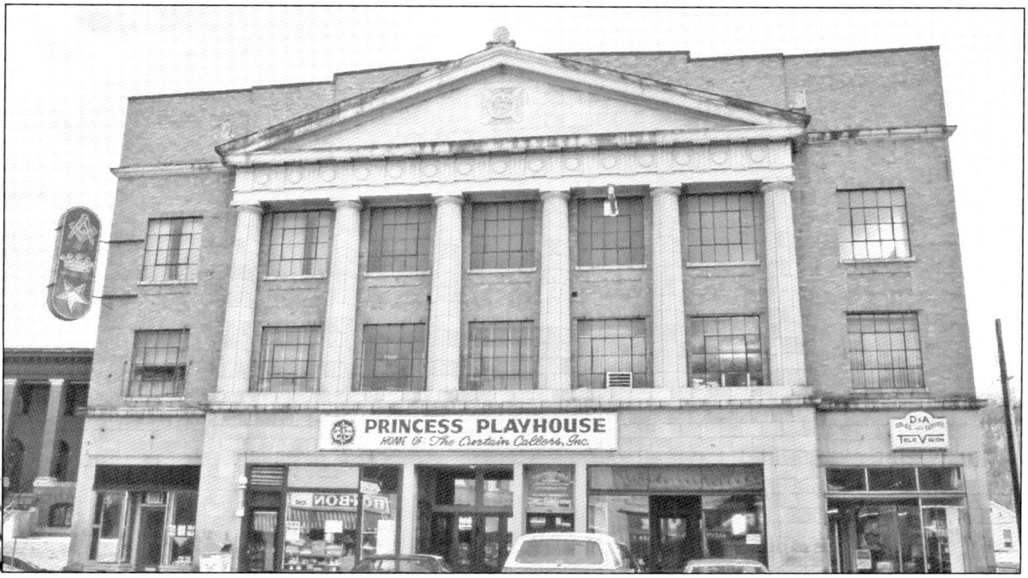

Mount Hope's Princess Theatre opened in 1928 inside the neoclassical Masonic Building. The 800-seat, first-floor auditorium, part of J. Woodrow Thomas's circuit, offered films and performances. In 1975, the Curtain Callers troupe made the space the Princess Playhouse (as this 1985 image shows). The Princess operated until 2004. The auditorium now holds the Princess Auction House, with goods for sale sitting amidst theatre seats. (Courtesy of American Classic Images.)

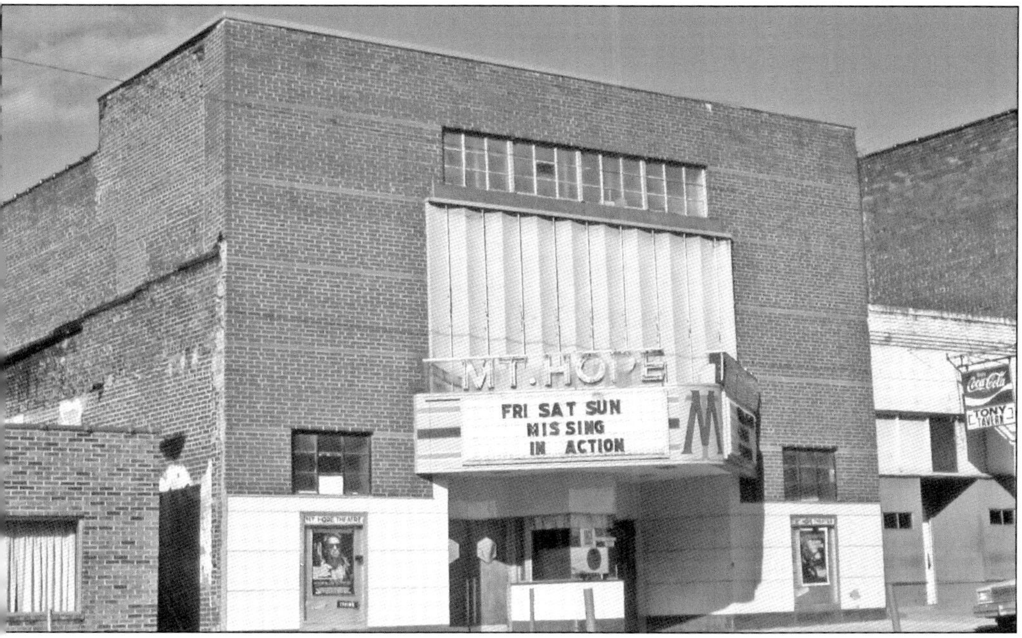

In 1945, Fayette County's worst arson fire destroyed Mount Hope's Royal Theatre. The Newbold-Keesling circuit's 506-seat Mount Hope Theatre—advertised as "modern, beautiful, luxurious"—opened on its site in April 1947. Alex Mahood's Art Deco design featured a facade of jade Vitrolite, greenstone, and red brick. At the time of this 1985 photograph, it was still open. The building is currently vacant and for sale. (Courtesy of American Classic Images.)

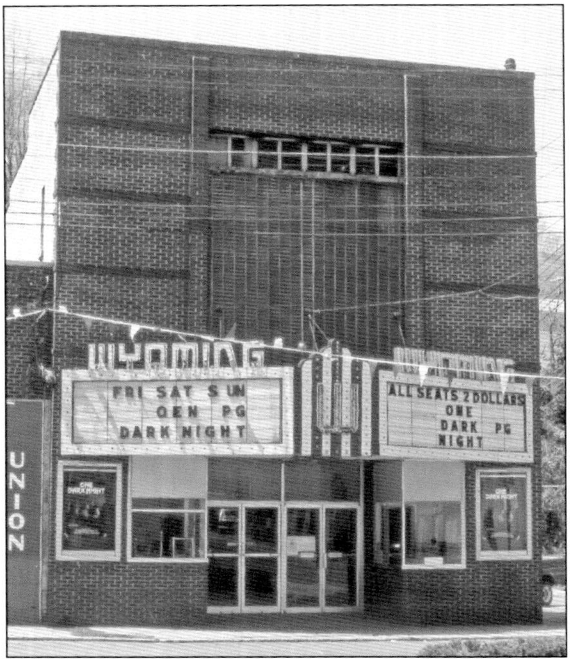

In the Wyoming County city of Mullens, the 500-seat Wyoming Theatre opened in 1919. The movie house upgraded in 1929, getting a new marquee, ticket booth, and Vitaphone sound equipment; manager C.E. Williams promoted the "gala opening of the talkies." The Wyoming was still operating when this 1983 photograph was taken. After a July 2001 flash flood devastated Mullens, the former Wyoming Theatre building was razed. (Courtesy of American Classic Images.)

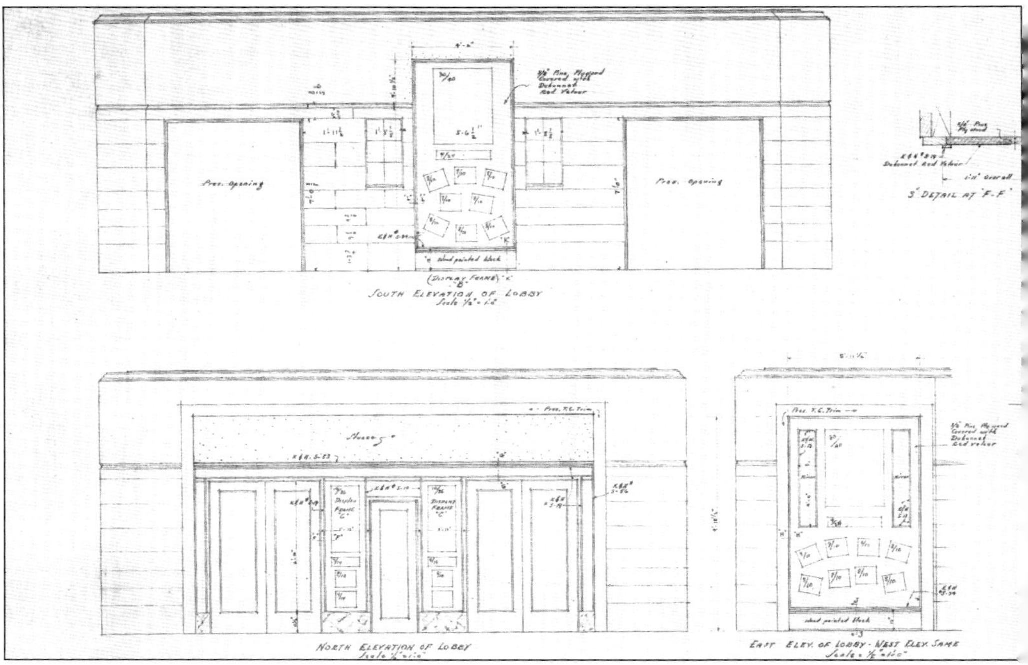

Northfork's Freeman Theatre opened in January 1928. The $100,000 McDowell County venu had a Wurlitzer pipe organ (which theatre owner J.C. Newbold later donated to Bramwel Presbyterian Church). Along with presenting film and vaudeville, it held various communit events. In 1942, the 600-seat Freeman remodeled; this blueprint shows architect Alex Mahood' plan for the lobby. The Freeman was showing movies until at least 1957. (Courtesy of Easter Regional Coal Archives.)

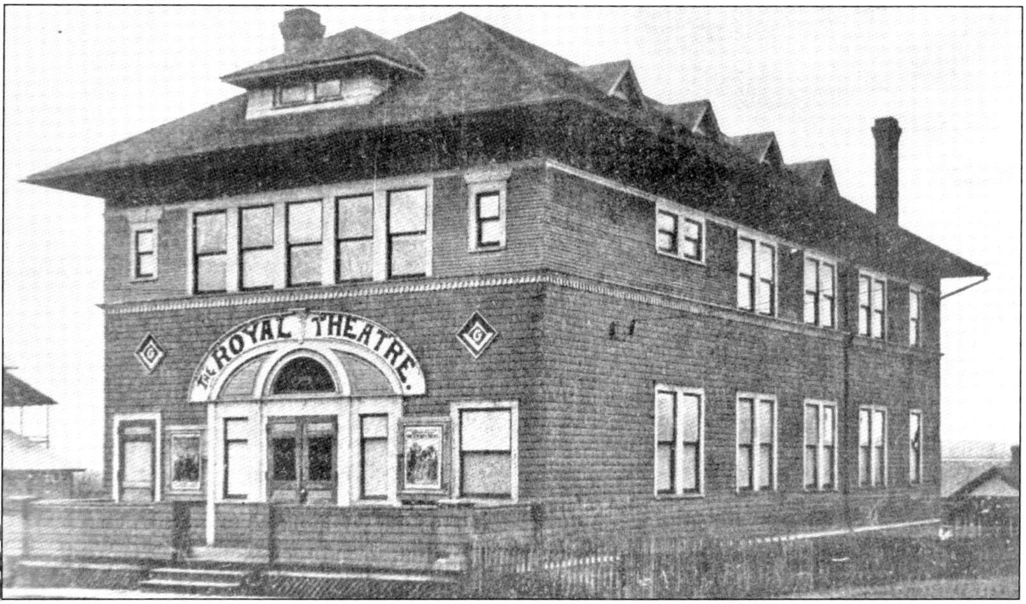

The Royal Theatre in Oak Hill was open and showing films by 1914. In 1920, it received a Simplex projector. The movie house stopped appearing in exhibition journals' annual listings after 1927; apparently, it did not last into the age of sound pictures. Located on the 300 block of Washington Street, the building was later reused as a church; today, it serves as a Masonic lodge. (Courtesy of Timothy A. Richardson.)

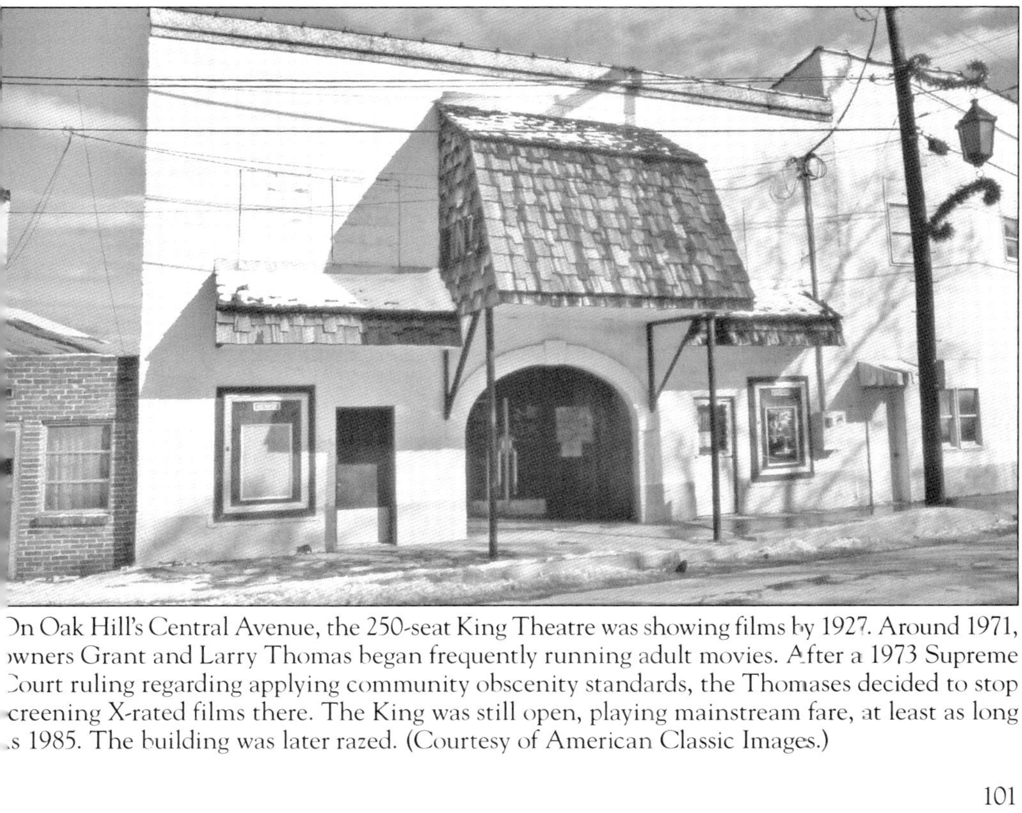

On Oak Hill's Central Avenue, the 250-seat King Theatre was showing films by 1927. Around 1971, owners Grant and Larry Thomas began frequently running adult movies. After a 1973 Supreme Court ruling regarding applying community obscenity standards, the Thomases decided to stop screening X-rated films there. The King was still open, playing mainstream fare, at least as long as 1985. The building was later razed. (Courtesy of American Classic Images.)

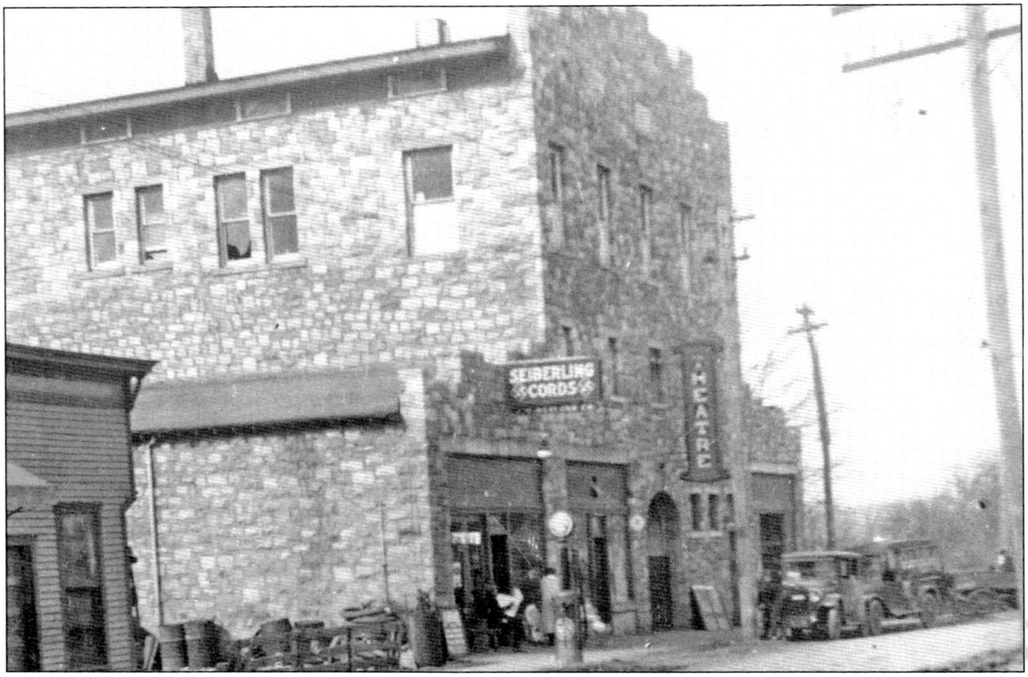

The 500-seat Lyric Theatre opened in Oak Hill's Knights of Pythias building around 1928. S.D. Morton bought it in 1937, renaming it the Mayfair Theatre. In 1945, the Mayfair suffered a major fire. The movie house reopened, operating until at least 1957 with 350 seats. By 1961, its stone structure on Main Street East's 300 block held commercial uses, which is still the case today. (Courtesy of Timothy A. Richardson.)

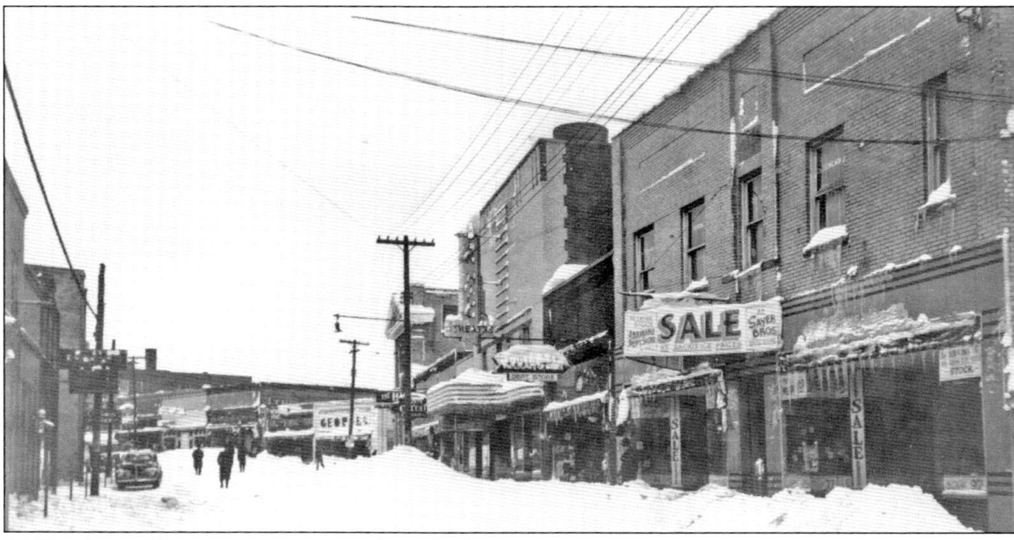

J. Woodrow Thomas's 600-seat Oak Hill Theatre opened on Main Street in Oak Hill in 1938. During World War II, Elizabeth Thomas ran the Art Deco movie house while her brother was in the military. Other Thomas relatives were still showcasing major movies there in 1973. The Oak Hill Theatre (seen here during the winter of 1941–1942) was demolished in 1975 for a bank expansion. (Courtesy of Timothy A. Richardson.)

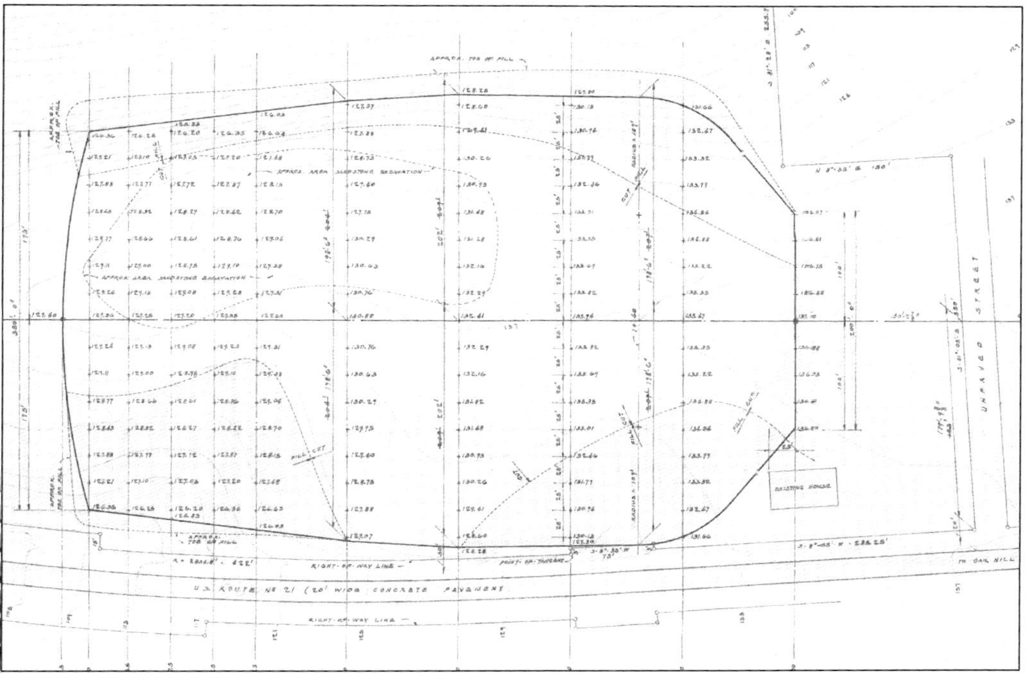

This blueprint shows Alex Mahood's layout for the Newbold-Keesling circuit's Skyline Drive-in Theatre. The 500-car venue's 1952 creation entailed mountaintop removal through blasting, and the Skyline's screen tower featured a mountain mural. The drive-in, on Fayetteville Road in eastern Oak Hill, included streamline moderne elements. By 1969, the year it stopped advertising, the Skyline was playing sexploitation films. Skyline Plaza replaced it in 1973. (Courtesy of Eastern Regional Coal Archives.)

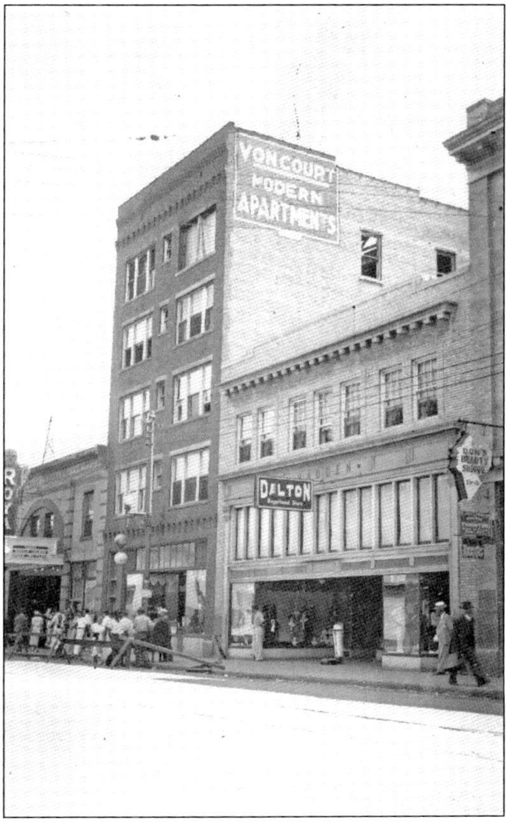

Princeton's Royal Theatre opened in 1911. During the Great Depression, F.F. Von Court expanded it to 900 seats and reduced admission to 10¢. In 1954, his relative Lawrence Von Court bought it, giving it a new marquee and renaming it the Lavon Theatre. It closed in 1983 and later hosted a church. The nonprofit Princeton Renaissance Project is currently rehabilitating it into a community venue. (Courtesy of Eastern Regional Coal Archives.)

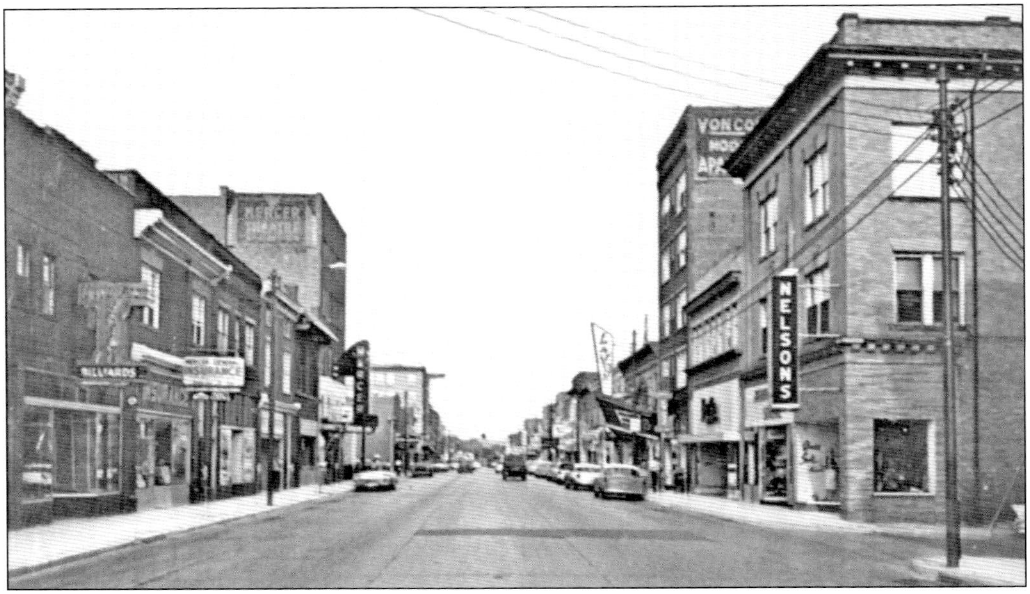

In 1937, F.F. Von Court opened the Mercer Theatre, located across Princeton's Mercer Street from his popular Royal Theatre (seen here during its Lavon Theatre era). The 450-seat Mercer, with its porcelain enamel facade of green and ivory, played X-rated movies throughout the 1970s. In 1977, after its adult films ended following controversy, a subsequent patronage decrease caused the venue's closure. Dick Copeland Town Square replaced it. (Author's collection.)

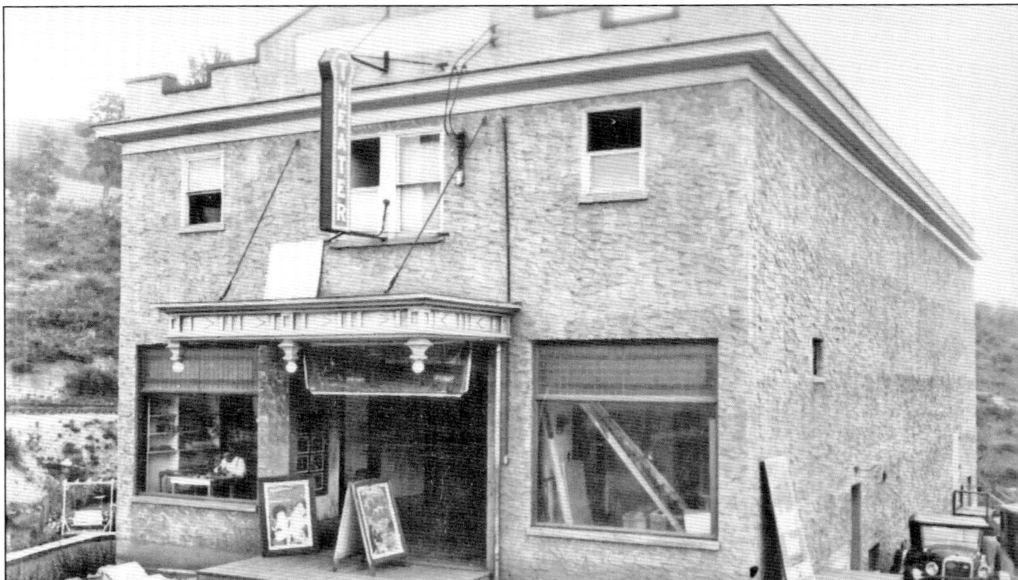

The 150-seat Quinwood Theatre opened in Quinwood, a Greenbrier County coal company town in 1921. At the time of this photograph, its freestanding advertising board showcased a poster fo *Gang War*, a 1928 movie notable because its accompanying cartoon was Walt Disney's pioneerin *Steamboat Willie*. J.B. Dobbins managed the movie house between at least 1940 and 1952. The Quinwood Theatre Company dissolved in 1955. (Courtesy of Greenbrier Historical Society.)

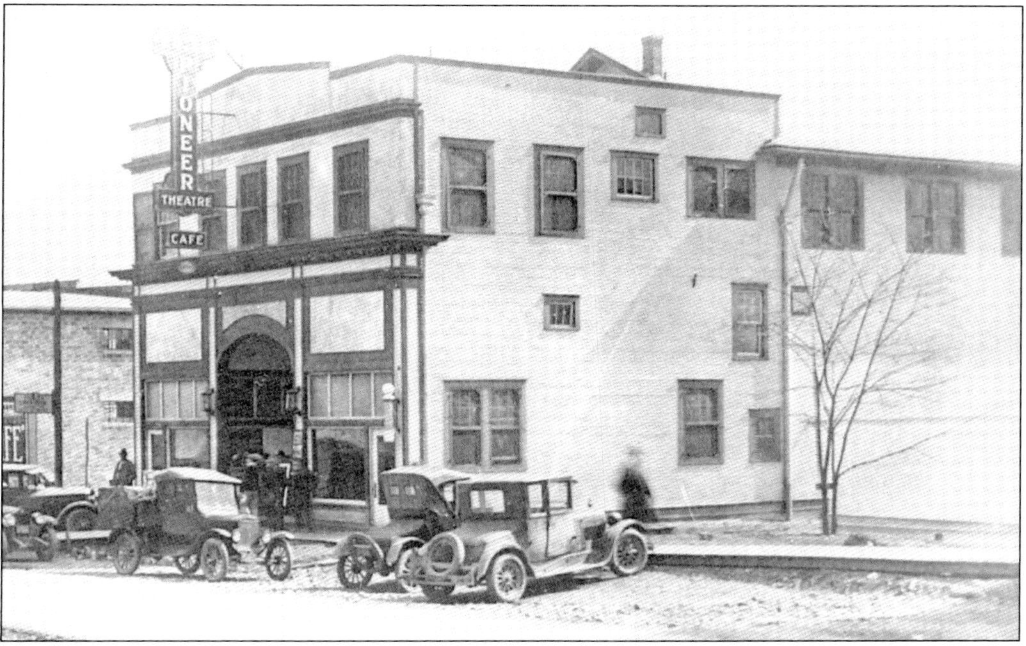

In 1923, Richard Raine and Howard Gray opened Rainelle's first movie theatre, the Pioneer, appropriately playing *The Covered Wagon*. The 500-seat venue did not outlast the silent film era, becoming an early example of adaptive reuse. The two-story building reopened in 1929 as the Pioneer Hotel, with 34 rooms. Its "theatre" sign remained, and the former auditorium served as the hotel lobby and restaurant. (Courtesy of Greenbrier Historical Society.)

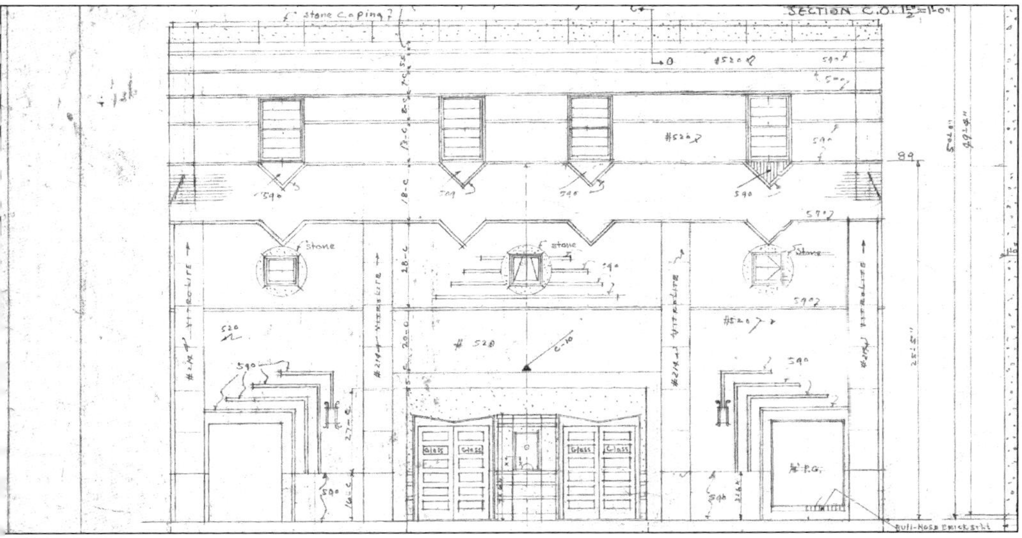

African American architect John C. Norman created this blueprint for Ronceverte's segregated Shanklin's Grand Theatre. The wooden 1910s Grand Theatre was demolished for J.C. Shanklin's 350-seat, concrete-and-steel movie house. Shanklin's Grand operated from 1937 into the 1960s. The roof has collapsed behind the long-vacant building's Art Deco enameled brick facade. The city is attempting to purchase it for renovation. (Courtesy of West Virginia State Archives, John C. Norman Sr. Collection.)

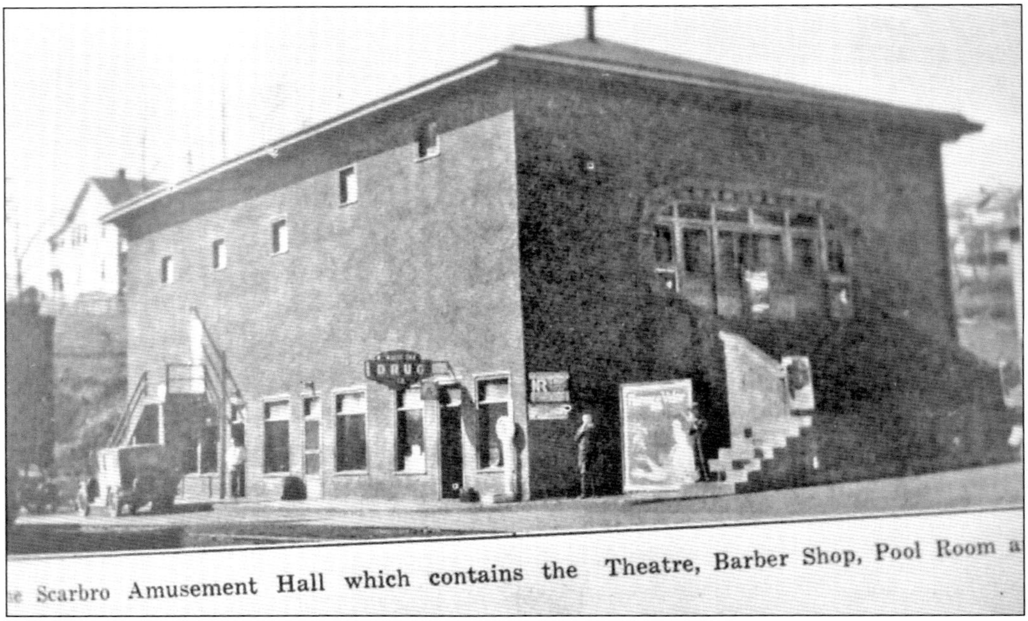

In Fayette County's Scarbro coal camp, beside the still-standing New River Company Store, the multipurpose Amusement Hall offered a 300-seat movie venue. Seen in this postcard, the second-floor Rialto Theatre was open as early as 1927. In 1930, C.D. Crawford sold it to E. Henderson. The Rialto showed films at least until 1957. Its building survived into the 1990s. (Courtesy of West Virginia & Regional History Center, WVU Libraries.)

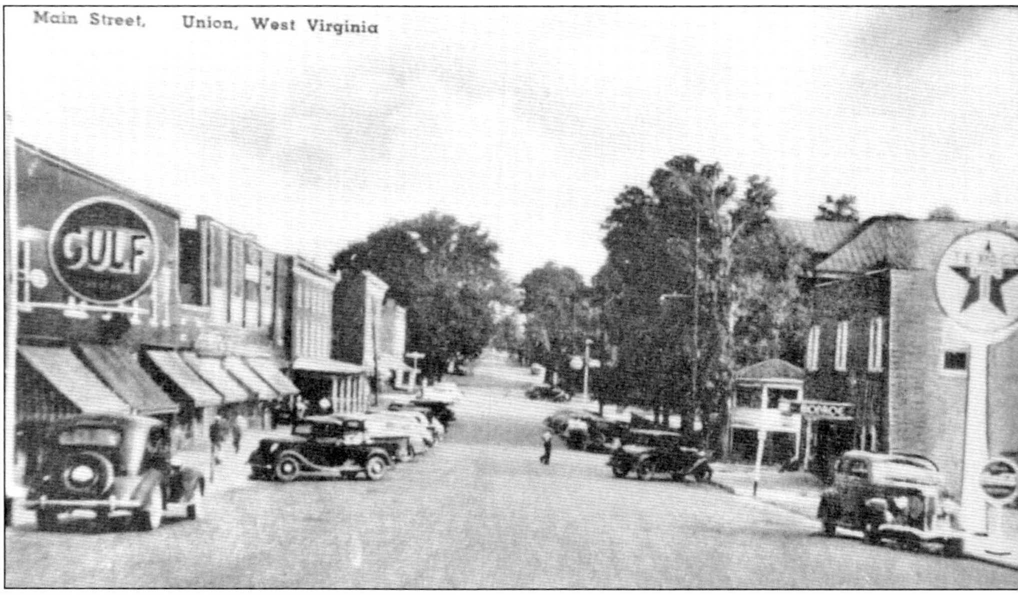

In Union in Monroe County, the 300-seat Monroe Theatre was built in 1941. The $15,000 brick-and-cinder-block building was located on the site of Gratton Gillespie's wooden Union Theatre which burned down in 1940. Closed sometime between 1957 and 1977, the Monroe Theatre ha been converted to office space. Except for a missing marquee, its exterior still looks as it does ir this postcard. (Courtesy of Monroe County Historical Society.)

This 1946 photograph shows Welch's Temple Theatre sitting across McDowell Street from its sibling, the Pocahontas Theatre (both owned by the Rogers circuit). The Temple opened in 1929 on the Odd Fellows temple's first floor. Locals remember the 470-seat movie venue for its Westerns and kids' matinees. It operated as late as 1956. The building is part of the Welch Commercial Historic District. (Courtesy of University of Kentucky Special Collections.)

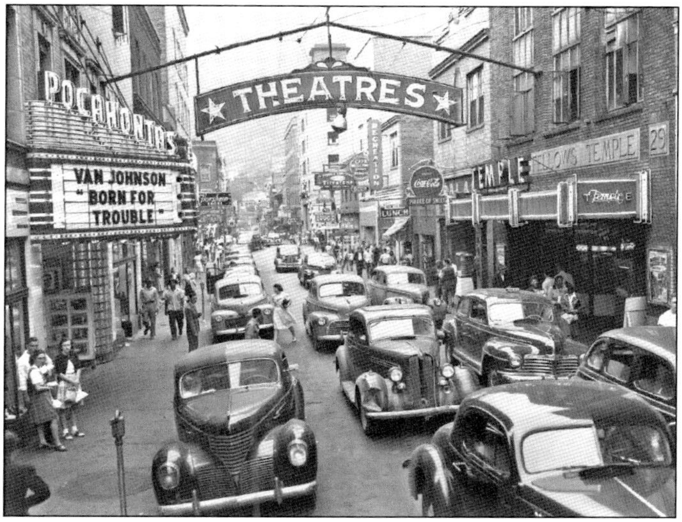

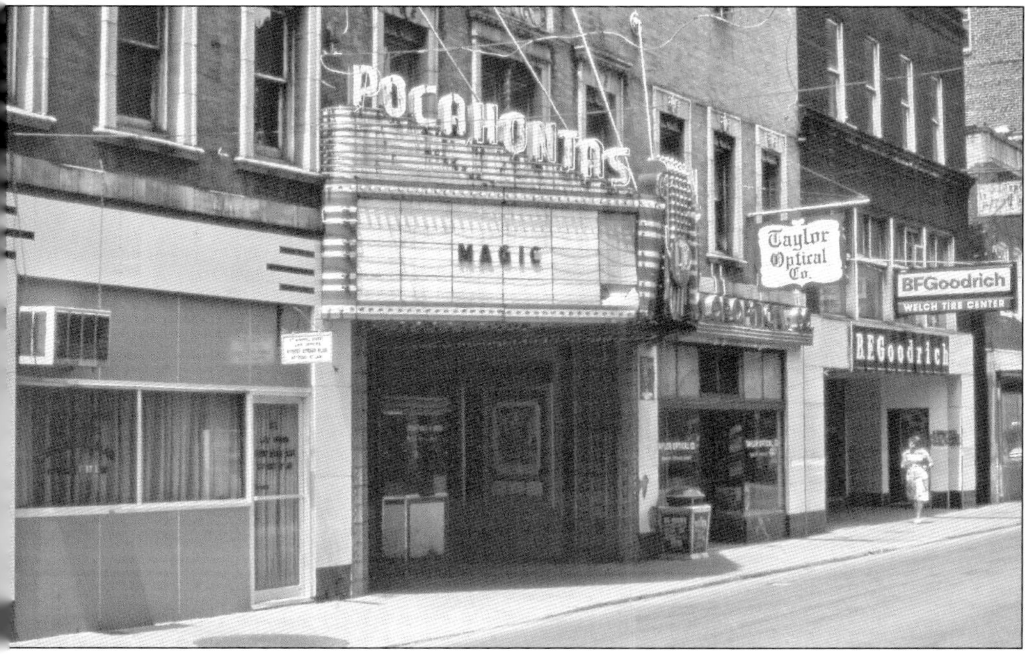

Welch's $100,000 Pocahontas Theatre opened on Christmas Day, 1928. Alex Mahood designed the elegant picture palace for Mayor John W. Blakely. It offered a Mighty Wurlitzer pipe organ and 1,264 seats (including 150 for "colored" patrons in the balcony). In the 1960s, WELC Radio hosted Saturday morning sock hops, with youths dancing onstage. The Pocahontas was still open in 1980, when a fire destroyed it. (Courtesy of American Classic Images.)

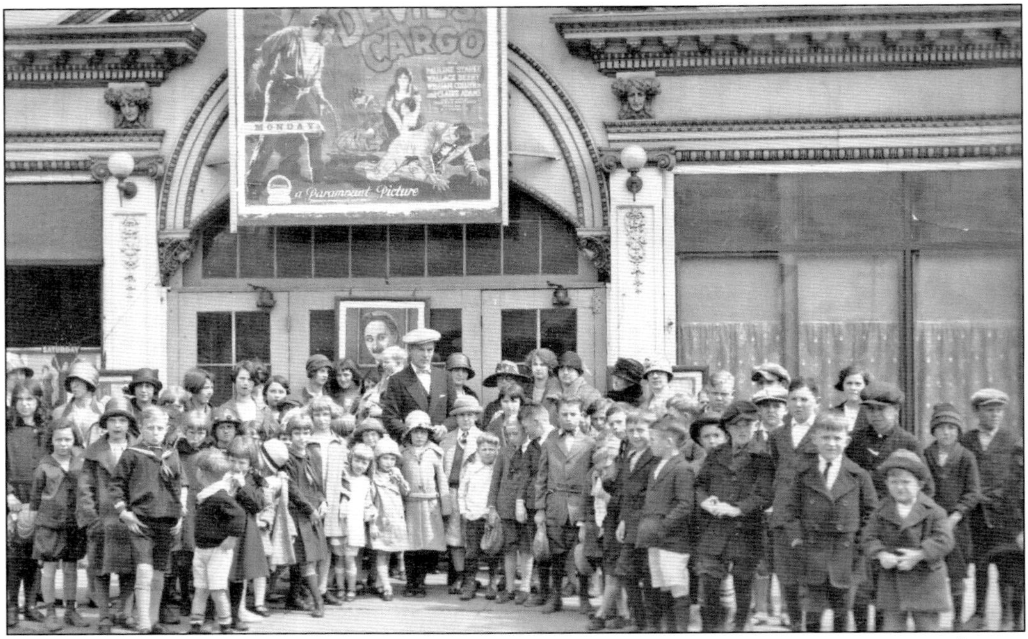

In White Sulphur Springs, W.B. Hines opened the Plaza Theatre on July 19, 1915. The $7,000 venue with 300 seats provided films and live entertainment, such as a 1932 performance by country music pioneer Fiddlin' Charlie Bowman. This 1925 photograph shows a group of children at the Plaza, which was showing *Devil's Cargo*. The Newbold-Keesling circuit ran the Plaza during the 1950s. It was demolished in 1969. (Courtesy of Greenbrier Historical Society.)

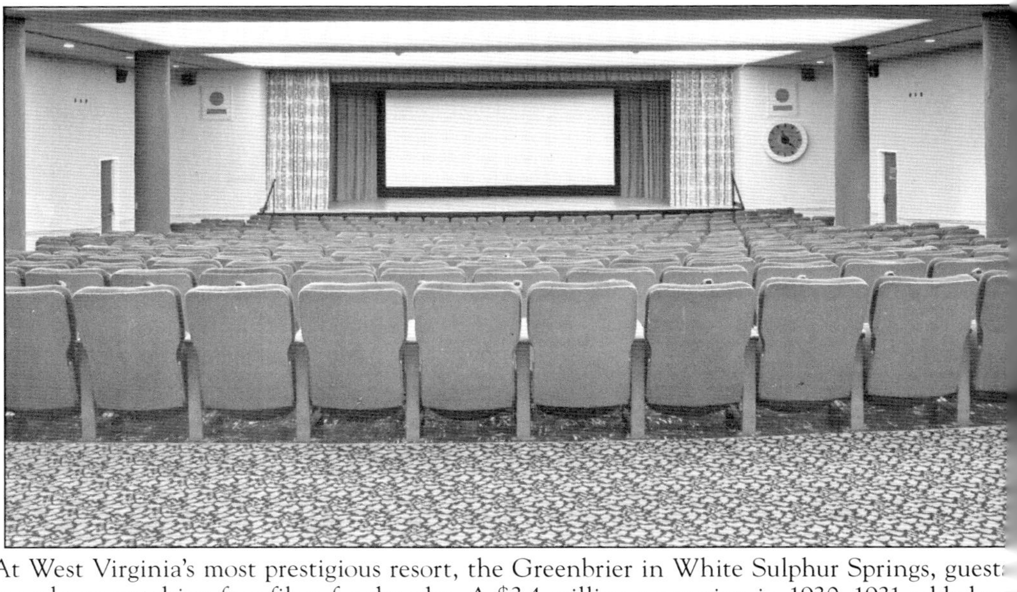

At West Virginia's most prestigious resort, the Greenbrier in White Sulphur Springs, guest have been watching free films for decades. A $3.4 million expansion in 1930–1931 added a auditorium, with flyers announcing " 'Talkies' every evening at 9:00." In 1954, movies moved t their current venue (seen here in 1969) inside a new addition. The theatre plays recent family-friendly DVDs nightly. Two Cinemascope-capable, carbon-arc projectors are still on-site. (Courtes of the Greenbrier.)

Eight

NORTHERN PANHANDLE

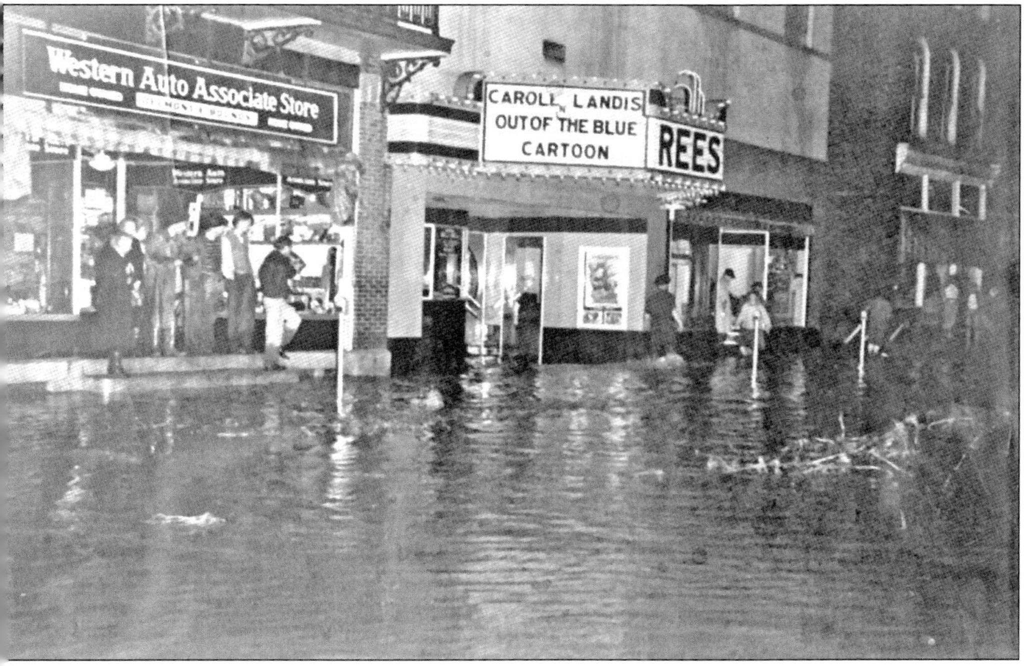

The Rees Theatre opened during the spring of 1940 in the Marshall County city of Cameron. Owned by Earl G. Rees and his wife, the 460-seat movie house survived the 1948 flood seen here. It operated until at least 1981, by which time the "Rees" lettering on its Art Deco marquee had vanished. On January 25, 1988, the theatre burned down. (Courtesy of West Virginia State Archives, Cameron Public Library Collection.)

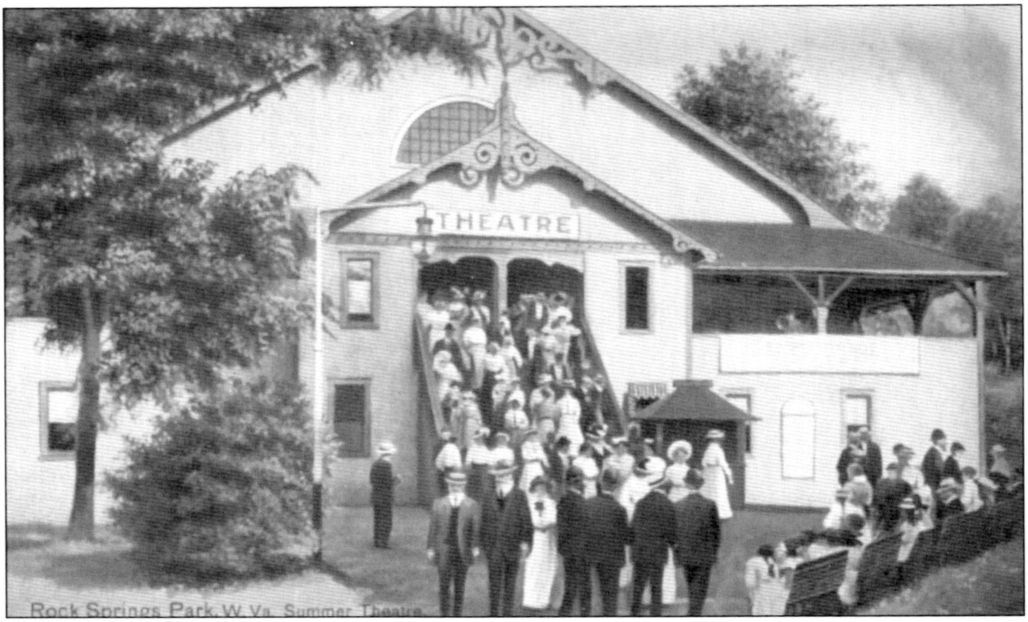

The Summer Theatre was part of Rock Springs Park, a popular amusement park at the West Virginia–Ohio border in Chester, which operated from 1897 to 1970. The seasonal venue, which park owner C.A. Smith opened in 1903, mainly held performances like the "refined vaudeville" noted on the sign on the right. However, it also played silent films frequently. Destroyed by fire in 1917, it was not rebuilt. (Author's collection.)

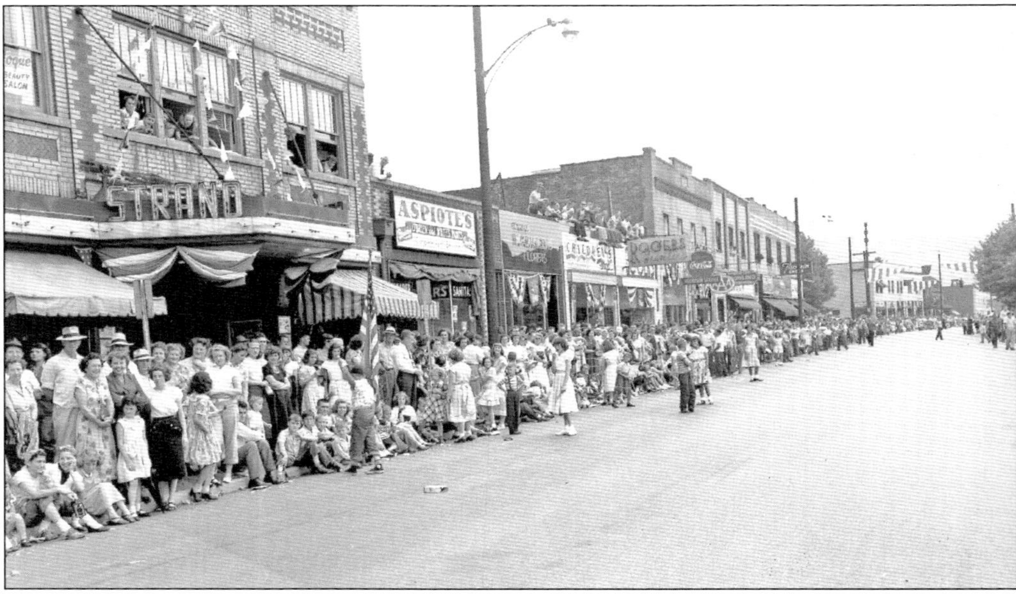

The Strand Theatre was operating prior to 1926 at 3216 Main Street in Hollidays Cove (ar incorporated city that later became part of Weirton). The 250-seat Strand was part of Nick Anas' circuit, soon known as Weir-Cove Enterprises. In this 1950 image, people wait outside the Stranc for a Fourth of July parade. The movie house closed between 1951 and 1954. The building is now gone. (Courtesy of Weirton Area Museum.)

In 1926, Nick Anas bought Hollidays Cove's closed Lincoln Theatre at 3405 Main Street. After Pittsburgh decorator William Naidenoff remodeled it, it reopened as the 500-seat Cove Theatre. This 1954 photograph shows the Cove's free preview screening of a documentary featuring Weirton Steel. In 1962, it was the Weir-Cove circuit's last operating indoor movie house. By 1964, a market was reusing the Art Deco building, later demolished. (Courtesy of Weirton Area Museum.)

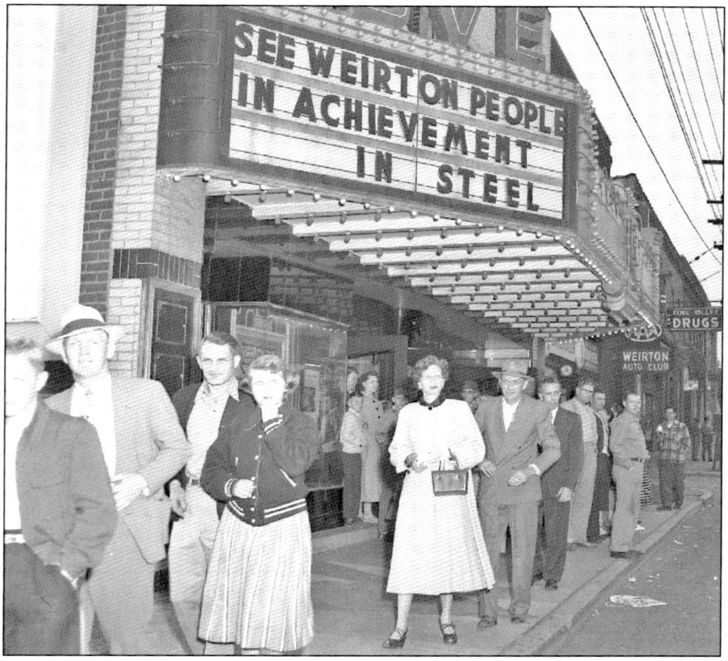

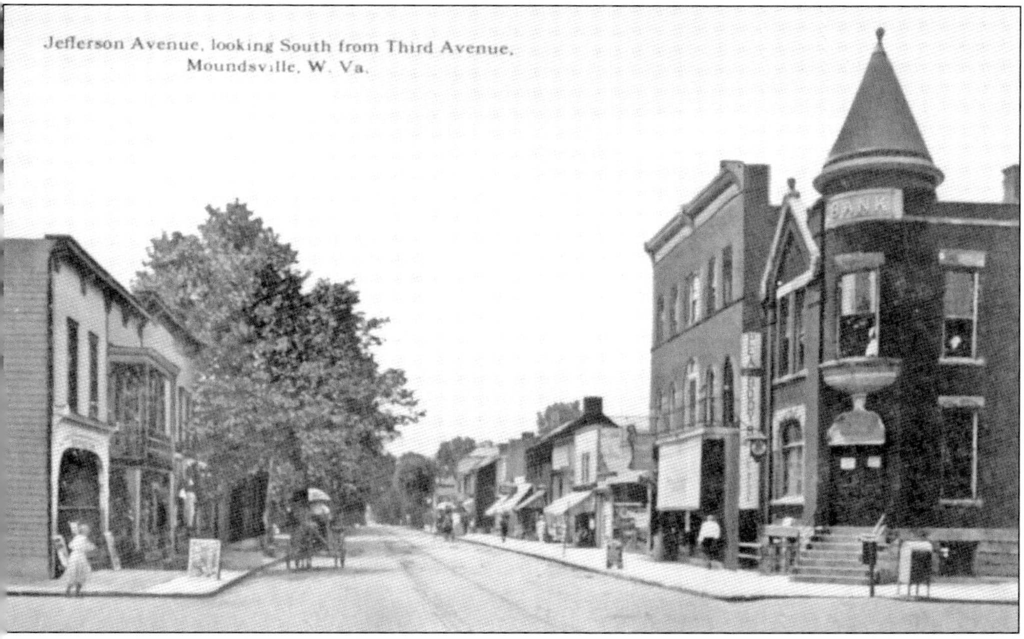

The Moundsville Orpheum Theatre opened on July 1, 1910. In 1912, the Orpheum's L.R. Thomas became secretary of the Motion Picture Operators' League of West Virginia. Advertisements promoted the Orpheum as offering vaudeville and "the latest, cleanest, and best photo plays," with "pictures changed daily." Safety was key, with the Orpheum said to disinfect daily and have a metal-lined projection booth for fire prevention. It no longer stands. (Author's collection.)

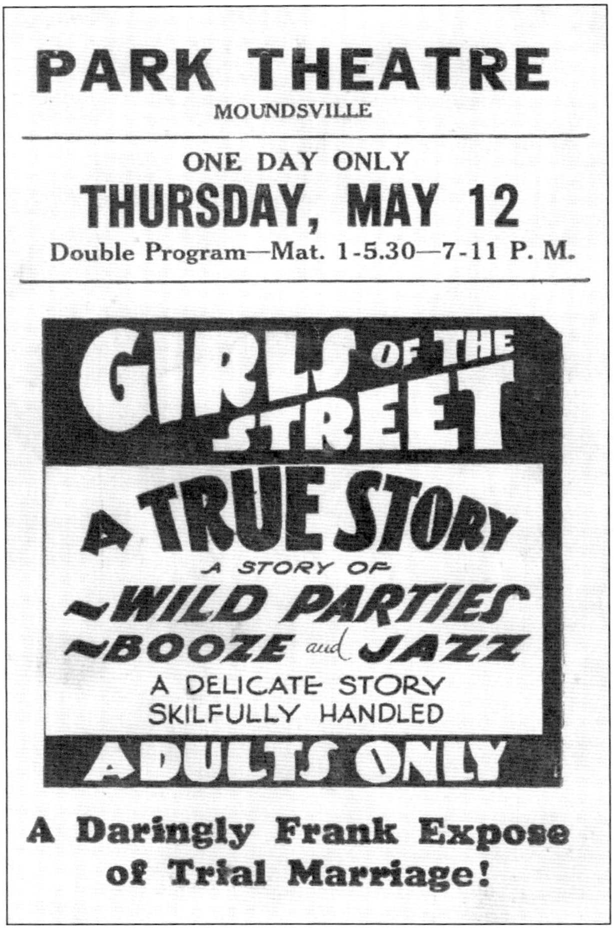

At 228 Jefferson Avenue, Moundsville's Park Theatre opened in 1912 as a movie house. Merton A. Sybert bought it in 1913, renovating it then and in 1916. In late 1918–early 1919, an influenza epidemic caused its closure for over 13 weeks. After Sybert's 1928 death, the 400-seat Park went through three more owners by 1931. The theatre operated until 1957 at least and was later destroyed. (Author's collection.)

The Branded Woman and *The Garage* were shown when Moundsville's 1,100-seat Strand Theatre opened in 1920. In owner Merton A. Sybert's $100,000 neoclassical steel structure, attendees enjoyed central heat and pipe organ music. Besides a closure between 1968 and 1976, the Strand showed first-run movies until 1996. In 2002, the Strand Theatre Preservation Society formed to restore and reopen the Strand as a performing arts venue—accomplished in 2014. (Courtesy of American Classic Images.)

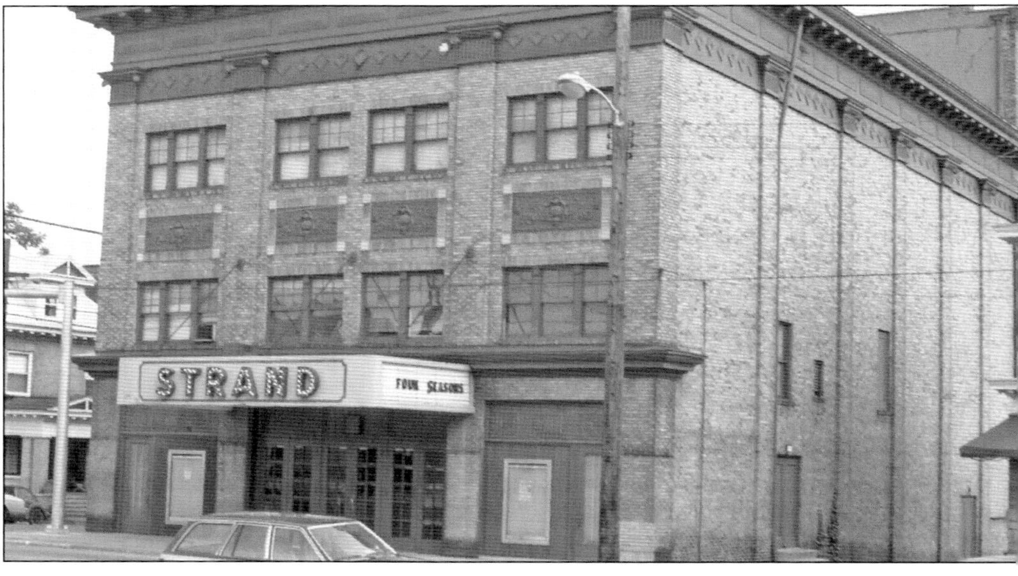

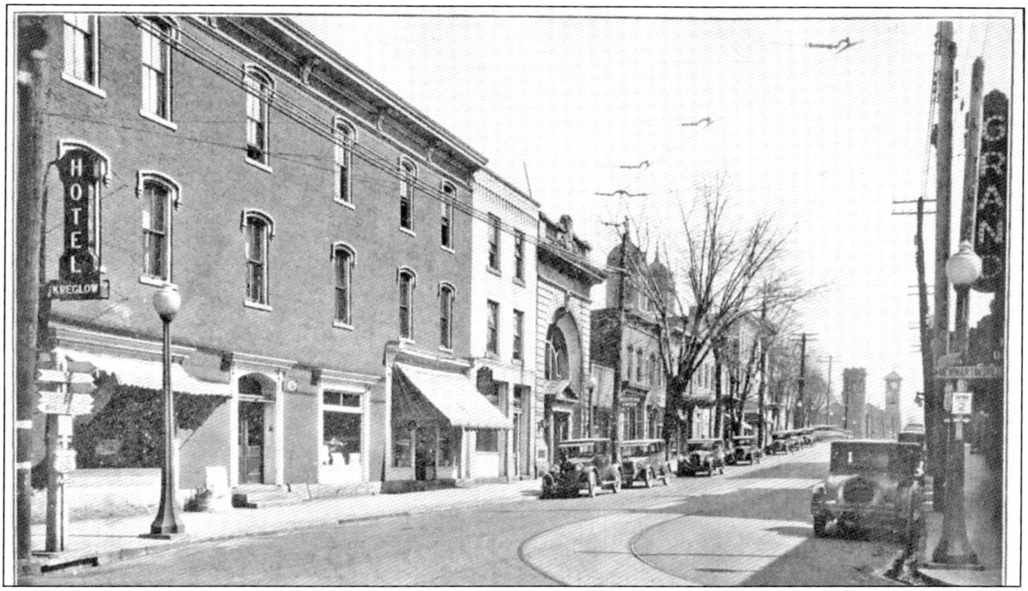

The Ferris brothers opened the Grand Theatre in 1927 on Seventh Street in Moundsville. After Vitaphone was installed, a 1929 directory advertisement touted that the Grand provided "the ultimate perfection of pictures that talk like human people." The Grand, which originally had 600 seats, was operated by Walter Kepple in 1960. Later converted to offices, it was demolished in the 1970s. (Courtesy of West Virginia State Archives, Becky Clutter Collection.)

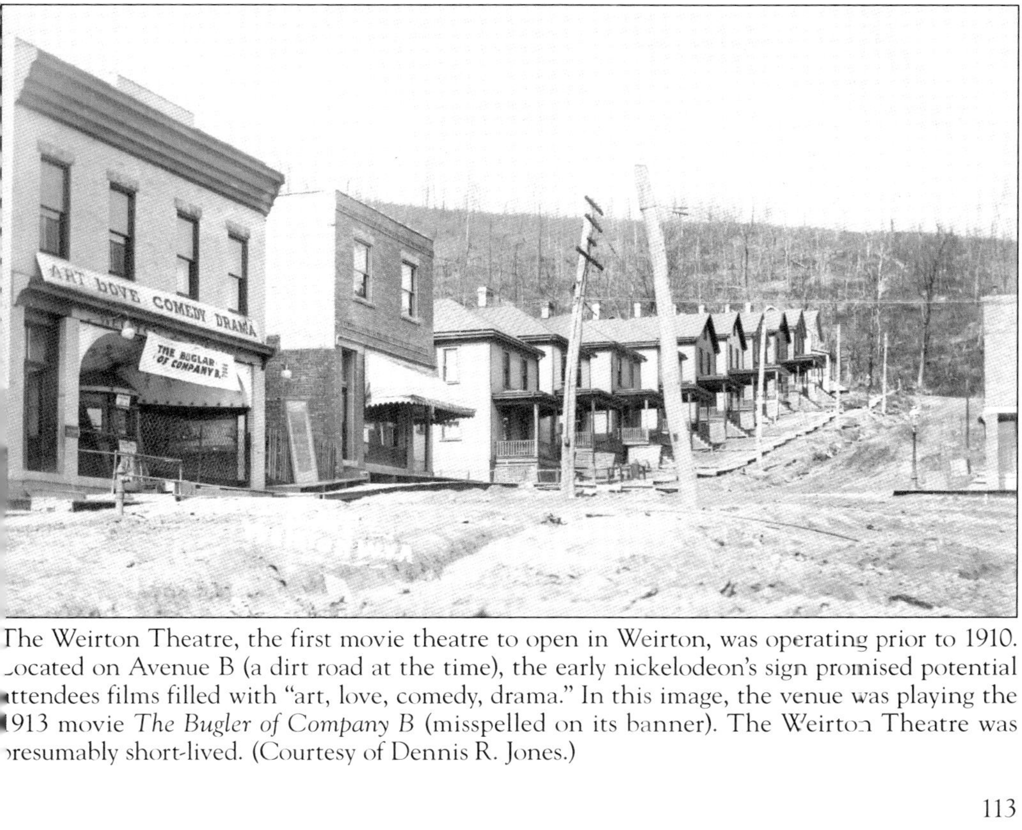

The Weirton Theatre, the first movie theatre to open in Weirton, was operating prior to 1910. Located on Avenue B (a dirt road at the time), the early nickelodeon's sign promised potential attendees films filled with "art, love, comedy, drama." In this image, the venue was playing the 1913 movie *The Bugler of Company B* (misspelled on its banner). The Weirton Theatre was presumably short-lived. (Courtesy of Dennis R. Jones.)

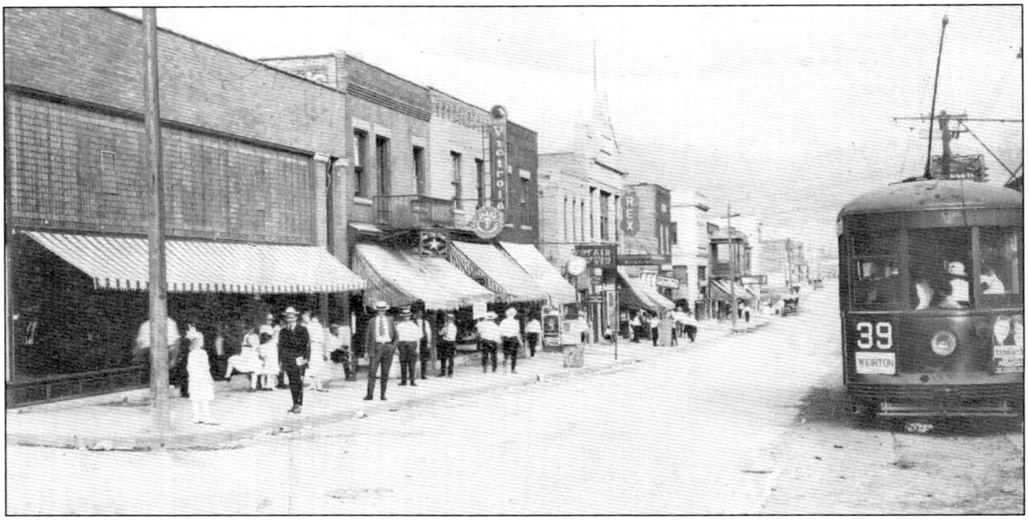

Weirton's Rex Theatre opened on Main Street's 1300 block in May 1917. *Moving Picture World* noted, "A program of high class features will be shown." The 500-seat movie house, seen in this c. 1921 image, was originally operated by George Velas and S. Stances. The Rex, which featured a Seeburg pipe organ, closed around 1931. Weirton Steel later covered the Rex's section of Main Street. (Courtesy of Dennis R. Jones.)

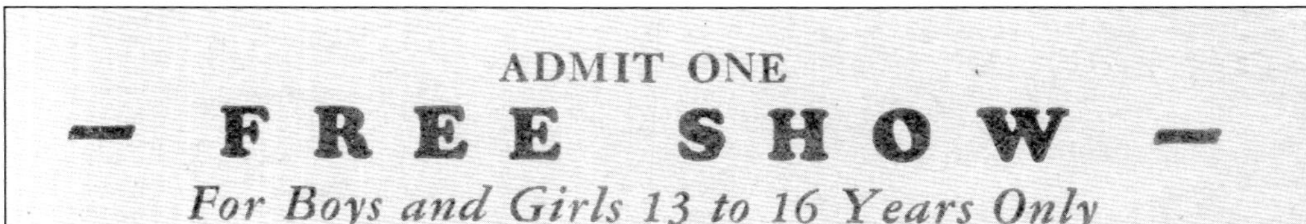

ADMIT ONE

— FREE SHOW —

For Boys and Girls 13 to 16 Years Only

MANOS THEATRE

Weirton, W. Va.

SATURDAY, FEBRUARY 9th, 1935

9:00 A. M. 5 Reels of Comedy

DOOR PRIZE (Must have Name below to Win)

Name ....

Address ....

Town ....

The Manas Theatre was open before 1927. Operated by the Anas family's Weir-Cove Enterprises circuit, it was on Weirton's Main Street, near Avenue E (now Weirton Steel). Misspellings were common, as seen with this free children's ticket for the "Manos" from 1935. In 1940, the 600-seat movie house was redecorated inside and out and renamed the Anas Theatre (which its new marquee proclaimed). It closed around 1956. (Courtesy of Weirton Area Museum.)

Weirton's 1970 Plaza Theatre, part of Weirton Heights Shopping Plaza, was rare—a single-screen movie house in a strip mall. The $125,000 venue offered 350 seats, free parking, and what the *Weirton Daily Times* called a "fully automated control system to draw the curtains and dim the lights." Donna Risbin operated it from 1976 to 2010. The Plaza closed in 2015 to remodel, reopening in 2017. (Courtesy of Weirton Area Museum.)

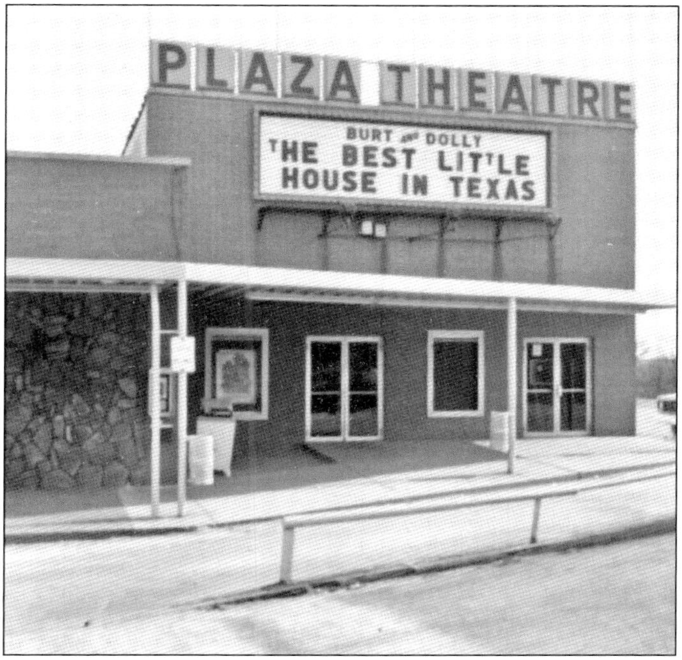

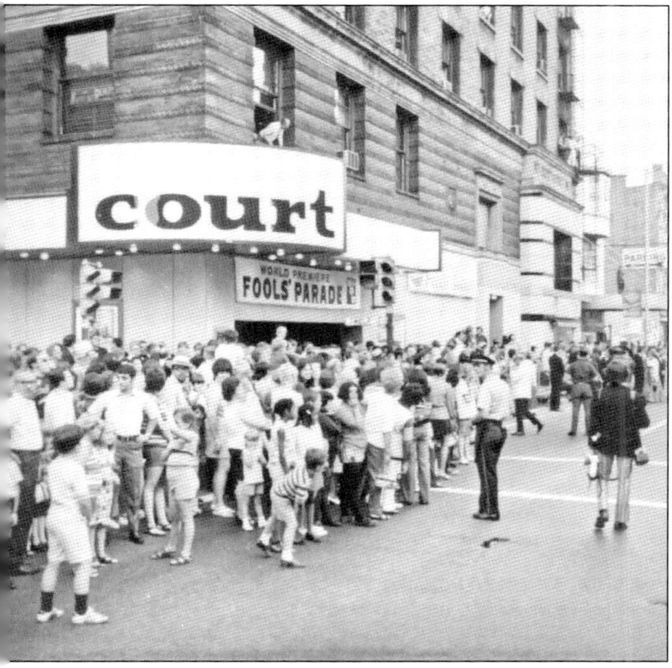

Edward Franzheim was the architect and first manager of the Court Theatre, opened in 1902 inside Wheeling's Board of Trade Building. In 1938, the sumptuous Court was heavily remodeled, becoming exclusively a movie house. This photograph is from the Court's 1971 world premiere of the James Stewart film *Fools' Parade* (shot in nearby Moundsville). The 1,200-seat Court closed in 1982. Its building still stands. (Courtesy of Ohio County Public Library Archives, Wheeling, West Virginia.)

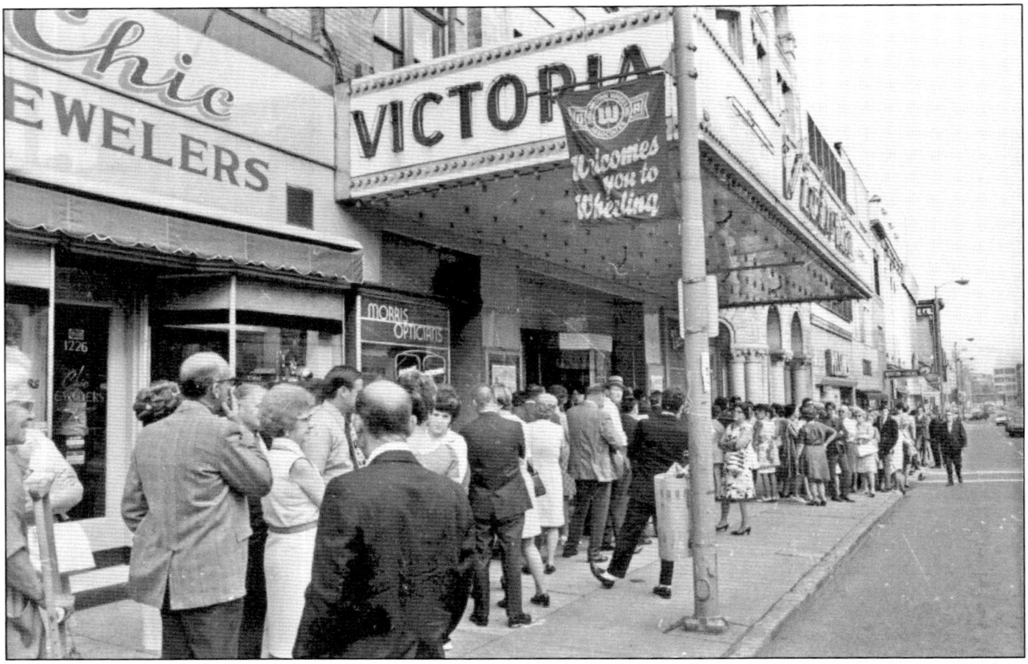

Opened by George Shafer in 1908, Wheeling's vaudeville-oriented Victoria Theatre expanded in 1919 and began playing films as early as 1921. The "Vic," with its streamline moderne marquee and its ornate interior filled with neoclassical plasterwork, stopped showing movies in 1986. Following preservation efforts and stints as a comedy club and church, the auditorium has hosted regular variety shows since 1996. (Courtesy of Ohio County Public Library Archives, Wheeling, West Virginia.)

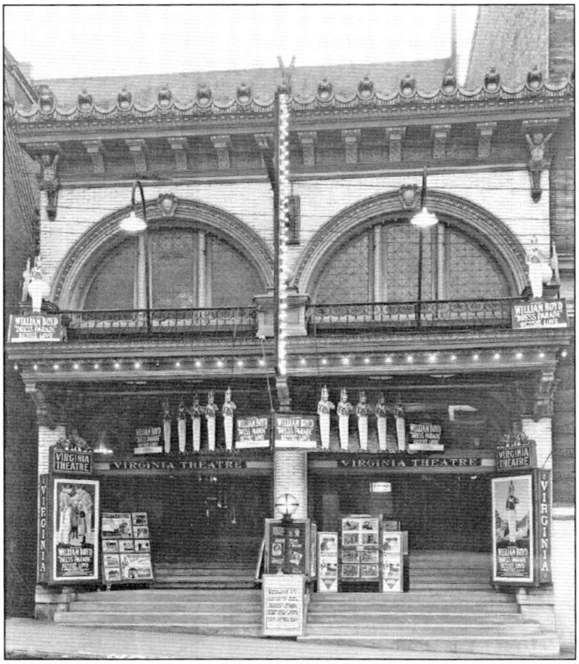

Wheeling's Virginia Theatre, containing the state's largest stage, opened on Twelfth Street in 1908. Charles A. Feinler's venue started showing movies in 1911. In 1923, Feinler gave delivery wagon owners movie passes for posting flyers on their vehicles (except "colored" wagon owners, who could not enter the Virginia; they received 50¢). The 1,340-seat theatre fell in 1962. (Courtesy of West Virginia State Archives, Wheeling Area Chamber of Commerce Collection.)

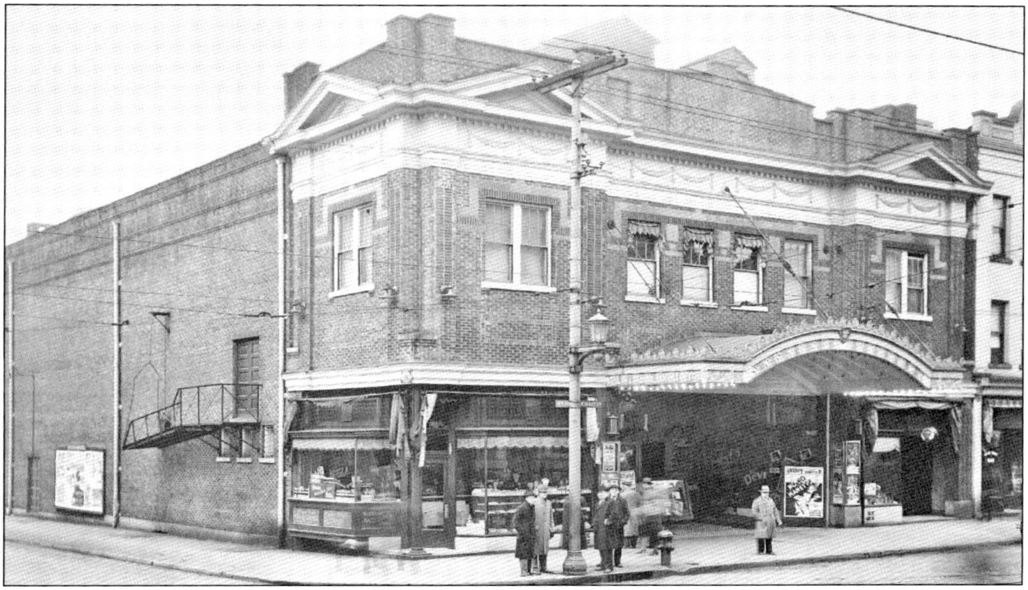

James Velas's Liberty Theatre opened in December 1917 with a screening of Norma Talmadge's *The Moth*. Designed by architect Charles D. McCarty, the venue was located on Market Street's 1500 block in Wheeling. In 1930, Warner Bros. bought it. During the 1940s, it was expanded from 800 to 1,080 seats. The Liberty closed around 1961; another building stands on its site. (West Virginia State Archives, Wheeling Area Chamber of Commerce Collection.)

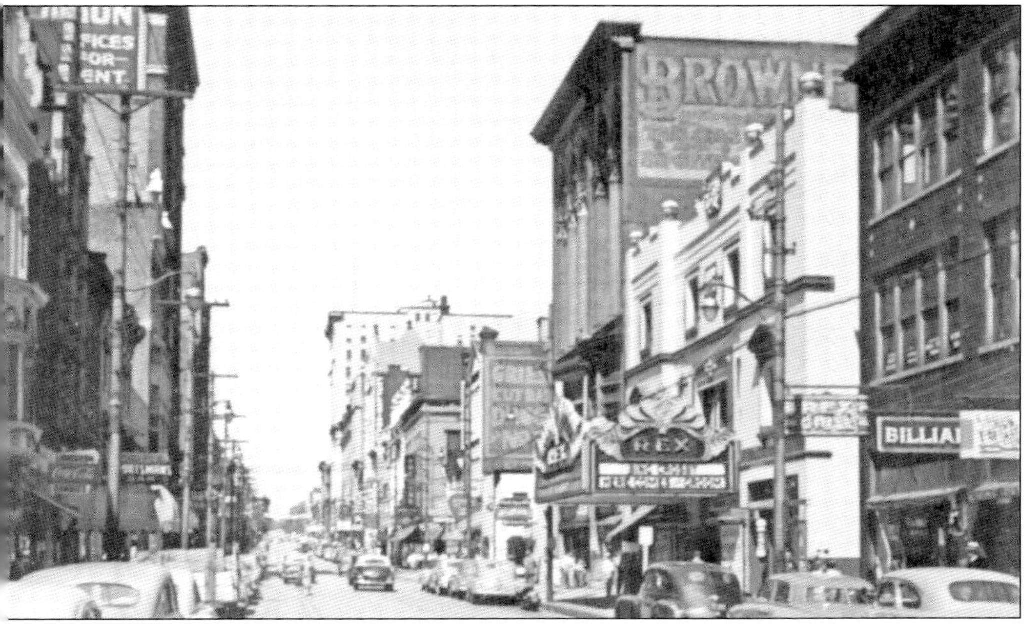

Wheeling's 1000-seat Rex Theatre opened in 1915, designed by Edward Franzheim. In 1925, it was listed as one of West Virginia's primary first-run movie houses. By 1981, the Rex was renamed the Coronet, with its elaborate marquee removed and its ornamented, stucco facade hidden under a metal slipcover. The Coronet closed in 1985. Despite a campaign by preservation organization Friends of Wheeling, it was destroyed in 1989. (Author's collection.)

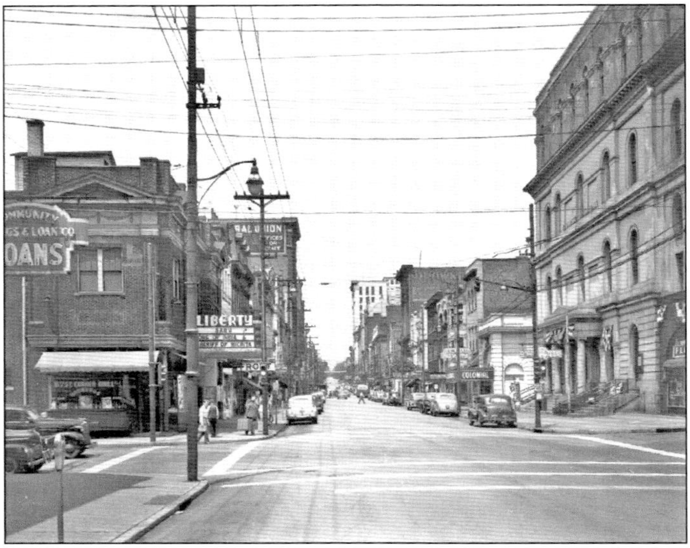

Charles A. Feinler's 900-seat Colonial Theatre was showing movies by 1914. The long, narrow Colonial's architecture took cues from its neighbor, Wheeling's Renaissance Revival–style West Virginia Independence Hall (right). Feinler remodeled its interior in 1920 and sold it to Sam Richblum in 1932. The Colonial was operated by the Dipson circuit into the early 1950s. Its building no longer exists. (Courtesy of Ohio County Public Library Archives, Wheeling, West Virginia.)

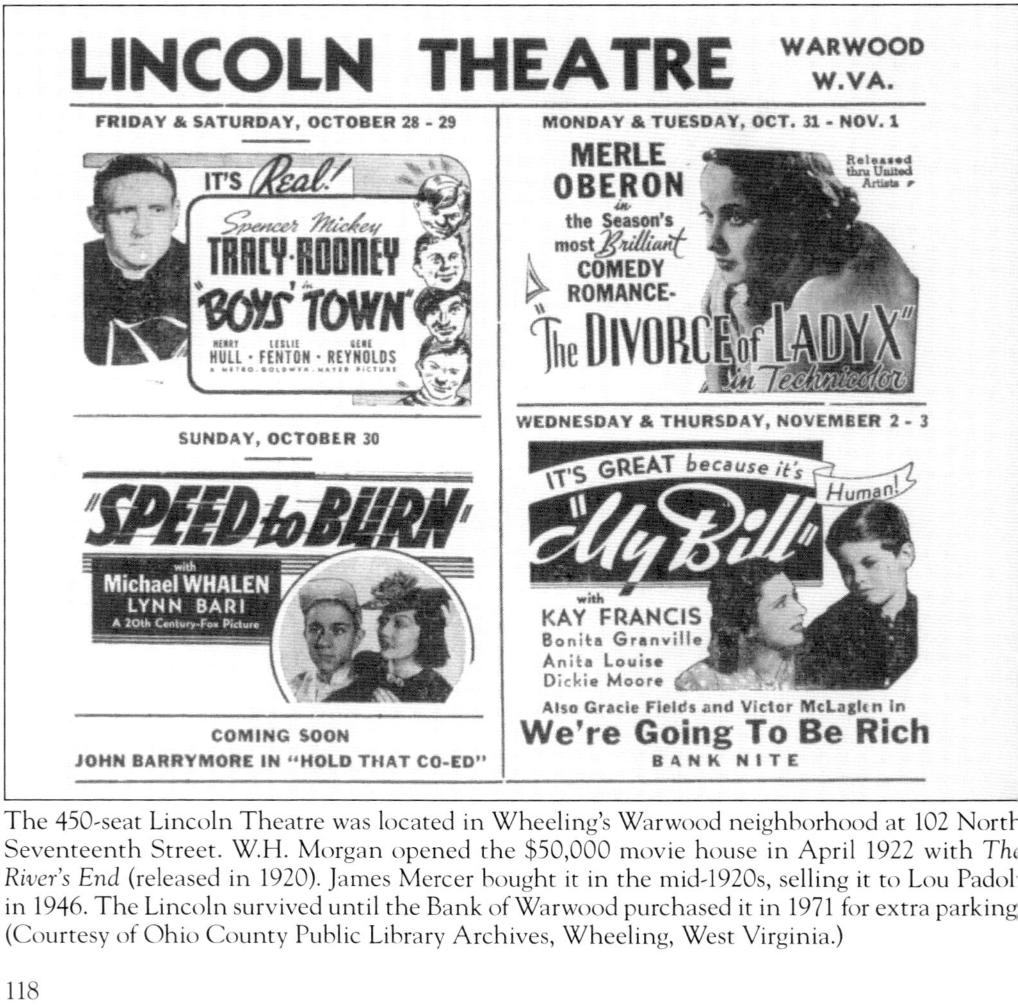

The 450-seat Lincoln Theatre was located in Wheeling's Warwood neighborhood at 102 North Seventeenth Street. W.H. Morgan opened the $50,000 movie house in April 1922 with *The River's End* (released in 1920). James Mercer bought it in the mid-1920s, selling it to Lou Padol in 1946. The Lincoln survived until the Bank of Warwood purchased it in 1971 for extra parking. (Courtesy of Ohio County Public Library Archives, Wheeling, West Virginia.)

Architect Frederick Faris designed Wheeling's 1,200-seat Plaza Theatre for owner George Zeppos. It opened on August 1, 1921, with a hospital-benefit screening of *Black Beauty*. In 1931, D.R. Kautz bought it, added sound, and renamed it the State Theatre. Operated by James Velas since at least 1940, the 900-seat State closed during the 1950s. Its 1114 Market Street structure is now gone. (Courtesy of West Virginia State Archives, George Neiman Collection.)

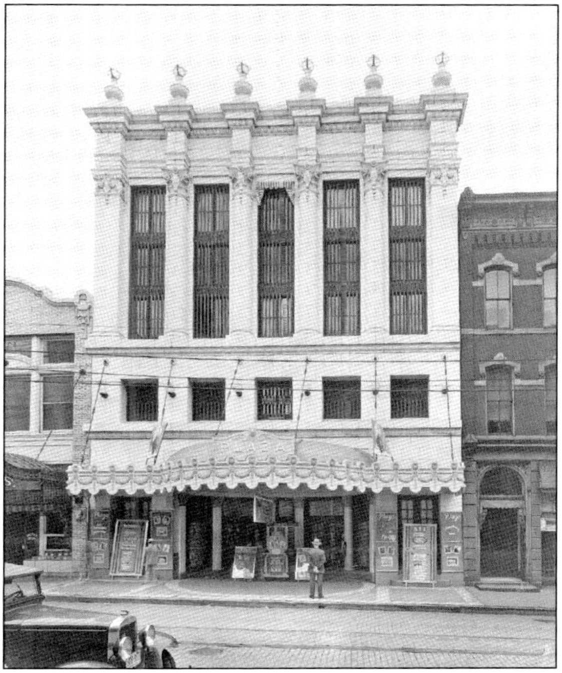

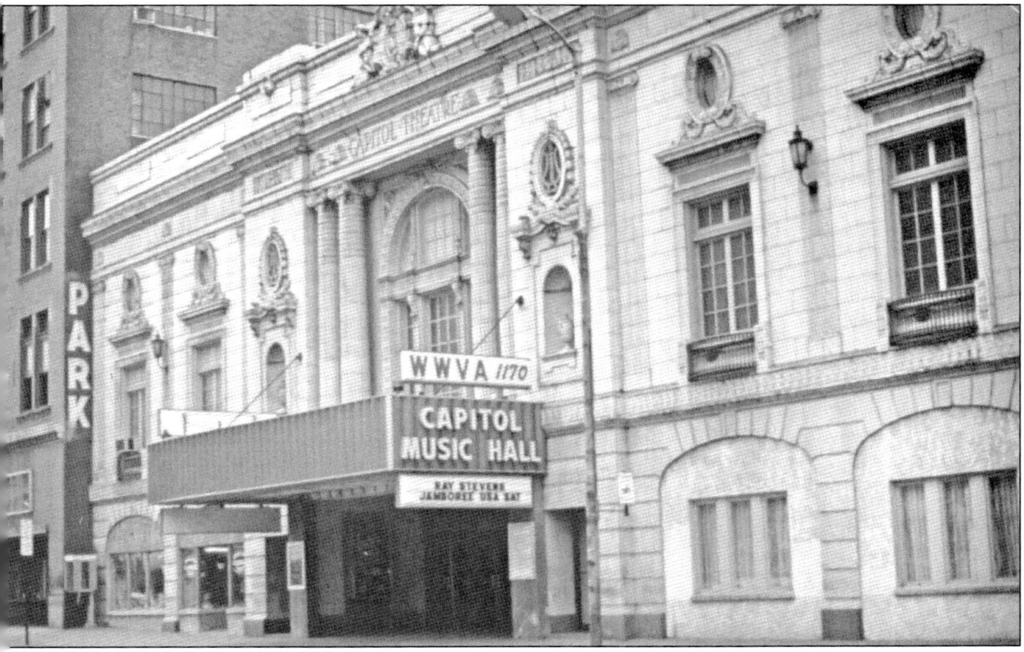

Wheeling's 3,000-seat Capitol Theatre opened on Thanksgiving, 1928. The Beaux-Arts–style, Charles W. Bates–designed picture palace cost $1 million. Its 1969 renaming as Capitol Music Hall signaled movies' end there. After two years' closure, the Wheeling Convention and Visitors Bureau purchased, renovated, and reopened it in 2009. Again called the Capitol Theatre, it is the region's primary performing arts center. (Courtesy of Ohio County Public Library Archives, Wheeling, West Virginia.)

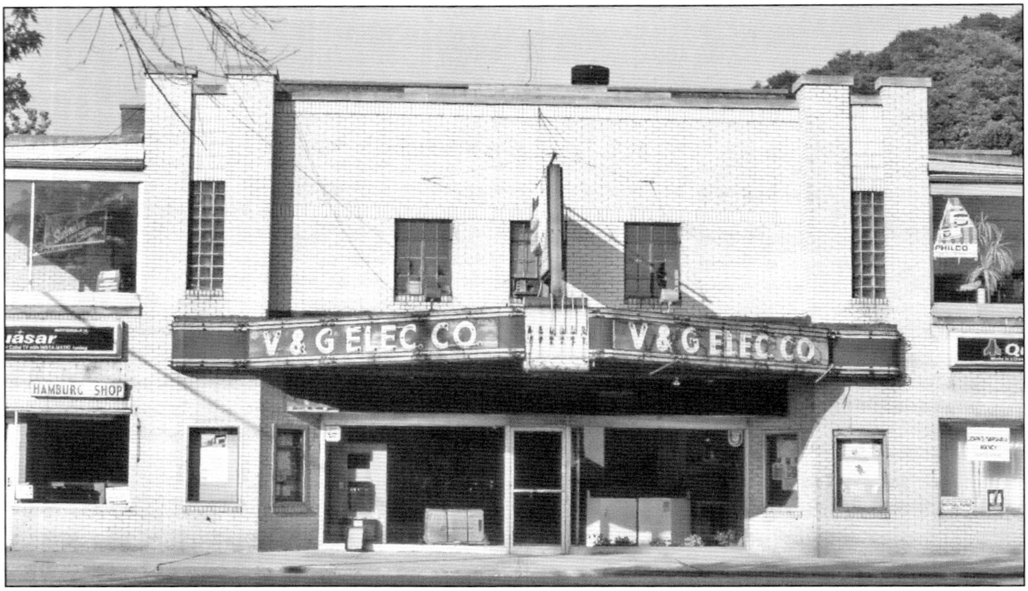

Chris Velas opened the Art Deco 850-seat Mayfair Theatre in late 1939. The $70,000 movie house was located at 1171 National Road in Wheeling's upscale Pleasant Valley neighborhood. By 1954, it had become part of the Dipson circuit. The Mayfair last appeared in city directories in 1959. The building was then adaptively reused, maintaining its key exterior features, as seen in this 1981 photograph. It was later demolished. (Courtesy of American Classic Images.)

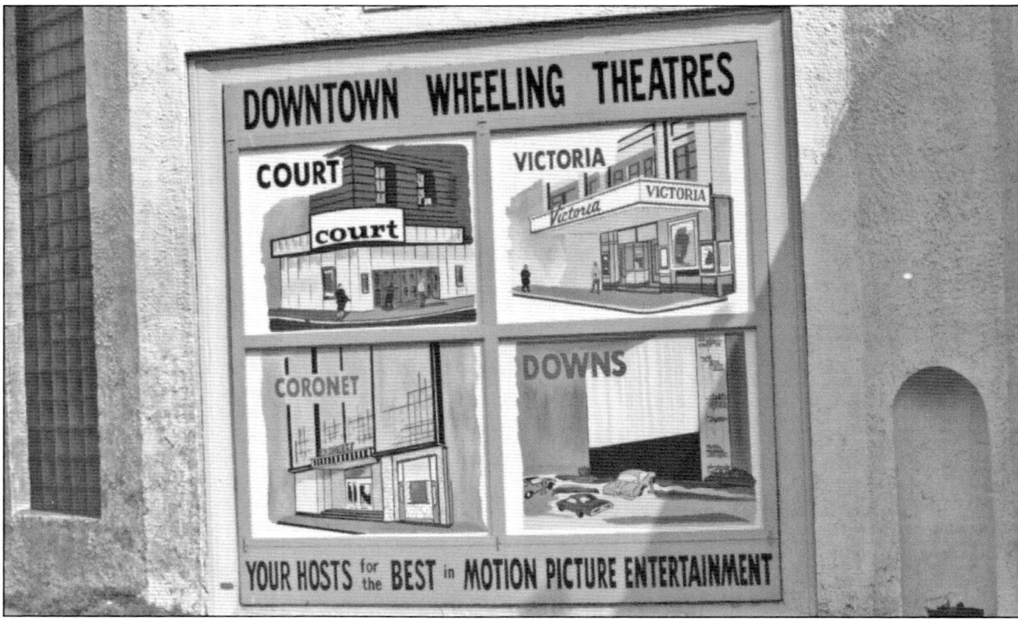

The Downs Drive-in Theatre, named after the nearby Wheeling Downs racetrack, opened o Wheeling Island in the late 1960s. It was part of Wheeling Theatres, Inc., in 1971, when i appeared on this poster on a downtown Wheeling wall. Later owned by the Cinemette chain, i had disappeared from newspaper advertisements by 1978. Its site is now a parking lot. (Courtes of Ohio County Public Library Archives, Wheeling, West Virginia.)

Nine

Potomac Highlands

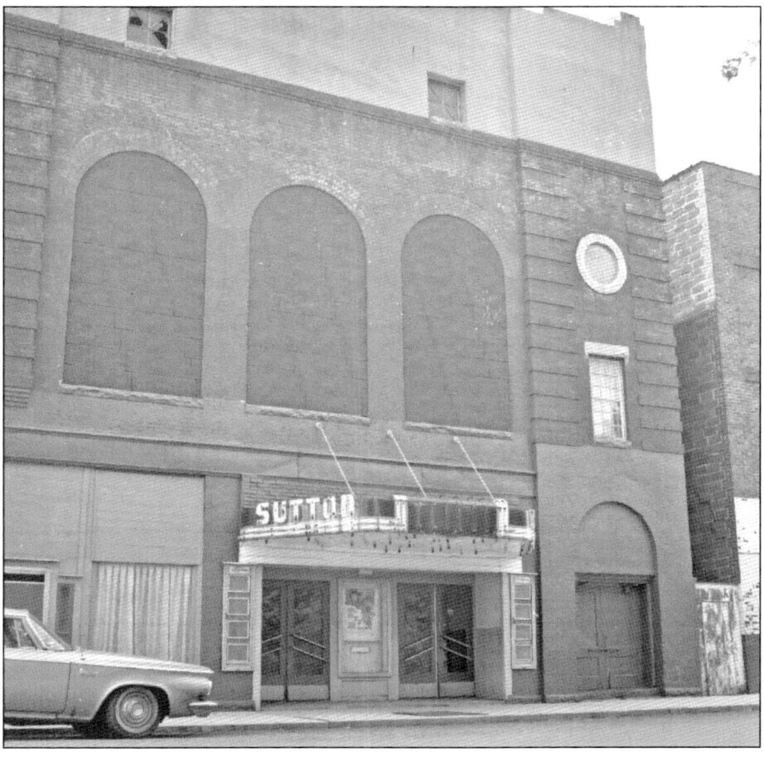

Hiram Cottrill's Opera House opened in 1902 in Thomas. Designed by Holmboe and Lafferty, the building included storefronts below a three-tier auditorium that played films starting in 1915. Decorator Billy ZeVan did an Art Deco interior remodel of the renamed Sutton Theatre in 1939. The 600-seat Sutton closed in 1972. Local organizations have been fundraising to restore and reopen it. (Courtesy of Theatre Historical Society of America, Negative Collection.)

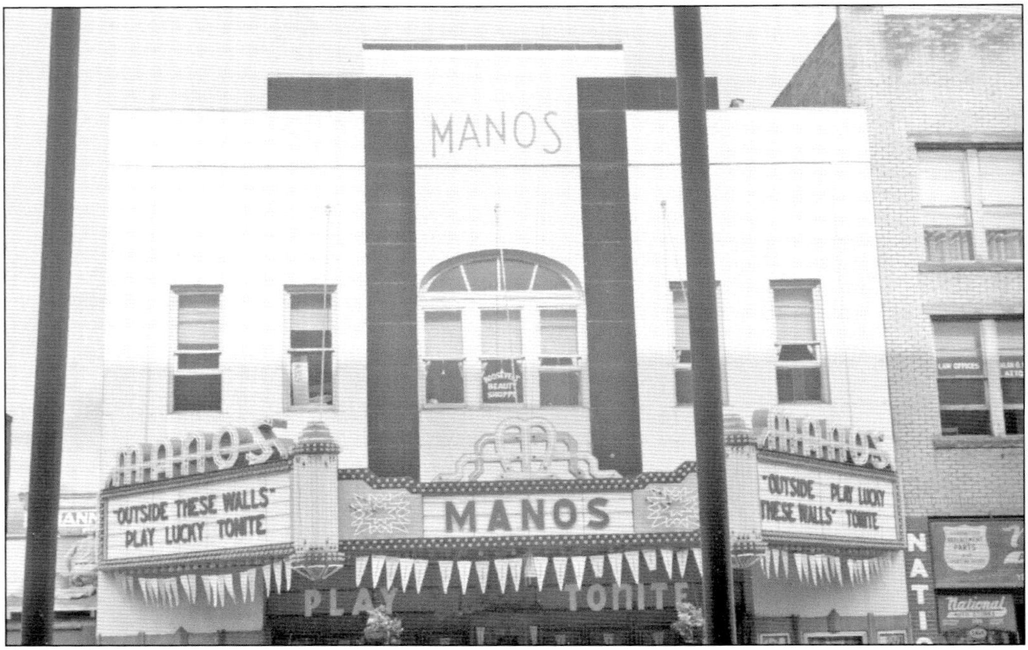

The 500-seat Grand Theatre in Elkins was built in 1909. It was renamed the Roosevelt in 1934, the year the Roosevelt administration's New Deal subsistence community, Tygart Valley Homesteads, was established about 10 miles away. In 1938, the movie house's new owner, Michael Manos, gave it an Art Deco makeover and the Manos Theatre name. The Manos closed around 1974. Today, the remodeled building hosts retail. (Courtesy of Library of Congress.)

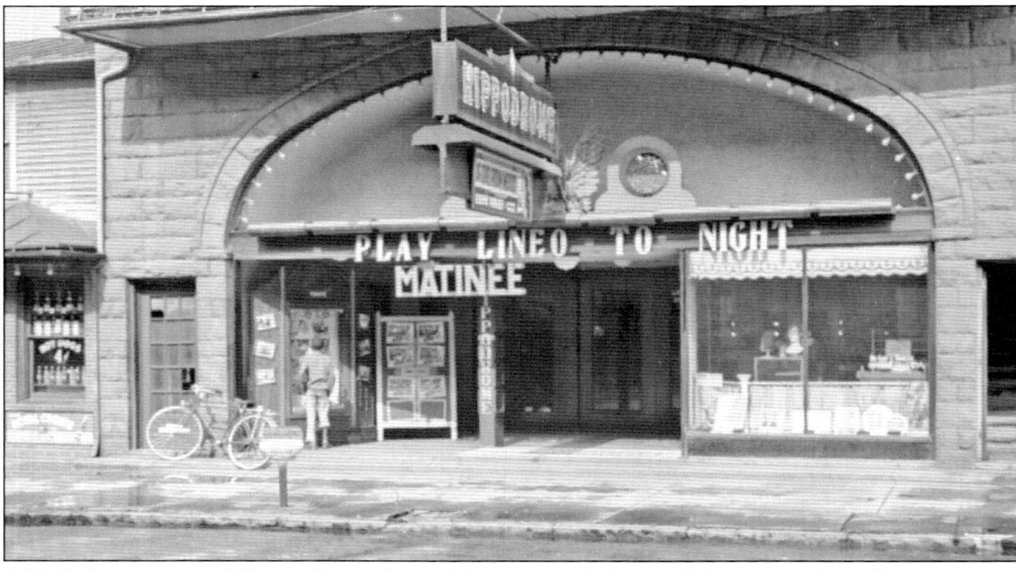

R.H. Talbott opened Elkins's Hippodrome Theatre in 1915. In 1922, it entered the Hymes circuit This 1939 image shows the Hippodrome offering attendees the opportunity to play Lineo, a game with monetary prizes. It was purchased in 1941 by the Manos family. Renamed the Elkins Theatre between 1957 and 1960, the Manos circuit's venue closed around 1967. Its Davis Avenue building is gone. (Courtesy of Library of Congress.)

The Music Hall in Keyser opened before 1901. Luther Carskadon was running it as a movie venue in 1919, when it burned. Located on the new building's second floor, above storefronts, the rebuilt, 500-seat Music Hall presented both vaudeville and films. The Carskadon family operated it until 1955, when they converted the auditorium to storage space—a function it retains today. (Courtesy of Theatre Historical Society of America, Negative Collection.)

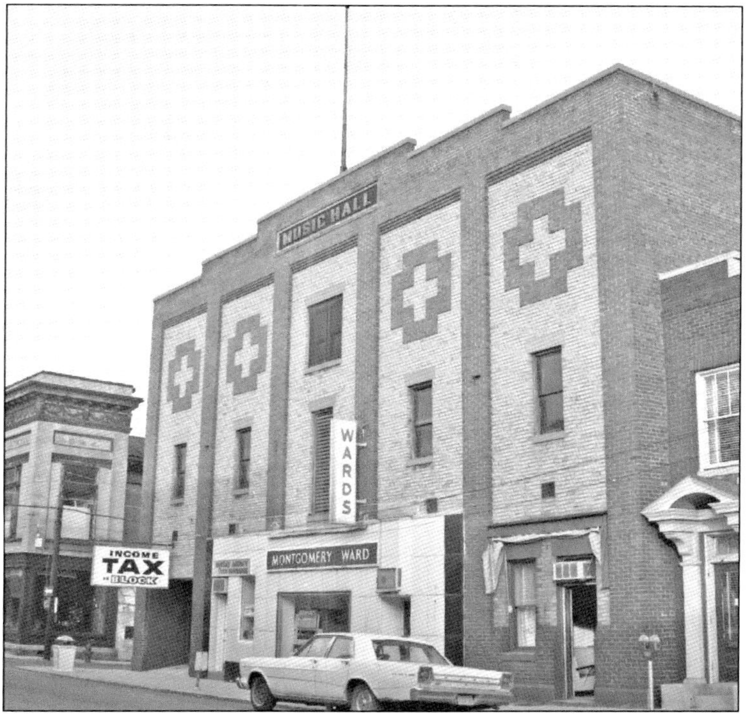

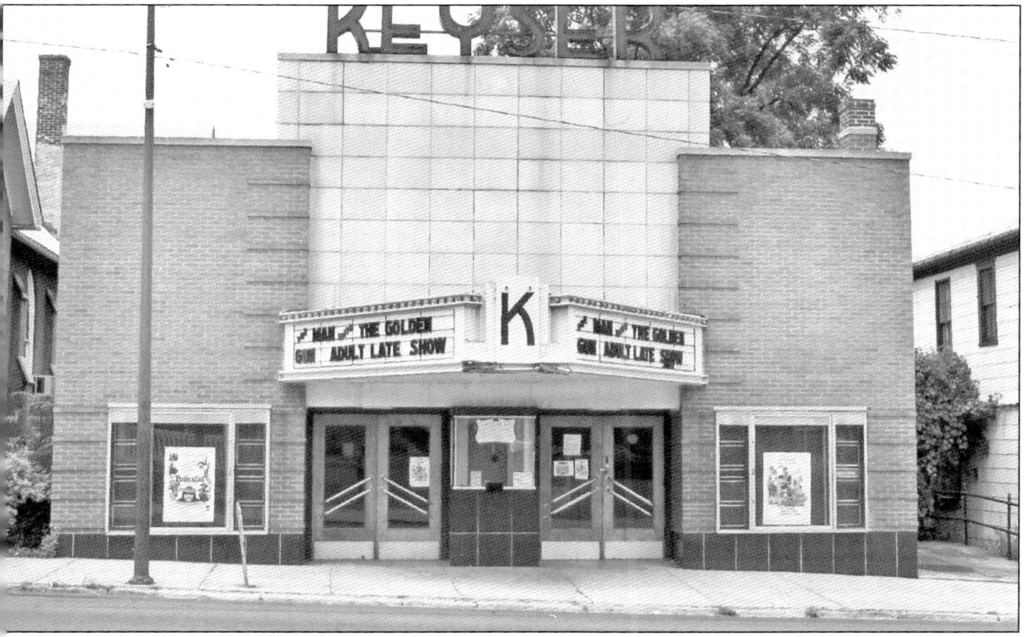

The 400-seat Keyser Theatre opened in September 1939, showing *In Name Only*. Advertised as "Ultra Modern," the Carskadon family's Keyser movie house featured Art Deco design inside and out. It closed in 1977. Various uses followed, including a church and skating rink. After a vacant period, it reopened in June 2017 as Indie on Main, a combination lounge, art center, music venue, and classic film showplace. (Courtesy of American Classic Images.)

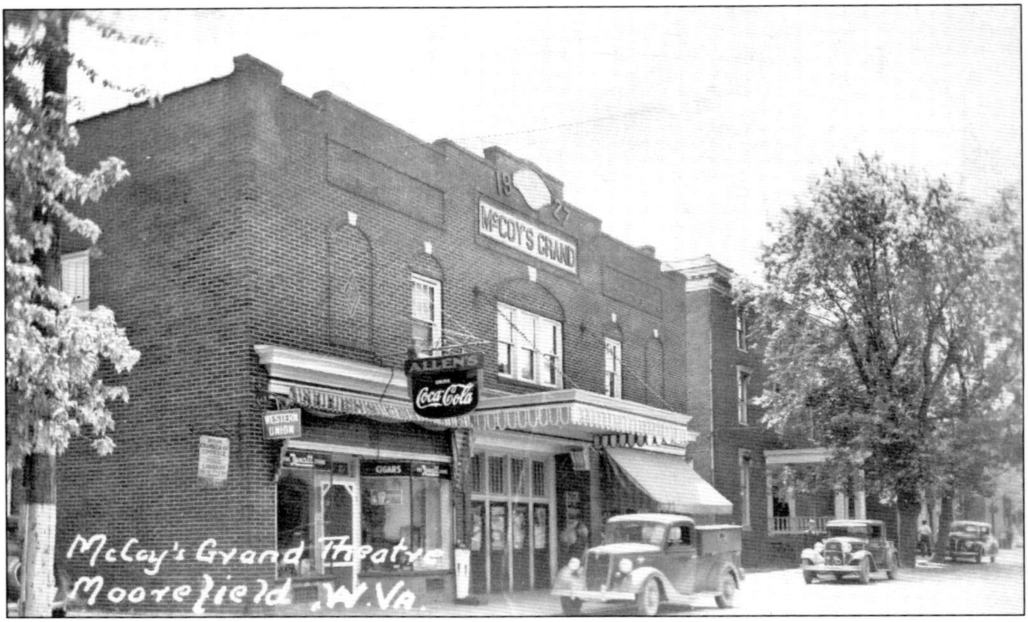

McCoy's Grand Theatre opened in February 1928 with a screening of *Wife Saver*. Until its early 1980s closure, the 400-seat Moorefield movie house was owned and operated by the McCoy family. A provision in Eunice McCoy's will ensured the theatre would not be demolished after her passing, and in 1983, her estate donated it to a nonprofit organization. McCoy's Grand has since functioned as a playhouse and small museum. (Author's collection.)

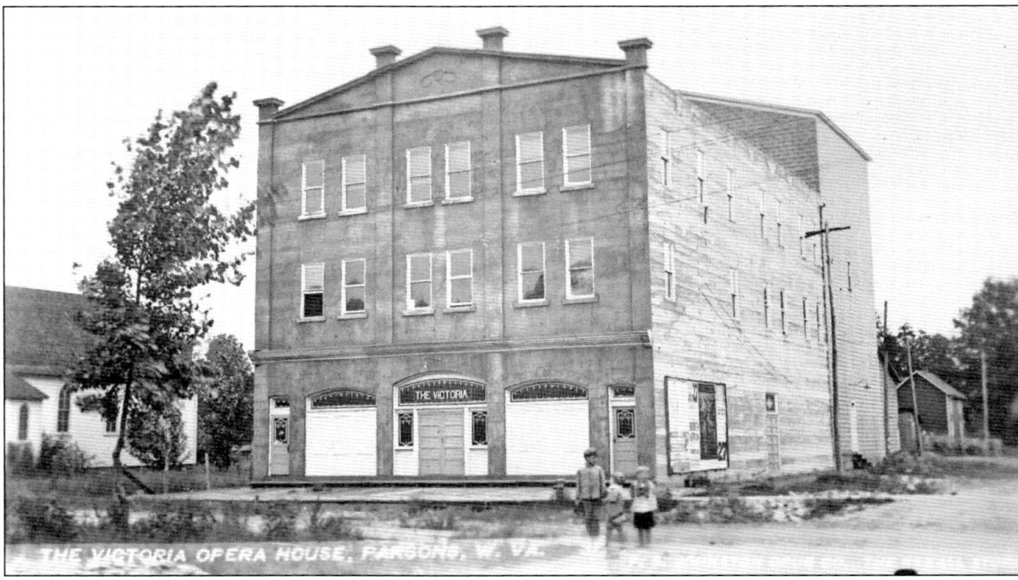

In the Tucker County seat of Parsons, the Victoria Opera House opened in 1909 on Walnu Street's 200 block. The large venue included not just a balcony but also a gallery and boxes. I was showing films by 1918; H.L. Bennett operated it during the 1920s. Later called the Victori Theatre, it played movies as least as late as 1959. (Courtesy of West Virginia State Archives, Mrs C.R. Taylor Collection.)

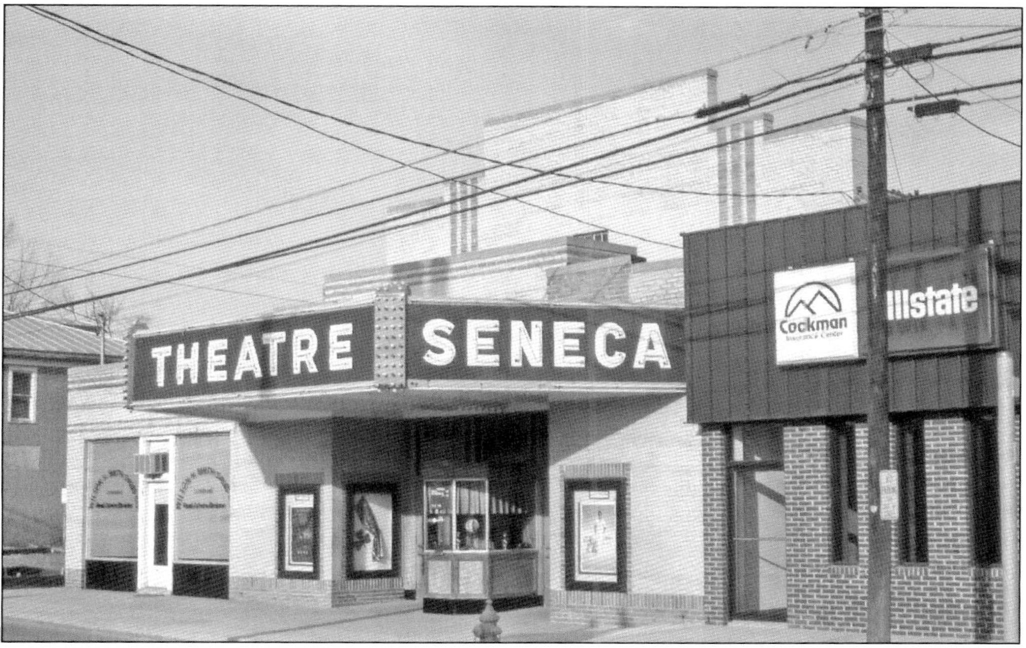

In 1942, the Alpine circuit opened Petersburg's Alpine Theatre. The 230-seat, Art Deco movie house, designed by prolific theatre architect John Zink, had a balcony for African Americans. In 1956, a wide screen and other equipment were installed for Cinemascope films. A year later, owner Elizabeth Smith took over the Alpine's management, remodeled, and renamed it the Seneca Theatre. The Seneca operated until at least 1989, showing major movies. (Courtesy of American Classic Images.)

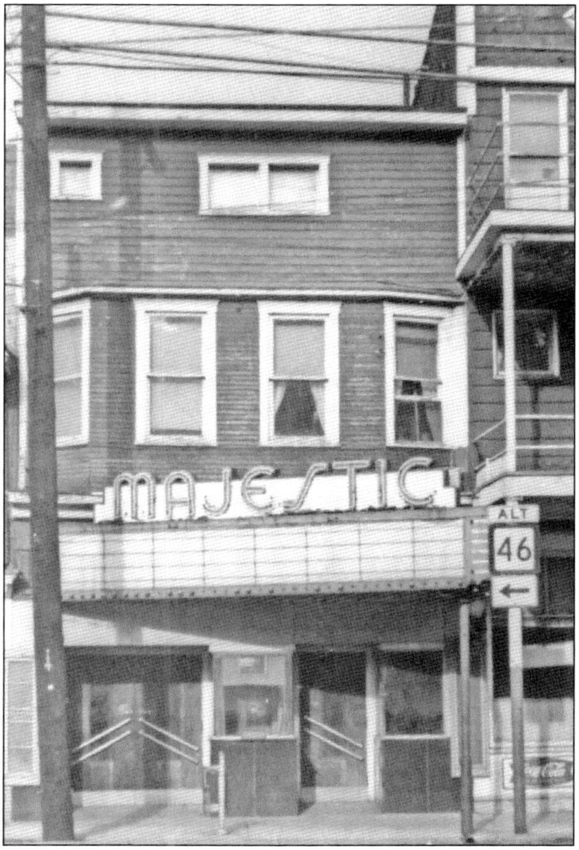

The 400-seat Majestic Theatre in Piedmont was open as early as 1926. Badly damaged by a 1930 fire, it sat closed for over six years while owner Floyd Lininger continued to operate Piedmont's other movie venue, the Opera House. In 1937, following a major remodeling and a decrease to 300 seats, Lininger finally reopened the Majestic. Still open in 1967, it was vacant when this 1979 image was taken. (Courtesy of American Classic Images.)

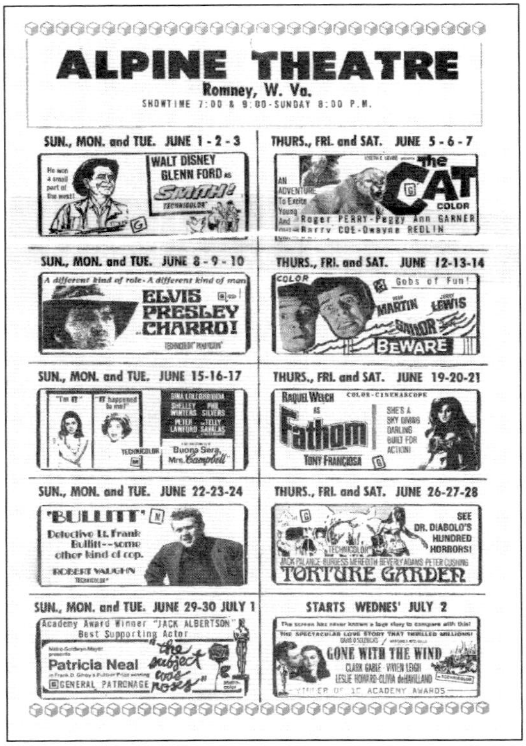

The Alpine theatre circuit purchased a car dealership in Romney in 1941. It turned the building into the 300-seat Alpine Theatre. In 1961, the circuit's owner sold the Romney Alpine—by then its last remaining movie house—to projectionist W. Roy Smith. Smith operated it, showing family-friendly films, until 1978. The theatre closed in 1985; its site is a parking lot. (Courtesy of Theatre Historical Society of America, Theatre File Collection.)

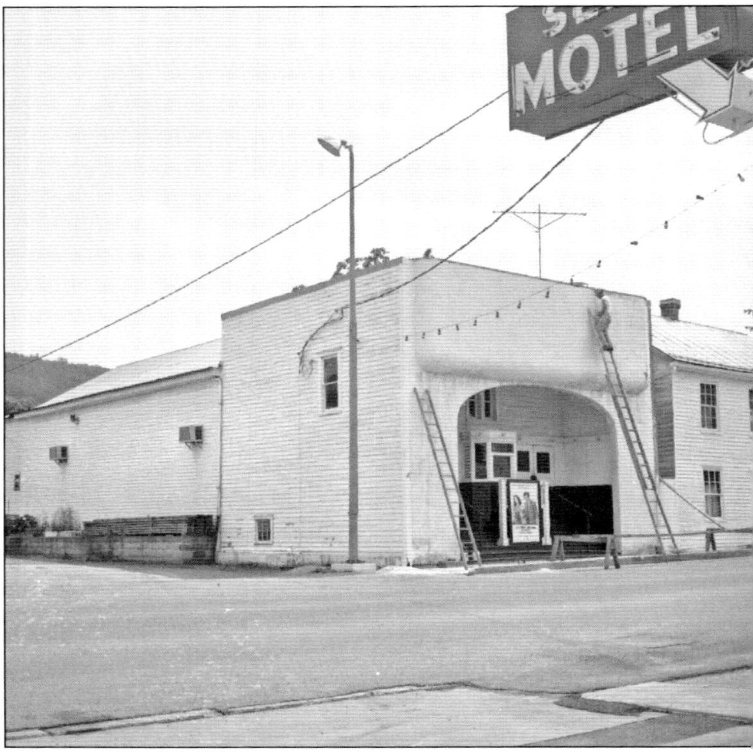

Charles and Ada Dellinger opened Wardensville's Doric Theatre around 1930 or 1931. Their daughter and granddaughter, Orpha and Marlene See, continued running the over-200-seat venue until 1978. The See family also opened See's Motel, visible across the street in this c. 1970 photograph (when the Doric was playing *The Out-of-Towners*). The Doric Theatre was later demolished, but See's Motel still operates. (Courtesy of Theatre Historical Society of America, Negative Collection.)

PRESERVATION ALLIANCE OF WEST VIRGINIA

The Preservation Alliance of West Virginia (PAWV) serves as the statewide grassroots organization dedicated to the support and promotion of historic preservation. With a commitment to preserve the state's unique cultural heritage, PAWV and its members work to save the past for the future, supporting and promoting historic preservation through education and outreach, advocacy, preservation tools, and heritage tourism. Since its founding by a group of dedicated volunteers in 1981, the nonprofit organization has continued to grow, focusing on how historic preservation can be a tool for economic and community development throughout the Mountain State.

One of PAWV's many programs is the West Virginia Historic Theatre Trail, a statewide thematic tour of operational historic theatres—encompassing both cinemas and live performance venues. All of the trail's theatres are listed in, or have been officially determined eligible for, the National Register of Historic Places (the list of the country's historic structures that the National Park Service has declared preservation-worthy). The trail promotes the rehabilitation and sustainable operation of the state's historic theatres for the enjoyment of the public. The trail was born in 2010 following a 2007 Preserve America grant award to the West Virginia Division of Culture and History's State Historic Preservation Office (SHPO), in partnership with PAWV, to develop statewide thematic tours to encourage heritage tourism in communities throughout the state. As of 2018, the trail includes nearly 30 member theatres. More information about the West Virginia Historic Theatre Trail can be found at wvhistorictheaters.com.

PAWV's other efforts include the Preserve WV AmeriCorps program (with its AmeriCorps members serving at historical organizations and agencies across the state); the biennial West Virginia Historic Preservation Conference; an annual Endangered Properties list; annual preservation awards; a variety of educational workshops; and a historic preservation loan fund (launched in 2018). Finally, PAWV was instrumental in the successful 2017 attempt to raise West Virginia's State Historic Tax Credit from 10 percent to 25 percent, encouraging the rehabilitation and reuse of historic buildings. To learn more about PAWV, please visit www.pawv.org.

Preservation Alliance of West Virginia

Consistent with our mission to preserve history on a local level, this book was printed in South Carolina on American-made paper and manufactured entirely in the United States. Products carrying the accredited Forest Stewardship Council (FSC) label are printed on 100 percent FSC-certified paper.

MADE IN THE USA